Religion in the Public Square

RELIGION IN THE PUBLIC SQUARE

Sheen, King, Falwell

James M. Patterson

PENN

UNIVERSITY OF PENNSYLVANIA PRESS

PHILADELPHIA

Published by
University of Pennsylvania Press
Philadelphia, Pennsylvania 19104-4112
www.upenn.edu/pennpress

Printed in the United States of America
on acid-free paper
1 3 5 7 9 10 8 6 4 2

Library of Congress Cataloging-in-Publication Data

Names: Patterson, James M. (James McGill), author.
Title: Religion in the public square: Sheen, King, Falwell / James M. Patterson.
Description: 1st edition. | Philadelphia: University of Pennsylvania Press, [2019] | Includes
    bibliographical references and index.
Identifiers: LCCN 2018045748 | ISBN 9780812250985 (hardcover)
Subjects: LCSH: Christianity and politics—United States—History—20th century. |
    Church and state—United States—History—20th century. | Sheen, Fulton J. (Fulton John),
    1895–1979. | King, Martin Luther, Jr., 1929–1968. | Falwell, Jerry. | United States—Politics
    and government—20th century. | United States—Religion—History—20th century.
Classification: LCC BR526.P375 2019 | DDC 261.70973/0904—dc23
LC record available at https://lccn.loc.gov/2018045748

Dedicated to
Maria Sedes Sapientiae

CONTENTS

INTRODUCTION

> Therefore, everyone who listens to these words of mine
> and acts on them will be like a sensible man who built his
> house on rock.
> Rain came down, floods rose, gales blew and hurled
> themselves against that house, and it did not fall: it was
> founded on rock.

—Matthew 7:24–25

During the early years of the twentieth century, a "Judeo-Christian consensus" formed the foundation for public discourse in the United States. At first, remnants of the old Protestant hegemony resisted integration of Catholics and Jews, but after the Second World War the new consensus had taken root. Catholics, Protestants, and Jews sought a shared dogma from which citizens could draw when debating political issues. Not only was it necessary that this dogma satisfy three faiths, it also had to square with the liberal principles of the Declaration of Independence and Constitution. The dogma of the Judeo-Christian consensus changed over time, and it was the priests, bishops, pastors, reverends, and rabbis who negotiated these changes and brought them to their congregations. When a new, more radical generation of secular progressives emerged during the late 1960s and advocated for the liberation of and equal respect for repressed groups, religious leaders continued to insist on the close tie between an adherence to a religious faith and the preservation of a free country. The prevailing view among those leading the Judeo-Christian consensus was that its tie to American liberalism required defending and, over time, such a defense would succeed. Thus began the "Culture War."

During the Culture War from the 1980s until the recent years, generations of defenders of the Judeo-Christian consensus made their stand, but at present the ranks are thinner and less certain. At the same time, their old secular, progressive opponents in the Culture War have more favorably appraised the Declaration of Independence. For example, Danielle Allen believes that religious faith is inessential to it. She explains, "You do not need to be a theist to accept the argument of the Declaration. You do, however, require an alternative ground for a maximally strong commitment to the right of other people to survive and to govern themselves" and that this commitment is "the achievement of equality," which "is the sole foundation on which we can build lasting and meaningful freedom."[1] In the past, conservative American Catholics would have vigorously disputed her position; however, conservative American Catholic Patrick Deneen agrees with Allen's assessment, arguing that the liberalism of the Declaration of Independence "was premised upon the limitation of government and the liberation of the individual from arbitrary political control," but those Americans now seeking liberation of individual have discovered the necessity of limitless government. Deneen claims, "remnants of associations historically charged with the cultivation of norms are increasingly seen as obstacles to autonomous liberty, and the apparatus of the state is directed toward the task of liberating individuals from such bonds."[2]

For Deneen, modern conservatism offers no help because conservatism was always a liberal project. Observing the state of conservative politics, he pronounces, "The dying gasps of a 'conservative' reaction to that disassembling [of preliberal institutions] only accelerated liberalism's self-destruction—including the demise of a 'conservatism' that by its nature could not conserve."[3] Rather than return to a theistic ground for the Declaration of Independence, he calls for America "to be founded again, now explicitly in departure from the philosophic principles that animated its liberal founding, appropriating those structures and even the language of liberty and rights to build anew a civilization worthy of preservation."[4] Precisely because the Declaration of Independence adheres to a liberal philosophical tradition and this tradition seeks liberation from all preliberal authority, religious Americans should found "intentional communities" that appear "nonthreatening to the liberal order's main business" from which "a viable postliberal political theory will arise."[5] Deneen, in other words, endorses what Rod Dreher has called "the Benedict Option."[6]

Deneen's position has two problems. First, Deneen stresses the agency of "liberalism" as a concept always lurking behind the scenes, usually "invisible" and becoming visible only when "its deformations are . . . too obvious to ignore."[7] Ideas matter but not because they are agents of political change. Politics remains a human activity performed by individual persons within a regime composed of laws and norms. Hence, for ideas to influence politics, persons must introduce them, defend them, and revise laws and norms according to them. Second, because Deneen mistakenly identifies ideas as agents, he condemns the ideas as if they were guilty of crimes, and he strangely exonerates liberal political actors as hostages to an ideological false consciousness.

Political actors are agents for ideas, and their agency is freely chosen, if not always free from external constraints. Chief among these political actors are the American clergy (who, oddly, receive no attention in Deneen's recent work), and since the founding of the United States many among them sought to limit the power of the state and redirect it to what they regarded as its proper moral ends and its proper limits in achieving those ends.[8] One critical decision the clergy have tried and too often failed to avoid was affiliating their faiths with a political party, since such a decision would then premise the success of the faith on the capricious outcomes of electoral politics. By the 1990s, however, leading members of clergy had declared their affiliation with the New Conservative Movement and its avatar the Republican Party. The GOP thereby increasingly became the party of religious conservatives as the Democratic Party began to become more secular—except for its African American Protestants. As a result, these churches then began to decline as existing and potential congregants regarded them merely as political entities instead of anchors of a local community, a source for human salvation, or a tradition connecting generations past, present, and future to the divine. Hence, Deneen's general idea of "liberalism" conceals more than it explains. Specifically, it conceals the political decisions that have led to so deep and numerous divisions over faith in American life. American churches, first among the "pre-liberal" institutions on which American liberalism depends, ceased to operate as independent, indirect influences on citizens and, instead, lowered themselves to merely ordinary political factions seeking to work their ministry through state coercion instead of grace or tradition. "Liberalism" is not the cause of the problems Deneen observes, since ideas lack agency. Rather, one of the most important defenses against the excesses of American liberalism, religious institutions, failed to remain independent of politics. In short, liberalism did not fail the church; the church failed liberalism.

To make this case, this book offers two claims. First, ideas make their way to the public by way of popularizers, and these popularizers have very often been clergy. Second, to remain persuasive to the public, clergy must focus their efforts on moral and religious education rather than direct participation in government or political parties.

While a small number of thinkers might do the difficult work of developing philosophies of life, a second, middle tier connects the thinkers and the people at large. Between these two worlds were popularizers that sought to connect the two groups, but it is wrong to regard popularizers as somehow merely derivative or pandering. The genius of the popularizer is in rendering difficult ideas into simple tenets with direct relevance to the everyday lives of regular people and, at the same time, elevating these everyday lives by joining them to a higher purpose than mere material consumption. During the twentieth century, many of these figures were members of clergy who sought to link their specific ideas about faith to a diverse religious population. Hence, they took for granted this diversity and sought to develop a consensus that satisfies the members of the several faiths. This consensus rested on a dogma, or a set of assumptions out of which popularizers could build arguments for ethical and political reform, and the consensus would remain robust if clergy generally understood their responsibility to be the preservation of its terms through persuasion, conversion, and tradition.

This book examines three cases illustrating this process. They are Ven. Fulton J. Sheen, Dr. Martin Luther King Jr., and Rev. Jerry Falwell.[9] The three were nationally recognizable figures who promulgated difficult ideas to a large, engaged American audience. The three figures are somewhat contemporaneous but spaced out over the course of the twentieth century. Sheen began his ministry during the 1920s to preach American Catholic patriotism and opposition to totalitarianism, and his television show *Life Is Worth Living* ran until 1957, the year after King had successfully led the Montgomery Bus Boycott. Falwell was a successful independent Baptist preacher in Lynchburg, Virginia, when, in 1965, he condemned King's political activism as antithetical to a preacher's job to save souls. Fifteen years later, he would reverse this position when he formed the Moral Majority to mobilize Evangelical and Fundamentalist Christians into the New Conservative Movement and increase its influence over the Republican Party. Throughout his career, Sheen avoided endorsing a political party or tying his ministry to a political ideology. Once a national figure, King had informal relationships with elected officials, but he carefully avoided making political overtures that would compromise his ability to influence members of both parties. Falwell, however, premised his moral and religious teaching on the direct sponsorship of an ideological movement within a political party, and it was this decisive break that has sundered liberalism in America from its traditional religious constraints.

To explain this position in greater detail, this introduction provides an explanation of the proper relationship between American religious and political institutions. This discussion will draw from the work of Alexis de Tocqueville, who argued that churches were the only institutions that could provide a religious dogma that could rival the dogma of American liberalism. To preserve the integrity of religious dogma, however, churches had to observe the separation of church and state, since direct church participation in politics would reduce the church to a mere political faction. The introduction then briefly examines previous scholarly efforts to define dogma within comprehensive "conceptual frames." The trouble with conceptual frames is how often they become agents rather than the political actors. Therefore, this introduction briefly explains how to use the concept of "foundations" to explain how popularizers borrow from traditions, improvise on them, and thereby influence American dogma. The introduction concludes with an explanation for the selection of cases and the order of the book.

Historical and Institutional Arrangements for Religious Consensus

Alexis de Tocqueville was a French aristocrat from Normandy, who visited America with his friend Gustave de Beaumont from 1831 until 1832. Upon returning he wrote one of the most perceptive treatments of American democracy ever written. Among his insights was the way that American religious institutions favored political freedom. The United States had unique historical and institutional arrangements that facilitated the formation of a religious dogma. In *Democracy in America*, Tocqueville observed the following:

Historical:
A Puritan founding that linked democratic self-government to religious discipline
An unbroken continuation of English traditions respecting individual rights
A diversity of sects with no one sufficiently dominant over national affairs

Institutional:
Religious disestablishment at the federal and (mostly) state level
Religious liberty guaranteed at federal and state level
Exclusion of clergy from public office[10]

The arrangements, in turn, shaped the popular assumptions about the role of clergy and the importance of political freedom. Tocqueville observed that congregations wanted their clergy to attend only to congregational matters, and these clergy publicly admitted to wanting this.[11] The clergy also adamantly favored religious liberty for all churches, despite believing that their own constituted the true church. The reason is what Tocqueville calls "self-interest well understood."[12] The clergy might want the establishment of their own faith as the one, true faith; however, no sect had the majority necessary to establish itself. Of course, the First Amendment prohibited an establishment at the federal level, but even if there were no such prohibition, the lack of a majority denomination precluded any single faith from securing the privilege. If no single church could monopolize the faith of Americans, then the second-best option was to provide religious free exercise for all faiths. That way, all churches would share the freedom normally only afforded to established faiths. In exchange, all faiths renounced efforts to claim state establishment. The renunciation bore a cost—no sect could depend on the state—but a cost equally borne by all sects.

Renouncing state sponsorship, Tocqueville stressed, carried with it a benefit that far exceeded the benefit of state sponsorship: the embrace of political freedom among clergy. Because clergy benefited from religious free exercise, they preached its blessings from pulpits, and the blessings were all too apparent to congregations aware of religious repression in other parts of the world. For Tocqueville, the result was something thought impossible in his native France: an alliance between "the spirit of religion" and "the spirit of liberty." In France, the Catholic Church remained strongly aligned with the French monarchy in the hope of protecting its establishment. Therefore, advocates of political freedom in France understood themselves as enemies of the Catholic Church, as well.[13] American historical and institutional arrangements had prevented such a division and even transformed churches into the greatest bulwarks of freedom.[14]

In America, religion defended political freedom but also set its limits. As Pierre Manent explains, on the one hand, religion for Tocqueville was "the premier political institution of the Americans, which guarantees and supports freedom in the best fashion, in preventing them from daring all," while on the other hand, "religion forbids Americans, much to their happiness, to conceive the idea of the unlimited power of society only by virtue of the reality of this very power!"[15] These limits provoked relief among citizens for whom, as Aristide Tessitore describes, "the possibility of limitless independence inspires fear and agitation."[16] Tocqueville called these religious limits to democratic power, "dogma." Manent explains that, for Tocqueville, the separation of church and state ensured the predominance of social power over religion, since: "Religion is the instrument of this shared opinion, the specific mode of expression of the social power of democracy. It is not dogma that comprises shared opinion; it is shared opinion that is dogma. It follows that the separation of church and state is largely an illusion if one means by this the establishment of their mutual independence. In the United States, this separation is the vehicle by which the submission of religion to a new political regime—the democratic regime—is established and expressed."[17] American clergy provided religious instruction to their congregations and thereby shaped their opinions. These congregations, when combined, form the people, and their shared opinions became dogma. The dogma had no constitutional or government power; rather, its power came from the people who acted on dogma in their every political decision.

By dogma, Tocqueville meant something different from specific sectarian commitments like the Augsburg Confession or the Baltimore Catechism. He disputed that one could avoid dogma at all, saying, "one cannot make it so that there are no dogmatic beliefs, that is, opinions men receive on trust without discussing them. If each understood himself to form all his opinions and to pursue the truth in isolation down paths cleared by him alone, it is not probable that a great number of men would ever united in any common belief."[18] As Alan S. Kahan explains, for Tocqueville, without dogma, "action would be impossible. If we had to constantly figure out, first individually, and then as a community, whether 'green' should mean 'go' and 'red' 'stop,' or with which hand one should a hold a knife, the only question left would be which would come first, death by automobile accident or death by starvation."[19] One should note that Kahan argues that, for Tocqueville, dogma was inescapable. He is not quite right. Tocqueville did argue that dogma was inescapable, but it could be either shared or individual. The absence of shared dogma, however, rendered a united public impossible. If one wanted a public capable of acting on united beliefs, one had to insist on dogma. Without dogma, individuals fell back into their own private lives to define terms in isolation from one another, a condition Tocqueville regarded as the precondition for despotism. Therefore, Tocqueville presented a choice between the "salutary servitude" of religious dogma or the smothering tutelage of despotic government.[20] Dogma, for Tocqueville, held together a consensus for public discourse in America. Americans depended on religion to provide "general ideas relative to God and human nature" in a regime "for which there is most to gain and least to lose in recognizing an authority."[21]

By "religion," Tocqueville meant Christianity, broadly understood. Christianity offered very little in the way of a political constitution. Tocqueville observed, "The Gospels . . . speak only of the general relations of men to God and among themselves. Outside of that they teach nothing and oblige nothing to be believed" and had proved adaptable to the changing political and social conditions where the Gospels persisted.[22] Moreover, Americans, being democrats, disliked ornate forms of religious observance. Therefore, even American Catholic priests had little "taste for small, individual observances, for extraordinary and particular methods of gaining salvation."[23] In this respect, Catholicism had reconciled itself to American democracy, if not theologically, at least socially, and the latter was more important for the preservation of political freedom in American democracy. Tocqueville observed that "Although Christians of America are divided into a multitude of sects, they all perceive their religion in the same light."[24]

The clergy accommodated the democratic tendency to enjoy material goods even as dogma curbed the power of democratic majorities and state power. Clergy "do not associate themselves with industry" but are "at least interested in its progress and applaud it . . . while constantly showing to the faithful the other world as the great object of their hopes and fears."[25] In the same way, "they do not mix in the quarrels of the parties, but they willingly adopt the general opinions of their country and time."[26] Instead, clergy "strive to correct their contemporaries."[27] The clergy did not fight with the people but guided them because, as Tocqueville stressed throughout his two volumes, democracy naturally produced a rival dogma: popular sovereignty. Religious dogmas could not avoid popular sovereignty; indeed, it was this dogma that grounded the American republic. However, if clergy retained their place detached from political life, Americans could remain adherents to dogma, and even those without faith would strive to imitate the outward appearance of obedience. Faithful or not, Americans agreed that the state simply did not have the authority beyond what dogma permitted, and Christian clergy could credibly guide the people away from complete submission to the state in favor of political freedom both because the clergy themselves enjoyed the benefits of political freedom and because the health of the churches themselves depended on it. Settling on this dogma, as well as the limits to the clergy in propagating it, provided the intellectual space for politics and material well-being.

The surest way to undo the salutary servitude to religious dogma would be for the clergy to take sides in partisan disputes. Tocqueville was concerned about clergy attaching themselves to transient political causes, since the effect was to associate religion with transience rather than eternity and divisive politics rather than shared dogma.[28] The tension in Tocqueville's thought is that he did not want religion, Christianity in particular, to enter into politics; however, Christians too often tended toward political indifference. Christianity found its cause "to form a human society outside all notional societies," and, hence, articulated "the duties of men toward each other as *citizens*, the obligations of the citizen to the fatherland, in a word the public virtues seem to me to be badly defined and pretty neglected in Christian morality."[29] The French aristocrat never found a resolution to the problem, but Tocqueville's best effort came in a curious speech by a Catholic priest.

The speech is strange. Tocqueville did not identify the priest by name or by town, preferring the anonymous description, "one of the largest towns of the Union."[30] The priest wore "his ecclesiastical habit" but spoke as an equal among an assortment of orators. Despite his appearing as an equal, the audience gave due respect to the priestly office by "removing their hats" and remaining "in silence."[31] The priest stressed the universality of the Christian religion yet spoke of the divine interventions in the lives of nations. He invoked martial terms when describing God's role in defending the rights of Americans: the "God of hosts! Thou who did maintain the hearts and guide the arms of our fathers when they sustained the sacred rights of their national independence; thou who made them triumph over an odious oppression and granted our people the benefits of peace and freedom."[32] The priest entreated God to "watch over the destiny of the Poles, render them worthy of being free," and he did not forget Tocqueville's homeland when prophesying: "arouse [Polish] allies to the sacred cause of right; make the French nation finally rise, and, leaving the repose in which its heads keep it, come to fight once again for the freedom of the world."[33] The priest stressed not just a common God but a common human nature. Americans, Poles, and the French constitute each an individual nation, yet are "created . . . on the same model," and he ended the speech with a benediction acceptable to nearly all Christians at the time and in a way that stressed Christian universality, "We ask this of thee in the name of thy much loved son, our Lord Jesus Christ, who died on the cross for the salvation of all men."[34] Perhaps the most explicit endorsement of Tocqueville's ideal, and perhaps most incredible to his contemporary French readers, was to quote this Catholic priest, "permit us always to be the most religious people as well as the most free."[35] This speech was Tocqueville's ideal prayer for how Christian dogma can offer salutary servitude to a democratic nation. The priest appealed to a common God to affirm sacred rights that shape the boundary of majority rule and state power and the connection of those rights to generations past. Tocqueville's priest did not direct the audience to agitate for an American intervention in Polish or French affairs but merely petitioned God for divine assistance out of respect for common humanity.[36] This priest had found the language for making Christianity no longer an indifferent or retreating remnant but instead a fighting faith in democratic politics. Tocqueville's priest demonstrated how religious dogma blessed and constrained liberal dogma, and he also revealed how clergy popularized religious dogma in a way that earns popular respect and assent.

Prior Conceptual Frames for the American Dogma

There are several prior efforts to understand how religious ideas influence American public life. There are three to discuss, albeit briefly: the American jeremiad, the American civil religion, and the "Great Denouement."

In his study of the New England Puritans, Perry Miller discussed how their clergy deployed the "jeremiad" as a narrative to encourage congregations to return to the moral and religious discipline necessary to preserve their community in the wilderness.[37] Sacvan Bercovitch expanded the application of the jeremiad from New England Puritans to American history up until the present, and more recent scholars in American political development, such as James Morone and Andrew Murphy, have innovated on the approach.[38] These scholars have argued that American clergy warn their congregations that the sins of the nation angered God. If such sin were to continue, God would punish them. The only way to avoid decline and eventual ruin is to repent and to return to the old Gospel teaching that God rewards nations for following.

There are two problems with the American jeremiad. First, the American jeremiad assumes that the diverse American clergy adhere to the same relationship between God and the nation, which is the one that the New England Puritans believed in. As one moves from the Puritans into the Protestant denominations of the nineteenth century, the jeremiad functions well enough; however, as Jews and Catholics worked their way into the national consensus, this view became less useful as both faiths rejected the Protestant assumptions at the heart of the jeremiad. Even twentieth-century Protestants offered more complicated views about the relationship between American religion and politics, as this book will argue in chapters on King and Falwell. Second, the American jeremiad suffers from something of an ideological bias. Bercovitch deployed the jeremiad to explain the failure of radical social change that he wished America would embrace.[39] Both Morone and Murphy dispute this conclusion only to argue that some cases of the American

jeremiad might work toward that very same social change Bercovitch envisioned.[40] Therefore, to study dogma through the lens of the American jeremiad is to presuppose, first, that American religions fundamentally agree
with the peculiar New England Puritan interpretation of the Reformed Protestant faith and, second, a commitment to repurposing religion to facilitate
radical social change. The first presupposition becomes more problematic as
America becomes less subject to Protestant hegemony, and the second presupposition pushes scholars to promote a political program that may skew
both the cases the scholars select and how the scholars treat those cases.

Scholars of the American civil religion examine how Americans honor
a parallel national creed alongside their revealed religions. Robert N. Bellah
introduced the concept in his seminal 1967 essay, "Civil Religion in America,"
and spawned a genre of scholarship of incredible verve and volume. Bellah
defined the civil religion as a "collection of beliefs, symbols, and rituals with
respect to sacred things and institutionalized in a collectivity," which in the
American context includes venerating the American founders, the Declaration of Independence, the Constitution, the martyrdom of Abraham Lincoln,
commemorating fallen soldiers, and other sacred tasks specific to the nation
rather than one faith.[41] Scholars like Peter Gardella and Philip Gorski have
recently explored the liturgical, mythological, and ceremonial uses of the
civil religion in public life with both searching for political circumstances
in which Americans could find in the civil religion a renewed consensus.[42]
Gorski wishes for return to the old Cold War civil religion of the vital center.
Gardella hopes for an American civil religion rendered less American and
more international, which he believes was a trend former president Barack
Obama had started during his presidency.

The difficulty with the American civil religion is its impermanence.
Despite Gardella's and Gorski's efforts to offer a comprehensive account of
it, other scholars have explained how the American civil religion always
seems to change in accordance with political and religious leadership. In a
recent volume, historians indicated how differently the civil religion operated under different presidents, as well as how different religious denominations responded to the American civil religion.[43] To the latter point, John D.
Wilsey has argued that the American civil religion is an institutional arti-
fact of religious disestablishment. Even as the civil expression of American
religion lacks denominational preference, Wilsey shows that "in many ways,
churches have served as agents of the civil religion to support it and advance
it. American clergy do not serve in political offices as an extension of their
ecclesial role, but they have historically served as mouthpieces for the civil

religion."[44] In short, the American civil religion remains dependent on American revealed religions as mediators and interpreters of it.[45] Of course, this difficulty does not indicate that the American civil religion does not exist but merely that it never exists as one set of beliefs. As Americans experience new events requiring historical commemoration, the civil religion must integrate those experiences into its canon, and differing political and religious leaders are the ones integrating them. As these leaders change, they not only integrate the new events but revise or even reverse the decisions of prior leaders.

Finally, the newest, least well-known of the three conceptual frames is Hugh Heclo's "Great Denouement" of American Christianity. He defines it as a "profound historical achievement, centuries in the making, [that] blended commitments to religious liberty and popular self-government" and "the political freedom of elected governments from control by religious authorities, and the religious freedom of individuals and groups from control by the government."[46] By Heclo's account, the superficial secularism of the American founding was merely a way "to avoid inviting sectarian disputes and diversions that might interfere with the ratification business at hand."[47] Instead, the founders hoped for "something like an *entente cordiale* between the forces of Christian faith and Enlightenment reason" in which "concepts revealed by the light of reason—inalienable rights of the individual, limited government, social compact theory—were no less evident to the Christian political theology developing out of the Puritan heritage."[48] Over time, what Heclo finds is an ever-increasing capacity for American faiths to bind together into a shared dogma that does not favor one sect over another but facilitates individual liberty even for those who belong to no sect at all.

The weakness in Heclo's theory of the Great Denouement comes with his description of its historical unfolding. To stress the continuity of a "Christian democracy" and a "democratic Christianity," he downplays the tremendous discontinuities that beset efforts to preserve Protestant hegemony during the nineteenth century.[49] The most notable omissions are the American Protestant responses to the rise of the Church of Jesus Christ of Latter Day Saints (LDS) and the arrival of Roman Catholics in large numbers. Anti-LDS and anti-Catholic discourse served as a way of preserving the Protestant hegemony even as Protestant churches multiplied sects and parachurch organizations. LDS members and Catholics provoked intense Protestant anger, since American Protestants understood their consensus as disestablished from government but nonetheless informally binding. LDS members and Catholics at the time broke with this view. Until the Second Vatican Council, the Catholic Church opposed the liberal and republican ideas at the heart of the American proposition. LDS founders originally wanted an explicitly theocratic republic, and some hoped to establish one in the Utah Territory. The issue was important enough to warrant the first platform for the Republican Party to refer to the LDS church as one of the twin evils in America— the other being slavery. The issue came to a head when LDS settlers in Utah, disguised as Native Americans, began attacking federal suppliers. In 1858, President James Buchanan sent out the army to suppress them. The "Utah War" was the culmination of decades of violence between LDS members and local, state, and federal officials since the founding of the church in 1830. Even though there was little bloodshed, the mobilization of federal power against a threat to Protestant hegemony demonstrates that there were very strict limits to the Great Denouement.

The American jeremiad, the American civil religion, and the Great Denouement each offers a deep insight into the nature of the dogmas that have held together a changing national consensus. However, too often, scholars treat their conceptual frames as fixed entities that act in history. The American jeremiad is an agent of religious reaction against radical social change. The American civil religion actively binds together citizens to serve a common aim. The Great Denouement is the spirit of religious reconciliation through Enlightenment reason and American democratic institutions. On the contrary, it has been the popular religious and political actors that seized upon these concepts and improvised on them to persuade audiences of whatever position those actors advocate.

This problem with conceptual frames is not new. No single conceptual frame can capture the fullness of American dogma; hence Donald S. Lutz warns that, for political scientists, one "unfortunate habit is to seek a single source that was decisive in the formation of American political thought"[50] and Rogers M. Smith has concluded, "I have also come to question whether we are sweeping too much into academic categories, some of which . . . were almost never used during hundreds of the years to which we apply them."[51] James W. Ceaser concurs, explaining that conceptual frames, which he calls "traditions," are "prefabricated essences . . . that analysts have imported from the outside in order to organize and make sense of the disparate ideas of American political life."[52] The strength of the approach is that "the breadth of this concept is what allows for a general characterization of the whole polity. But it is also its weakness, since few have bothered to define what a tradition is. It is a rule of logic that you get out of an inquiry only what you put into it. If scholars begin by looking for traditions in the study of American political development, then this is what they will find. But if parts of a tradition change, at what point does it cease to be the same thing?"[53] At its worst, the approach merely becomes efforts "to 'score' ideas based on which traditions they fall into" without concern about the origins, applicability, or historicity of the conceptual frames themselves.[54] Therefore, this book avoids identifying one single conceptual frame as an explanation or solution. Instead, the argument of this book rests on the constant political debate over the tenets of an American dogma and the consensus that holds it together. In the past, American clergy have served both as agents for settling on dogma and representatives of that consensus, and it should be clear why. They become the public voice for a congregation or sect, and what clergy preach can also form the "religious foundation" for the political positions the preacher advocates.

The term "religious foundation" has a specific meaning. Ceaser defines the role of a political foundation as "an idea offered in political discourse as a first cause or ultimate justification for a general political position or orientation. It is usually presented as requiring no further argument, since it is thought to contain within itself its first premise. It supplies the answer to the question 'Why,' beyond which any further response is thought unnecessary."[55] A religious foundation posits a divine authority as the source for right judgment on public policy. As shown in subsequent chapters, all three clergy members studied in this book explicitly invoke the term "foundation" when presenting their fundamental beliefs about American politics. America rests on popular sovereignty as the source for legitimacy, but the people require dogma to unify and act politically. Clergy seek to provide their religious foundations to define that dogma to set moral limits on the dogma of popular sovereignty. In sum, successful foundations become dogma.[56] Religious foundations are the source for the views that Americans use in politics, but they are not conceptual frames themselves. Clergy offer religious foundations by incorporating multiple views of America to persuade an audience, but the foundations are what the clergy hope to make American dogma, or the limits Americans agree to place on their own sovereignty. Hence, the study of religion and politics in America should begin with those foundations.

The Origins of the Judeo-Christian Consensus

Instead of Americans living through a slow and steady assimilation of religious faiths into a great denouement, they have experienced the unstable, dynamic, and sometimes violent conflict over who can determine American dogma and what that dogma taught. The first consensus was the Protestant hegemony.[57] Throughout the nineteenth century, American Protestants of all sects were a sufficiently large majority to establish the dogma of political decision-making.[58] Because Protestant rights of conscience were essential to their faith and because no Protestant sect had sufficient numbers to violate conscience rights, they established and preserved a separation of church and state. Even so, the social state in America remained decidedly Protestant. Upper-class Protestants raised funds to establish missions, passed legislation for Protestant public schools to Americanize immigrants, and campaigned to end the buying and selling of alcohol to improve the moral and even biological composition of the nation. From the pleading sermons of Lyman Beecher to the paranoid scribblings of *The Menace*, what held together this broad Protestant worldview was a unified understanding of decentralized religious authority among pastors, congregations, and denominational organizations in opposition to the conspiracies of Rome.[59] Anti-Catholicism, and to a lesser extent anti-LDS sentiment, had served as the "last acceptable prejudices" because American Protestants drank deeply from the theological traditions preserved in the storied divinity schools of Ivy League institutions that taught the origins of the Reformation in opposition to the papacy, the persecutions commanded by Queen Mary Tudor, and the great revival of true religion and civil liberties that sprang from the victory of the Gospel and self-government in 1688. Even during the American Civil War, the two sides did not divide between Protestant and secular but between regional divisions in parachurch organizations. As Abraham Lincoln himself noted, the North and South read the same Bible and prayed to the same God.[60]

The Judeo-Christian consensus slowly replaced Protestant hegemony but operated in the same way. Beginning with the 1920s, Catholics, Protestants, and Jews committed themselves to dogmas of religious liberty, civil rights, and traditional morality to express limits on majority tyranny and state power.[61] In the earliest stages of the Judeo-Christian consensus, American Catholics and Jews carved out a place for themselves as religious minorities with the help of liberal Protestants with a common commitment to preserving the right of free exercise among religious peoples at home and abroad. During the heyday of the Civil Rights Movement, the Judeo-Christian consensus applied these rights to the specific case of African Americans, whose church leaders invoked a prophetic tradition that challenged white clergy and, for a time, claimed the moral leadership of a nation, black and white. It was precisely when the Judeo-Christian consensus embraced the dogma of popular sovereignty that its members experienced political decline. When the Judeo-Christian consensus became, by attribution, the "moral majority," its religious dogma became indistinguishable from the tendency for democracies to embrace majority tyranny and limitless state power. What many Evangelical and Fundamentalist Christians during the 1980s failed to understand was that this language was fundamentally at odds with the Judeo-Christian consensus itself, since no single congregation ever constituted most Americans.

The fatal blow to the Judeo-Christian consensus was its transformation into the Religious Right. Protestants, Catholics, and Jews are not, theologically speaking, natural friends. To hold them together required a political consensus, but the late twentieth-century secularist challenge forced the Judeo-Christian consensus to decide on whether to preserve its political alliance by direct participation in politics or split up to minister to the unique challenges faced by the terminal decline of liberal Protestantism, the dramatic reforms of the Second Vatican Council among Catholics, and the fractious battles among Jews over Zionism, tradition, and social integration. The fate of churches became tied to the fate of the Judeo-Christian consensus, which was itself tied to the fate of the New Conservative Movement and the Republican Party. Because partisanship and ideology rise and fall, so did the several faiths committed to preserving their influence with direct political participation. Rather than find a new way to speak to all Americans indirectly, the clergy found themselves speaking to a shrinking number of stakeholders, campaign staffers, and elected officials interested less in the Gospel or Torah and more in donations, voter registration, and campaign volunteers.

Selection of Cases

There are other qualified cases for analysis not considered in this book. Instead of Sheen, this book could consider the work of Monsignor John A. Ryan, or "Monsignor New Deal," who tied his work on moral theology to policies such as the living wage and federal public works programs. In the same vein, another candidate could have been Dorothy Day. Day pioneered trade unions as religious and patriotic organizations. A somewhat later example could be Fr. Thomas Merton, OCSO, whose 1948 *The Seven Storey Mountain* appealed to the spiritual lives of Americans of many faiths. Finally, the most obvious alternative would be Fr. John Courtney Murray, SJ. His *We Hold These Truths* and later participation in the Second Vatican Council brought the American conciliarist position into the heart of Catholic social teaching. Why not any of these figures?

Sheen stands out from these examples in several respects. First, his career in apologetics was much longer than Ryan's, and his influence extended into more national issues than Day's. Murray left a great intellectual legacy. *We Hold These Truths* remains a formidable work. However, Sheen's career—begun in the aftermath of the 1928 anti-Catholic rages against Al Smith and his presidential campaign—had generated public sympathy, acceptance, and even conversions. Murray had his influence in largely intellectual and clerical circles, but to shape a national consensus required the broader appeal to national audiences. Sheen exceeded Murray at this objective in every respect; indeed, it was Sheen's job. He was National Director of the Society for the Propagation of the Faith from 1951 until 1965. None of this is to say that Ryan, Day, Merton, and Murray did not contribute to the formation of the Judeo-Christian consensus. It is only to explain the selection of Sheen for this book.

Dr. Martin Luther King Jr. is something of an easier choice. Many black church contemporaries of King's either worked for him or worked with him. King was the only pastor among the "Big Six" African American civil rights leaders of the 1950s and 1960s. The other five—James Farmer, John Lewis, A. Philip Randolph, Roy Wilkins, and Whitney Young—worked as leaders of political pressure groups. Other leaders defined themselves, in many respects, by contrasting themselves with King. Malcolm X, James Baldwin, Ella Baker, Stokely Carmichael—to name a few—each found something in King's traditional black church hierarchy and nonviolent direct action to censure. Of course, leaders like Baldwin and Baker had much to say in their own right, but placing them within the Judeo-Christian consensus would be a category error.

Falwell is perhaps (for once) the least controversial choice, though he emerged at the same time as many other conservative Fundamentalist Christians, including James Dobson and James Robison, as well as the Religious Roundtable founded by Ed McAteer. The reason for choosing Falwell is the same as with Sheen and King; Falwell was the figure with the greatest popular reach and strongest political message. Another figure, Marion "Pat" Robertson, peaked higher in influence with the Christian Coalition of the 1990s than Falwell but only after Falwell had broken the taboo of Fundamentalist and Evangelical Protestant participation in conservative Republican politics. Fundamentalists were "separatists," or rejected national politics as fraught with sinfulness decent Christians had to avoid. Falwell's popular televised sermons directly challenged that prevailing orthodoxy, as did his books—right down to the titles, *America Can Be Saved* and *Listen, America!*

One might notice that the Judeo-Christian consensus contains, presumably, some number of Jews, yet no Jewish leader is the subject for this study. There are a few reasons for this. First, no Jewish leader ever reached the same notoriety and influence of Sheen, King, and Falwell. The two who came closest were Rabbi Joshua Loth Liebman, author of the 1946 book *Peace of Mind*, who tragically died young. The other is the storied Rabbi Abraham Heschel who passionately allied with the Civil Rights Movement. In civil rights, however, Heschel was, like Rabbi Joachim Prinz of the World Jewish Congress, strongly tied to King, and they sought to ground America in the same Beloved Community that King prophesied.[62] Hence, treating Heschel would merely reiterate the study of the more foundational figure in King. Second, American Jews were part of a consensus and, hence, did not require a Jewish leader to lead them. Indeed, Sheen, King, and Falwell each believed himself to be a national moral leader for Jews as much as Christians, while no renowned Jewish leader sought to speak definitively as the leader of the Judeo-Christian consensus. Indeed, one feature of the "Judeo-Christian" consensus was that it tended to be much more "Christian" than "Judeo." Sheen was on good terms with Jews and publicly condemned anti-Semitism.[63] King experienced great support not only from Heschel as well as among American Jews in the South.[64] Falwell, on the other hand, had a compromised claim to leading Jews, though he made efforts to earn Jewish trust.[65] Finally, the relationship of Jews to Protestant hegemony and the Judeo-Christian consensus has its own political development, which is beyond the scope of this book.[66]

Outline of the Book

Chapter 1 illustrates how Sheen defined a political foundation he called "Americanism." As early as the 1930s, Sheen insisted that the Catholic Church provided the true moral leadership to face secular totalitarian ideology, especially as the Soviet Union emerged as an existential threat. The Church also provided the proper moral instruction for citizens and the proper standard for social and economic life. Sheen's opposition to totalitarianism reverses the old anti-Catholic fears of Romish plots against a Protestant republic. Rome was not an enemy but an ally against the true conspirators: the Communist, Fascist, and Nazi conspiracies against religious freedom. Sheen also preached that Americans should view themselves as congregations enjoying religious free exercise with a duty of liberating those who did not. Finally, the chapter explains the three primary ways Sheen made this effort: public conversions, public acts of patriotic piety, and direct political interventions.

Chapter 2 examines King. The first part of the chapter strips away recent efforts to render King's "Beloved Community" a Christian-inflected variety of social democracy. King advocated a federal intervention against state-sponsored racial segregation that would usher in a closer approximation of the Kingdom of God on earth. The Beloved Community depended on *agape*, a conversion of the soul to the good community and nation and ultimately the cross on which all citizens suffered to redeem the sins of Jim Crow and northern segregation. This chapter then examines how King used prophetic language to refound the nation in a pluralistic covenant that obliged elected officials in Congress and the presidency to take immediate action to usher this Beloved Community into the world. Finally, this chapter examines how political officials adopted religious language to show support and justify the legal action they took in response to his pressure.

Chapter 3 moves on to Falwell, one of those who originally opposed King and the Civil Rights Movement more broadly. Falwell grounded this opposition in separation of church and state but reversed his position after the Civil Rights Movement fragmented into more aggressively secular movements that succeeded in separating the church and state in the way that he opposed. This chapter finds in Falwell's political sermons of the late 1970s and 1980s some use of the jeremiad, but his sermons relied much more on the neglected "nehemiad," or narrative of religious perseverance to do the "great work" of religion. Like the biblical Nehemiah, American Protestants, Catholics, and Jews had to rebuild the moral walls that kept the nation safe, but they faced the Sanballat, Tobiah, and Geshem of the secular press, pornographers, and most of all liberal Democrats. Falwell's narrative choice mirrored his political one: he closed off Protestants, Catholics, and Jews as a party who must not "go down to the plains of Ono" and leave the great work unfinished. Instead, to complete the great work required joining the faithful to those in the Republican Party who might otherwise be less interested in the common mission that the Judeo-Christian consensus needed. Finally, the chapter examines Falwell's partial political success, despite the amateur operation of the Moral Majority and the fateful and fatal retrenchment of the Judeo-Christian consensus into a single political party.

This book concludes with an assessment of the Judeo-Christian tradition as a spent force and the rise of ersatz creeds that compete to secure a majority to wield the power of the state against enemies. This outcome Tocqueville anticipated—and feared.

CHAPTER 1

Americanism

Fulton J. Sheen, Catholic Patriotism,
and the Fight Against Totalitarianism

> The tempter approached and said to him, "If you are
> the Son of God, command that these stones become loaves
> of bread."
>
> [Jesus] said in reply, "It is written: 'One does not live by
> bread alone, but by every word that comes forth from the
> mouth of God.'"
>
> —Matthew 4:2–3

In one of his many sermons against totalitarianism, Ven. Fulton J. Sheen offered his audience a choice, pronouncing, "There is no such thing as living without a cross. We are free only to choose between crosses. Will it be the Cross of Christ which redeems us from our sins, or will it be the Double-Cross, the Swastika, the hammer and sickle, the fasces?"[1] The "Double-Cross" referred to more than the images on totalitarian flags. Sheen believed totalitarian ideologies promised an earthly paradise, which every Fascist, Nazi, and Communist party would inevitably betray. However, the only other choice—the cross—was a hard one. The cross dispelled totalitarian dreams in favor of the reality of human fallenness, its need for redemption, and religious liberty to pursue that redemption. For America to choose the cross was only hard at first, he preached, since upon choosing the cross the nation and its citizens would experience the blessing of fulfilling its role in defending religious liberty at home and extending it to repressed nations abroad. According to Sheen, Catholics in the US chose the cross and, by choosing it, affirmed the defense of American religious liberty and their commitment to restoring it to the rest of the world double-crossed by totalitarian ideology. By choosing the cross, Americans also chose their country.

For the first half of the twentieth century, Sheen was one of America's most famous and beloved Catholic priests. Most American Catholics today remember him for his theological instruction, consoling sermons, and his thoughts on the priesthood—as well as for his penetrating stare into the television camera. However, Sheen also had a political mission to persuade America of the dangers posed by totalitarian regimes, as well as to demonstrate American Catholic patriotism in opposing them. He argued that the Catholic Church was the spiritual authority that provided the moral education necessary for guiding Americans of all faiths away from totalitarianism. For this reason, he rejected American exceptionalism, regarding the Church as the "city on the hill" rather than America.

These positions are striking considering American religious history. Since the colonial period, anti-Catholicism was a mainstay of American politics. After the anti-Catholicism provoked by the 1928 candidacy of Democratic presidential candidate Al Smith—a "wet" on Prohibition and a Catholic— Catholic leaders sought to exploit new mass media technologies to improve public opinion of the faith. One of those enlisted was Sheen, who demonstrated Catholic patriotism by appropriating traditionally Protestant anti-Catholic narratives and repurposing them to combat totalitarianism instead. Just as Samuel Morse and Lyman Beecher had warned nineteenth-century Americans about Rome, Sheen railed against an aggressive, tyrannical, foreign power. For Sheen, the threat was not the foreign prince in Rome. On the contrary, the Church was America's best ally against totalitarian ideologies of Fascism, Nazism, and, with the end of the Second World War, Communism in particular. Sheen thereby sought to prove the Catholic commitment to religious liberty in America and abroad by condemning repression of religious liberty in totalitarian nations.

To make this case, Sheen grounded his Catholic patriotism and antitotalitarianism in what he called "Americanism." Americanism defined citizenship in terms of membership in a religious congregation or as people of conscience. Sheen's version began with the observation that America was a liberal democracy, which depended on the people for its legitimacy. For Sheen, no people unaided by religious instruction were sufficiently moral to establish good government, defined above all as one protecting religious liberty. An irreligious people would create a government that they hoped would feed them, no matter the cost to their personal liberties. This kind of government inevitably tyrannized the people. Therefore, the Church preceded the people in importance to found a government. While in the old days, the Church crowned kings, now, as Sheen preached, the Church placed the crown on the people by providing religious education about the priority of spiritual ends to material means as well as the necessary limits and moral obligations of the state.

Americanism Redefined

Peter "Fulton" John Sheen was born in 1895 to an Irish Catholic family in El Paso, Illinois, as the oldest of four boys. He had an older half-sister, Eva Natalie Sheen, born in 1886 to his father, Newton Sheen, a lapsed Catholic, and his first wife, Ida Clara von Buttear, a descendent of German Protestants. Von Buttear died suddenly a few years into the marriage. When Newton Sheen married Fulton's mother, the devout Catholic Delia Fulton, he returned to the Church—at which point the Von Buttear family had Eva removed from the Sheen family to be raised according to her late mother's faith. Early in life, Sheen wanted to become a priest and entered the seminary at St. Viator's College and Seminary, from which he graduated in 1919. He was then ordained a priest and sent to Catholic University of America (CUA), where he received a canon law degree in 1921. With strong backing from some American bishops, Sheen then attended the Catholic University of Louvain, Belgium, where he received a doctorate in 1922 and, in 1925, received the highest academic honor granted at the university: a "Very High Distinction" in the elite "*agrégé* in philosophy." After Louvain, Sheen became an assistant professor of theology and, after a spate of clashes with colleagues, moved into the Philosophy Department in 1931 and then the School of Scholastic Philosophy in 1936.[2] Though Sheen remained a faculty member at CUA until 1950, he spent much of his time away from the university, giving lectures and retreats, and penning both academic and popular publications.

In 1930, the National Council of Catholic Men started *Catholic Hour*, a nationally syndicated radio program, to combat anti-Catholicism stirred up during Al Smith's presidential campaign. Sheen was invited to be one of its chief contributors. Over the next two decades, Sheen also gave public sermons, led mass rallies of American Catholics, and published numerous bestselling books, including *Communism and the Conscience of the West* in 1948 and *Peace of Soul* in 1949.[3] After Sheen's mass media success, Pope Pius XII consecrated him a bishop in 1951 and appointed him to lead the Society for the Propagation of the Faith in the United States. While serving in this capacity, Sheen would also serve as an auxiliary bishop to Cardinal Francis Joseph Spellman of the Archdiocese of New York, the most powerful Church prelate in the United States. Sheen then became the official public face of the Catholic Church in America and led fundraising efforts for missions. The following year, the Dumont Television Network began airing Sheen's program *Life Is Worth Living* (it moved to the American Broadcasting Company in 1955). A surprise hit, the show earned Sheen the Emmy for Best Television Personality in 1953. His national renown and tenacious anti-Communism led to an appearance detailing the "ideological defects of communism" for the House Committee on Un-American Activities and several gatherings with top state and federal officials, including meetings—public and private—with President Dwight D. Eisenhower to discuss the role of American faith in defeating the Soviets and saving the Russian people.[4]

When Sheen first began his career as a priest, he faced populist anti-Catholicism found in the Ku Klux Klan and periodicals such as *The Menace*.[5] Significant parts of the American population regarded American Catholics as moral, physical, and racial inferiors with a slavish devotion to an absolute, arbitrary, and foreign dictator—the pope.[6] They feared the pope would, if he could, tyrannize Americans with forced conversions to Catholicism.[7] Much of this hysteria was grounded in anxiety over the rapidly changing ethnic and economic conditions, but much of it was also grounded in long-held, common beliefs that had once united disparate American Protestant denominations together when little else could. As already discussed, the "Protestant hegemony" treated American democracy as dependent on a consensus of Protestant confessions united in defense of republican liberty.[8] Sheen made efforts to redefine the Protestant consensus to include Catholics and Jews, what became the new "Judeo-Christian consensus." For the old Protestant hegemony, a chief threat to republican liberty was the Holy See, which rejected liberty of conscience with a policy of establishing the Catholic Church as the faith of all sovereign states. With the rise of the Judeo-Christian consensus, however, Sheen preached that Jews and Catholics wanted religious liberty as much as their Protestant neighbors, especially considering the totalitarian repression of the faithful in Europe. Sheen wrote in 1948, "Jews, Protestants, and Catholics alike, and all men of good will are realizing that the world is serving their souls an awful summons" in the fight against Communism. Jews, Protestants, and Catholics "may not be able to meet in the same pew— would to God we could—but we can meet on our *knees*."[9]

Sheen referred to this refounding of religious consensus as "Americanism," which he defined in the following way:

Americanism, as understood by our Founding Fathers, is the political expression of the Catholic doctrine concerning man. Firstly, his rights come from God, and therefore cannot be taken away; secondly, the State exists to preserve them.... The recognition of the inalienable rights of the human person is Americanism, or, to put it another way, an affirmation of the inherent dignity and worth of man.... As a political document, [the Declaration of Independence] affirms what the Gospel affirms as religion: the worth of man. Christ died on a cross for him, and governments are founded on account of him. He is the object of love theologically and politically—the source of rights, inalienable and sacred because when duly protected and safeguarded, he helps in the creation of a kingdom of Caesar which is the stepping-stone to the Kingdom of God.[10]

This definition, offered the year before the United States entered the Second World War, was part of a long tradition of American Catholics finding their place in the American founding.[11] Sheen's position was, like American Catholics before and after him, to find a kind of "accidental Thomism" among the Protestants and Deists who fought the War for Independence. If persuasive, Sheen could credibly claim that American anti-Catholicism was not merely bigoted but contrary to the nation's founding. American Protestants had fought the wrong enemy in the Catholic Church, and now the mutual enemy of American religious peoples was rising in the east. As he said in a 1939 address:

True Americanism means two things—positively, the recognition of the sovereign, inalienable rights of man, and negatively, unqualified opposition to all totalitarian forms—whether they be NAZI, FASCIST, or COMMUNIST—which deny these rights. There is irreconcilable opposition between the regimes of Russia, Germany, and Italy.

Over there, the state is the source of rights; here man is the source of rights. Over there, freedom resides in the collectivity: in the race as in Germany, in the nation as in Italy, and in the class as in Russia; over here, freedom resides in man.[12]

Sheen replaced Protestant hegemony with the Judeo-Christian consensus, and he replaced the old enemy in the Vatican with the new one in totalitarianism; in short, Sheen appropriated old anti-Catholic discourse for Catholic ends.

Two factors enabled Sheen's appropriation of anti-Catholic discourse to argue for its reinterpretation as Americanism. First, many moderate

Protestants experienced genuine alarm at the paranoid, illiberal rhetoric among hardline Protestant preachers and Klansmen. In response, they began an interfaith dialogue that introduced a new concept to Americans: the "Judeo-Christian heritage" that supported the "American way of life."[13] The central idea was an extension of the logic that had once defended disparate Protestants in the nineteenth century—that the differences across denominations mattered less than the similarities. Sheen by no means invented this idea, but he certainly expanded upon it as a rhetorical strategy for legitimating American Catholic citizens and political representatives, as well as making Catholic appeals against totalitarianism. The second factor was the difference between the anti-Catholic fears of "Romish" tyranny and Catholic-led fears of totalitarian tyranny. The difference was that, unlike the anti-Catholic Thomas Nast's fever dreams of alligator-mitered bishops crossing the Atlantic, the fears of Communist suppression of religious liberty were well-grounded in recent events.

One should note that Sheen chose an embattled term for his description of church-state relations. "Americanism" had, at the time, two directly contradictory meanings. For Catholics at the time, "Americanism" referred to the attempt, first made by American priest and founder of the Paulists, Isaac Hecker, to reconcile American liberalism with the Church. One of Hecker's principal admirers in Europe was the French priest Felix Klein, who popularized Hecker's ideas in a controversial effort to reconcile French Catholicism with the Third Republic. Soon after, Americanism became a "phantom heresy" somewhat condemned by Pope Leo XIII in the 1899 encyclical *Testem Benevolentiae Nostrae*. While this chapter cannot describe the intricacies of the dispute, it suffices to say that the Americanism controversy hinged precisely on the issues of church and state relations that Sheen portrays as settled.[14] Many Catholic bishops, including American ones, disputed the very idea that American liberalism and its disestablishmentarianism were compatible with Catholic teaching. Without addressing the controversy, or what was left of it, Sheen strongly endorsed Americanism and then popularized it with his superior Cardinal Francis Spellman, who used the term himself.[15] By 1951, Klein's retrospective on Americanism appeared in an English abridgement in America.[16]

"Americanism" had also been the term for the doctrine of Nativists during the middle of the nineteenth century. Indeed, central to the cause of Nativism was religious liberty understood to mean the absence of the "Romish" threat to Protestant conscience. Early examples from the 1830s include Lyman Beecher's *Plea for the West* and Samuel Morse's *Foreign Conspiracy*, which fed anti-Catholic violence in major cities, such as the 1834 Ursuline Convent riots in Boston and the 1844 Bible riots of Philadelphia.[17] In 1848, Pope Pius IX rejected the formation of an Italian republic, prompting American Protestants to renew their hostility toward all things papist. As the Whig Party collapsed during the early 1850s, one major faction to emerge was the "American Party." An example of its views is found in the 1856 work by Methodist minister James L. Chapman, who published a book dramatizing the battle between "Americanism" and "Romanism." Throughout, he described Catholics as agents of the foreign prince in Rome against whom every true native American fought to preserve republican liberty. In a typical passage, he warned of "foreign-born citizens representing America in distant lands" and "foreigners murdering American citizens" and "foreign legions organized to vote down American-born citizens at the polls."[18] In response, he demanded, "an American party organized to carry out American principles, and in its own way to correct evident abuses in these particulars—let no man complain; it is but Americanism struggling for original principles of policy, and for a wise and just application of them to men and measures" to "check and crush the growing and corrupting power of Romanism in this country."[19] Chapman merely expressed what had become a common ideology within the "Know-Nothing" or "Nativist" Movement that crusaded against Irish Catholic immigrants, though they often included the LDS church as an additional threat.[20]

At first, it is hard to imagine why Sheen would adopt a term tinged with heresy and laden with anti-Catholicism, but "Americanism" was a good fit for Sheen's approach. Sheen identified totalitarian ideologies, most of all Communism, as ideological threats to American religious liberty. These threats required vigilance inspired by commitment to constitutional government supported by a disestablished yet publicly confessed faith. The danger was not the pope but Mussolini, Hitler, and most of all Stalin and his successors. In a 1955 episode of *Life Is Worth Living*, Sheen explained that during the Second World War, when "Russia was praised as 'one of the great democracies of the world,' . . . Communists were worming their way into schools, universities, government, and offices of columnists."[21] The purpose was to use institutions to spread messages of "peace" to dupe the American public. Sheen continued:

The insinuation of Communists into American institutions by peaceful tactics were [sic] merely putting into practice the Communist theory of peace. Communism took over Russia, Stalin explained, by using peace tactics. In *Problems of Leninism*, Stalin said, "We used

the mighty weapon of peace. It created mass sympathy for our revolution, both in the West among the workers and in the East among
oppressed people." . . . Fellow citizens, be not deceived. Remember,
when Russia talks peace, it is a tactic, and a preparation for war. Russia says it wants peace. The peace it wants is a piece of China, a piece
of Hungary, a piece of Poland. A peace overture of Russia will be the
beginning of another Pearl Harbor.[22]

Sheen even told of a close encounter with Soviet espionage, when a Soviet
agent contacted him to spread propaganda for the Soviet Union, ending the
story with the following: "As soon as he left, I called up the F.B.I. and said, 'I
have a Soviet agent who has just visited me, and this is his name. Will you
look up his record?' Half an hour later, the F.B.I. called me up and said, 'Yes,
he is one of their most dangerous agents. We had traced him to Manchuria,
then to China, and then into the Philippines. We did not know he was in the
United States . . . your life could be in danger. Give us his address and tele-
phone number, and we will take over.' "[23] While Sheen approved of coercion,
he preferred persuasion as the better method for stopping Communism.
Sheen used violent language in persuading his listeners and viewers, but the
violence he recommended was against moral and spiritual errors. Sheen's
favorite image for moral persuasion was of the Apostle Peter in the Garden
of Gethsemane. Sheen invoked the version from the Gospel of John[24] as well
as from Matthew.[25] The image of the sword was crucial to Sheen's view that
war resulted from problems of the spirit. Sheen said during the middle of the
Second World War: "Are we in America like Peter? Do we think of our times
solely in terms of war? Do we think of the Nazis and the Japs as being only
our enemies? If so, as Our Lord told Peter, the sword is enough! But suppose
they are only symptoms of evil and sin; then will the sword be enough? No,
we must keep watch and pray."[26] In a book also published during the war,
Sheen preached, "The violence of Christianity is against pride, egotism, self-
ishness, greed, avarices, concupiscence, and hate. The Communist purges his
neighbor; the Christian mortifies himself."[27] Self-mortification purged one of
moral corruption and, thus, introduced the precondition for personal peace.
Sheen told a story to illuminate his point:

This idea can be illustrated by the story of two monks, one of whom
was attempting to explain to the others how quarrels arose in capitalist countries and how purges arose in Soviet Fascist and other Fascist
countries over property. One thumped down a stone and said: "This

stone is mine." The other, full of a spirit of charity said: "All right, take it." The other said, "Oh, no. You must say, 'it is mine'; then we can quarrel about it and have our class conflict." So the second monk said: "It is mine," and the first answered, "All right, take it," and the whole fight ceased because there was charity. Both of them had been so used to using violence against themselves, that they were incapable of using it against their neighbor.[28]

For Sheen, spiritual happiness was only possible when one has forced sin and temptation out of one's life, by using a spiritual sword to cut out vice from one's soul.

Sheen redefined Americanism in terms of a common commitment to religious liberty endangered by a foreign threat. In this sense, he repurposed Americanism for his religious opposition to totalitarianism. That he, and other Catholic leaders like Monsignor John Ryan, did so by linking the old Nativist Americanism to the old Catholic quasi-heretical Americanism was an act of tremendous irony and rhetorical ingenuity.[29] Indeed, in 1949, the American Legion of New York awarded Sheen a gold medal for his "exemplary work on behalf of Americanism."[30]

Americanism and the "Primacy of the Spiritual"

The appropriation of the old Nativist narrative enabled Sheen to explain the American commitment to religious liberty not as fundamentally anti-Catholic but as the defense of conscience against totalitarian persecution. To make that case, Sheen adopted Americanism to promote Catholicism as patriotic and to condemn totalitarian ideology generally and Communism specifically. Americanism had three core principles: (1) that human beings must above all pursue spiritual ends and that these ends only came through religious institutions; (2) that the state existed to protect the pursuit of spiritual ends and the freedom of religious institutions to provide them; and (3) that totalitarian states were the greatest enemies of religious institutions and wished violence against religious people, thereby embodying what Sheen called the "spirit of the anti-Christ."

In Sheen's view, the first task of religious institutions was to provide for the spiritual needs of the people. Much of Sheen's public ministry was on spiritual issues. He preached on traditional Catholic themes, such as the lives of the saints and reverence for the Blessed Virgin Mary, as well as on more general subjects like alcoholism and what books to read. The effect was to display common values among Catholics and other American religious denominations. Throughout these sermons, Sheen specified spiritual happiness as the proper end of human life: "After silence and the reflection that God is the end of all and the only peace and rest for souls, there comes the sudden and certain recognition of the primacy of the spiritual, which is the essence of the true Christian life. The primacy of the spiritual means that there is nothing in the world that really matters except the salvation of our soul, and that in its salvation the spiritual must reign over the temporal, the soul over the body, grace over nature, and God over the world. Religion means this or it means nothing."[31] On his television show *Life Is Worth Living*, Sheen described happiness more ecumenically, although still in strongly Catholic terms: "Our reason tells us that we, if we are to find Life and Truth and Love, must go to a Life that is not mingled with its shadow, death; to a Truth that is not mingled with its shadow, error; and to a Love that is not mingled with its shadow, hate. We must go out to something that is Pure Life, Pure Truth, and Pure Love; that is the definition of God, and the possession of God is happiness."[32]

The second part of Sheen's Americanism was to explain the state's responsibility to protect religious liberty, because such liberty was necessary to live a spiritual life in peace. Christopher Lynch refers to Sheen's metaphor of the medieval city "whose center is a majestic cathedral" to explain Sheen's view. According to Lynch, for Sheen "the cathedral connected the heavens and the earth and became a meeting place for king and bishop, providing legitimacy to civic life."[33] Political authority—the king—found its moral bearings within the church among fellow congregants at the center of civic life. Sheen's concession to American liberalism was to meet with public leaders not in the cathedral but on more ecumenical grounds, such as political rallies or even the White House. Still, the cathedral was, for Sheen, the physical manifestation of the common commitment to spiritual happiness, and it should direct American economics, education, and politics. In the medieval city, political life was the city guard patrolling the walls—that protected the city but was often the farthest from the center. In a modern liberal state, however, institutions could not be arranged as they were within the ideal medieval village. For Sheen, the Church remained necessary for good government, but the Church could only produce good government by means of spiritual instruction rather than direct political control. Sheen explained: "The primary business of religion is God; to bring man to God and God to man. Religion's service to democracy is secondary and indirect; that is, by concentrating on spiritualizing the souls of men, it will diffuse through political society an

increased service of justice and charity rooted in God. . . . The root of democracy is the recognition of the value of a person as a creature of God."[34] A dedication to the spiritual necessarily improved the virtue of citizens and, with it,
the regime itself.

By resting the regime on the spiritual, Americans naturally prioritized
religious liberty. Sheen preached:

> Unlike the beasts of the field, man does not exist for the sake of the
> species, for these individuals die that the species may survive. Rather
> each person is a possessor of a unitary value, which not even the State
> absorbs, for the State exists for man, not man for the State. Man has
> rights anterior to any State, which the State may recognize, but not
> create. The human person and his family, being prior to the State,
> have inalienable rights, such as the maximum of personal liberty and
> economic well-being consonant with the laws of God. Such is the tra-
> ditional concept of the source of rights which is today the essence of
> Catholic social teaching and the basis of Americanism.[35]

As many American Catholic thinkers had before him, Sheen detected in the
Preamble of the Declaration of Independence, specifically in the divine origins of individual rights, a commitment to the Americanism he promoted.
However, this sublime cooperation between the two separate yet comple-
mentary kingdoms of heaven and earth only functioned well when religious
education addressed not just spiritual happiness but how best to understand
political life in light of the primacy of the spiritual:

> It is religious education, whether it be Catholic or Protestant or Jew-
> ish, which is contributing most to the preservation of Americanism,
> for religion and the rights of man go hand in hand. The decline of
> human liberty in the world is in direct ratio with the decline of reli-
> gion. Religion and tyranny grow in indirect ratio. That is why those
> States which are most antireligious, are most antihuman. Nazism and
> Communism know they cannot control man and make him subservi-
> ent either to the race or the class until they strangle the Church which
> says that man has rights independent of any race or any class.[36]

For Sheen, only churches prepared citizens for liberty and the proper role
of the state.[37] Therefore, Sheen's view of church and state was not quite what
Mark S. Massa has described, borrowing from H. Richard Niebuhr, as "Christ

above Culture" or one in which the Church attempted to synthesize religious teaching and cultural practices.[38] Instead, Sheen offered a view that
was "Christ under Culture," meaning that religious education through the
Church was the foundation on which the American social and political edi-
fice rested. Sheen practiced what he preached. He appeared in print, on the
radio, and on the television to bring religious instruction to the people who
then relied on that instruction when selecting their representatives.

The third part of Americanism was opposition to the "spirit of the anti-
Christ." He spoke of it often and in apocalyptic terms. For example, during
the Second World War, he wrote:

> Something is rotten with the world; and that rottenness is so radical
> and universal that it can be explained not by things, but by a spirit—
> the spirit of evil. It is our blindness not to know there is evil, because
> we denied its existence. A man without eyes can be persuaded night
> is day and day is night. So too the modern world which has lost both
> its eyes of faith and its eyes of reason can be made to believe the spirit
> of anti-Christ is not here, for having forgotten Christ, who shall per-
> suade it there is an anti-Christ? . . . Men think that evil must come in
> the disguise of a germ, or a bomb, or a raid, or an explosion, or a train
> wreck, or a bank failure, forgetful that the greatest grief can come to
> man under the disguise of human ideas. It is under the masquerade
> of a progress which denies sin and guilt that anti-Christ parades the
> world today, sits in our lecture rooms, writes in our magazines, struts
> across our stages, promising to redeem man when he has left the
> Cross and penance behind, but only completing man's enslavement
> when it is already too late to free himself.[39]

Sheen regarded the anti-Christ as a spiritual emptiness that possessed totalitarian states when their people wished to abandon spiritual life to live on
bread alone. He described a sharp distinction between spiritual and material ends. For a materialist, evil was the deprivation of the means for enjoying utility—the sick body, the destruction or seizure of goods, or the loss
of money. Sheen believed the proper definition of progress was to improve
the ability to protect and maintain the health of the body as well as access to
goods and money to acquire them, but for Sheen progress required orienting
improved material well-being toward improving human spiritual lives.

The spirit of the anti-Christ redefined progress as strictly material. It
was the orientation of the person or society away from the spiritual ends in

the Church toward the material happiness promised by the marketplace or the state. Sheen supported the sort of liberalism he described as "a philosophy which believes in the progressive achievement of civil, social, political, economic, and religious liberties within the framework of a moral law."[40] However, he opposed liberalism understood as "an attitude which denies all standards extrinsic to man himself, measures freedom as a physical power rather than a moral power and identifies progress by the height of the pile of discarded moral and religious traditions" and "as an ideology generally identified with the doctrine of *laissez faire*."[41] He called the latter two "historical liberalism," which he understood to be the halfway house of descent from Christendom to Communism.[42] His view of totalitarianism was one which began with the Christian concept of the human person. The plural of the human person was the "people" who are the sovereign people named in the Declaration of Independence and the Constitution. Historical liberalism reduced the human person to merely an individual or a human without personality, wherein any individual could substitute for another. Such a distorted view of the human person easily became the Communist concept of the "mass" in which the collection of individuals had superior claim to power than any individual. Sheen explained:

> The danger is that the American people may degenerate into a "mass." They do this when they lose their sense of personal responsibility and, instead of being self-determined, allow *themselves* to be determined . . . , thus becoming slaves to an alien force outside of them. The more people become enslaved to evil habits, the more ready they are to be enslaved to another. Losing a sense of soul . . . , they are capable of being herded like little pigs into a collective pigsty. Reading the same books, the same newspapers, listening to the same slant on world events, they unconsciously become automata, thus losing their inner freedom.[43]

A brutal regime is the natural result of the dehumanization, starting with the devaluation of the human person to a mere individual among a collective.

Sheen regarded totalitarian ideologues with hostility, but he regarded Communism as the greatest of the three threats because it drew directly from the moral weaknesses of liberalism and promised a hideous simulacrum of Christianity. Sheen argued that Communism drew from the spirit of the anti-Christ, but was also a historical consequence of an extended corruption of the Western moral order. Of note is Sheen's refusal to equate Americanism with capitalism—far from it. He criticized laissez-faire capitalism as the origin of the intellectual and material conditions for the rise of Communism:

> The truth of the matter is: Communism is related to our materialistic Western civilization as putrefaction is to disease. Many of the ideas which our bourgeois civilization has sold at retail, communism sells at wholesale; what the Western world has subscribed to in isolated and uncorrelated tidbits, communism has integrated into a complete philosophy of life. . . . Both believe in egotism; our Western civilization believing in individual egotism; communism believing it should be collective. Our Western bourgeois world is un-Christian; Communism is anti-Christian.[44]

The spirit of the anti-Christ began with historical liberalism in the nineteenth century, which meant that Sheen charted the movement of Western opinion away from spiritual happiness to material happiness and the intellectual commitment to privatize religious questions to establish religious tolerance. Sheen believed tolerance was rooted not in a commitment to a peaceful resolution of spiritual questions but rather in the West's choice to get rich and to regard religion as merely an "addendum to life, a pious extra, a morale builder for the individual but of no social relevance, an ambulance that took care of the wrecks of the social order until science reached a point where there would be no more wrecks, and which called on God only as a defender of national ideals, or as a silent partner whose name was used by the firm to give respectability but who had nothing to say about how the business should be run."[45]

The laissez-faire West did not deny the opportunity for citizens so inclined to spend their Saturdays and Sundays at religious services, but it admitted no reasons other than personal preference to demand such attendance. Sheen thought the persistence of religious mores kept the spirit of the anti-Christ at bay, although materialism could quickly wear them away.[46] According to Sheen, few in the nineteenth century achieved wealth; the remaining poor believed in wealth as the path to happiness and became greatly resentful of the rich: "Every Communist is a capitalist without any cash in his pockets. He is the involuntary capitalist—but his heart is just as set on materialities as the economic baron whom he would replace."[47] Sheen did not mock Communists for being bad at capitalism; he condemned both systems as fundamentally dehumanizing. To return the human element to work life in America, Sheen recommended labor directly receive a portion of the profits companies generated, the formation of an "industrial council" in which labor and management would negotiate compensation, and the installation of worship spaces with breaks for religious services to ensure that both labor and management experience their equality under God and the fraternity that came from worshiping together.[48]

Sheen explained Communism as the synthesis of historical liberal errors, achieving an anti-Christian "complete philosophy of life." He explained that Communism "has a theory and a practice; it wishes to be not only a state but a church judging the consciences of men; it is a doctrine of salvation and as such claims the whole man, body and soul, and in this sense is totalitarian."[49] Because Communism was a philosophy of life, Sheen argued that it bore a resemblance to Christianity, but only as the spiritually barren opposite:

> Communism has its Bible, which is Das Kapital of Karl Marx; it has its original sin which is Capitalism; it has its chosen people which is the Classless Class; it has its Messianic hope which is the World Proletariat; it has its sermon on the mount which is its false appeal to the poor and oppressed; it has its monasticism which hid the infiltration of its doctrines through the "cells"; it has its Gospel which is the Gospel of Class War. . . . It persecutes all religions because it claims to be the one true religion and hence can suffer no other; it is the religion of the Kingdom of Earth, the religion which renders to Caesar even the things that are God's; it is the body of the elect; the new Israel; the ape of Christianity in all externals. It differs only in its soul, for its spirit is the spirit of the serpent; it is the Mystical Body of Anti-Christ.[50]

Communism was right that wealth should be used to help those who need it most. However, Communism retained a commitment to wealth as the source of happiness. In fact, Communism used this commitment to claim its legitimacy, because only the Soviets could redistribute wealth in a way to make everyone happy, rather than the laissez-faire elite who had exploited the poor. Yet, because Communism severed itself from any spiritual concern, it lacked any moral position on how to establish the redistribution of wealth. Instead, moral questions became strategic questions—when and how best to use force for creating a Communist state.[51]

Whenever Communists finally seized control of a state, according to Sheen, they exploited the people in the same fashion as capitalists had in a liberal state, but the material and spiritual conditions were always much worse. The Communists in the party did not merely seek to marginalize God to an hour or so on the weekends but to stamp God out of memory, because the Communist state proved inadequate to provide happiness for the people. State violence was not merely the practical attempt to control the people but was primarily an expression of frustration with human limitation. Sheen believed that the misery of the Russian people was a daily reminder to the Communist leaders not just that the revolution failed, not just that Communism failed, but that Party leaders could not become like gods and recreate the world. Sheen saw Soviet violence as primarily a rage against God, thus explaining why the first strike of a revolution was always against the Church. He said of Vladimir Lenin, "Just before the assassination, Julius Caesar compared himself to a god, as Stalin had compared Lenin to God, and later on allowed himself to be deified."[52]

Sheen believed that the United States and the Catholic Church were the two states capable of opposing Communism. He divided the labor between the Church, which provided moral and spiritual guidance, and the United States, which followed it well enough to defend religious liberty in the West. Provided that the United States retained its religious liberty, American citizens would have the religious education necessary for spiritual happiness, thus immunizing Americans from the "bread alone" appeals of Communism. However, that education was not merely about the value of a spiritual life but also about how to protect it on earth. What the Church offered was the moral basis for human freedom from state control over matters of conscience.

Under Church instruction, Americans had to do everything they could to stop Communism, by both coercion and persuasion. Sheen explained the goal this way: "Our country has always had a great mission. In the beginning of our history we were a sanctuary for the oppressed. In our times we became an arsenal for democracy. In the last few years we have been the pantry for the starving world. Each year we send millions of dollars to the distressed and hungry of the world. In the near future, we may be called upon to roll up the curtain of the Eastern world, that is, to give to the East the prosperity, peace, and fraternity with the other nations of the earth which it so ardently desires."[53] Sheen endorsed American use of economic and military power against the Soviets and demanded vigilance against domestic infiltration.

In Communism, America experienced the spirit of the anti-Christ. America could expect to use the sword but should never believe that the sword was enough. Furthermore, because America wielded only the sword, the true power to defeat the anti-Christ was the Church itself—the choice between Christian purification and Communist purges. It came down to the Cross or the Double-Cross. There was no third option.

Catholic Exceptionalism

While Sheen spoke of America's great mission, he resisted any notion that this mission somehow rendered America exceptional. He elevated the Church as the city on a hill and demoted America, to avoid elevating the state as quasi-divine, as the Soviets did. The exceptional nation, for Sheen, was the Holy See, headed by the Bishop of Rome who spoke with apostolic authority on matters of faith and morals and occupied, as a result, the proper place in mediating international affairs.

Jonathan P. Herzog has situated Sheen in the broader anti-Communist rhetoric of the 1950s, with religious leaders like Revs. Billy Graham and Carl McIntire, and the John Birch Society.[54] What holds these figures together is a process of "sacralization," which Herzog contrasts to secularization. Sacralization is the restoration of religious faith to citizens and institutions by way of religious foundations. The logic of sacralization is the following: "Communism is a spiritual threat that weapons alone could not defeat. Secular democracy will fail in defeating the Red scourge, but democracy grounded in a religious foundation will triumph. Religious Americans are immune from Communist infiltration. All major faiths need to unite against a common spiritual enemy. The Soviet Union's greatest fear is not American nuclear attack but American religious revival."[55] Sacralization describes the common traits shared between Sheen and other religious and political leaders during the 1950s, but it does not describe the traits that Sheen did not share with secular, Jewish, and Protestant leaders. Sheen encouraged a common ground for religious opposition to Communism, but he did so on behalf of the Catholic Church.

Sheen used widely shared images and language to make a strongly Catholic appeal to a broad American audience. As Massa explained, "What many media commentators and most non-Catholic viewers took to be ecumenical and nondenominational 'inspirational' chats were actually profoundly Catholic reflections on the cultural state of the American union."[56] Sheen derived his positions from papal encyclicals and grounded them in the neo-Thomism of the early twentieth-century Catholic Church, yet he had a keen ear for developing these arguments in language that ordinary Americans could understand. After all, if Americanism relied on religious education, then much depended on religious authorities to educate the people effectively. Hence, Massa observes, "Dressed up by Sheen in homely metaphors and accessible stories, natural law Thomism . . . sounded amazingly up-beat and fresh."[57]

Also, Herzog's view underestimates the degree to which American Catholics still lacked public respectability. Sheen's plea for an interdenominational alliance was part of a broader effort to bring the Church into the nation and, once there, to bring the nation closer to the Church. Kathleen L. Riley explained Sheen's use of anti-Communism as "essentially ideological, not political. And although this ideology was primarily Catholic and Christian, it was also very American. By speaking out as an American citizen, he assisted the Church in making its adjustment into the mainstream of American life, and facilitated its assimilation."[58] Sheen's tremendous popularity ensured that his effort to repurpose Americanism would succeed, and its success "helped to pave the way for the Catholic Church's greater participation in American life."[59]

Part of that participation was to introduce to Americans the moral and spiritual authority of the institutional Church. This Church taught America its mission; hence, America owed the Church its obedience—and not only America. Sheen did not shy away from asserting the universal authority of the Church for all nations. Indeed, for Sheen, the Church was the true "city on the hill."[60] Sheen's most explicit statement on the exceptional nature of the Church was the following: "The Church therefore is to save the world by being in it, but not of it; it is to be a city set on a hill toward which men may turn their eyes to know the secret of their strength, but it is not the hill. . . . Above all else, it is a fellowship, a spiritual Communism, based not on the laws of society, nor the ties of blood, nor the necessities of economics, but on the re-ordering of the whole field of human relations in a spirit of charity, and a cohesion of shattered and despised mankind under the leadership of Christ."[61] Sheen understood the Church on the hill to be the central institution for rebuilding Europe after the end of the Second World War. He insisted:

When [the Second World War] is over, the Church which will be the only institution to organically survive it, as it has survived all wars in the past, will go to the wounded and bleeding nations and say, "Here, my sons, are the principles of immutable justice, the rejection of which brought you into war." Whether or not the nations will accept those principles as the foundation upon which they will reconstruct a just national order, remains to be seen. But they can be sure of this: if they continue to exile morality and justice in the next postwar generation as they did in the last, they will only prepare for another dirty mess wherein apostate democracies by progressive demoralization will outbid one another in the surrender of the last vestige of Christianity.[62]

Americanism did not include elevating America as the chief spiritual authority in the world. On the contrary, America was as subject to Church authority
as any other nation.

What made America worth praising was its fidelity to Church teaching,
the "immutable principles of justice" that Sheen himself was responsible for
teaching to his audience. Sheen denied that there was any true "freedom
from authority," since any claim of liberation implicitly rested on an authority for liberation; hence, the "real problem is not whether we will accept law
and authority, but rather, which law and authority we will accept."[63] Sheen
argued in favor of the spiritual authority of the Catholic Church and in terms
explicitly opposed to secular and Protestant views of Church authority as
"oppressive" of conscience. In a 1932 parable concerning the Reformation
and Enlightenment, Sheen described an island where children played safely
within the stone walls of the Church, when, "With the dawning of the day of
False Freedom, there came to an island a group of men who argued with the
children in some language such as this: 'Why have you permitted the Church
of Rome to surround you with all her laws and dogmas? . . . Throw off the
obstacles and be free.' "[64] The children complied but found that their freedom
rendered them "afraid to move, afraid to play, afraid to dance, afraid of falling into the sea."[65] In contrast, Sheen described the Church as "Peter's bark"
sailing the seas and, by the grace of God, surviving the "sands of humanism,"
"the depths of determinism," and "the mists of Fundamentalism."[66] Throughout its passage, those on Peter's bark saw those who were not so favored:
"Before her she can see the shipwrecked rafts of Masterless men looking for
the Master Peter who is not for one time but all time."[67] Those aboard Peter's
bark will make a safe passage and arrive at its destination, when "they will
understand why it avoided the snares and pitfalls—because as Peter stood at
the helm of his bark, there rested on his hands the invisible, eternal hands of
Christ, whom the winds and seas obey."[68] Sheen extended this argument in
a 1941 book in which he predicted the betrayal of the Soviets against the rest
of the Allies by appealing to the example of Pope Benedict XV and placing
hope in the certainty that "there is only one thing we do know, and that is, the
one thing which will right the world is the one thing which the world today
believes to be wrong—the risen Christ and His Church!"[69]

In contrast, Sheen demoted the importance of democratic principles.
They were merely an instrument for governing and depended on the moral
and spiritual authority revealed by the Church. Sheen insisted that the
Church was "the only authority that is right, not when the world is right,
but right when the world is wrong. Trust in that religious authority would

reverse the present order and inaugurate a reign where, instead of politics setting limits to morality and religion, morality and religion would begin to set limits to politics."[70] To those who hoped secular democracy might offer a way forward, Sheen responded with strong dissent:

> Too long have men taught that God must serve democracy; it is now time to affirm the contrary. Democracy should serve religion—likewise indirectly, of course, in the sense that it will be obedient to a justice born of God and not of expediency; that it will give equal economic opportunities to all, provide the normal comforts of life, guarantee employment in order that citizens being freed from economic or political injustices will be free to serve their God. Democracy serves religion indirectly by removing those obstacles and disadvantages which stand in the way of man achieving the more glorious liberty of the children of God. . . . In the hour that is dawning the Church must defend democracy not only from those who enslave it from without, but even from those who would betray it from within. And the enemy from within is he who teaches that freedom of speech, habeas corpus, freedom of press, and academic freedom, constitute the essence of democracy. They do not. Given a freedom which is independent of the moral law, independent of inalienable rights as the endowment of the Divine Spirit, America could vote itself out of democracy tomorrow. How can we continue to be free unless we keep the traditions, the grounds, and the roots upon which freedom is founded? We could not call our soul our own unless God exists. Why, we would not even have a soul![71]

The American constitutional tradition was good only because it already rested on the Christian religion. What made a regime truly democratic was the foundation on which the regime rested and the ends to which its citizens used those procedures. The Church set those ends as policies meant to provide the material comforts necessary for free worship. If citizens failed to pursue ends the Church set, they would deny themselves their proper ends and truly democratic government. Were Americans to mistake democratic principles as sufficient, they would soon lose sight of the moral limits God sets on human activity and subsequently rest all power in the majority, which would by then lack religious instruction about the proper ends of government.

By replacing the city on the hill with the Church, Sheen treated American "Providence" as obedience to divine law. Sheen defined knowledge of divine law as the primary instrument for the Christian understanding of history.

Human history was composed of events that resulted from either fidelity or infidelity to divine law. For example, Sheen responded to the common question of how God could allow the horrors of the Second World War by answering that it was "for exactly the same reason God allows us to cut our fingers if we wantonly clutch a razor. Our bleeding fingers are the red witness to our rebellion against the laws of reason, for reason should have told us the razor would cut. Multiply that rebellion against the Divine Reason by millions and you have this war."[72] God had favored the American undertaking only because it had largely been in conformity with God's moral laws.[73] If Americans failed to follow divine law, Providence could be rather an awful thing. Providence, for Sheen, was also the judgment of nations. One of Sheen's most important sermons was "War as Judgment from God," which he preached and published several times over his career. In it, he defined the judgment of nations the same way each time: "To the extent that we obey God's will, we are happy and at peace; to the extent that we freely disobey it, we hurt ourselves—and this consequence we call judgment."[74]

Scholars have treated "judgment of God" as part of the jeremiad, which interpreted negative events as the consequence of Americans' departing from the terms of a special covenant God had made with America, as well as punishment for failing to meet the terms of the covenant.[75] Sheen demurred and offered a Catholic reinterpretation of the "judgment" against the American Protestant jeremiad. Judgment from God came from disobedience of the natural and the moral law: "Judgments are clear in the natural order. For example, a headache is a judgment on my refusal to eat, which is a law of nature. . . . No one who overdrinks wills the headache, but he gets one; no man who sins wills frustration or loneliness of soul, but he feels it. In breaking a law we always suffer certain consequences which we never intended. . . . When calamity comes upon us, as a consequence of our neglect or defiance of God's will, that is what we call the judgment of God."[76] Starvation, hangovers, and bleeding fingers were all consequences of disobeying natural laws, and alienation from God was the consequence of disobeying the moral law. Sheen emphasized individual moral freedom rather than the divine sovereignty central to the jeremiad.[77] Because these laws were everywhere and always the same, the judgment one experienced in America was no different from that in the Soviet Union. America was not bound in a unique bargain with God that explained natural and manmade disasters as divine wrath. Rather, Americans, like all persons, possessed moral freedom they could use to choose either spiritual goods to become happy and virtuous, or material goods at the expense of the spiritual, thus embracing the spirit of the anti-Christ. The consequences for these choices were built into creation.

Sheen regarded submission to the authority of the Church as the height of American patriotism. He knew very well that such a view was a tough sell, but he nonetheless advocated it throughout his career. As Massa concludes, "Sheen remained a committed devotee of Thomistic ultramontanism . . . [and] never wavered in his firm belief that Catholicism provided the best— and very possibly the *only*—answer to the question of human existence." Indeed, one Vatican official referred to Sheen as "our right arm in the U.S."[78]

The Apostle to the Rich and Famous

In 1956, Sheen appeared on the popular variety show *What's My Line* on the Columbia Broadcasting System (CBS). The show featured him as the "mystery celebrity" during a segment when a panel of other celebrities would blindfold themselves and ask questions of the mystery celebrity to determine his or her identity. The host, John Charles Daly, asked Sheen to sign in, which he did after writing "JMJ" on a blackboard, the initials representing the Holy Family of Jesus, Mary, and Joseph. The first panelist and cofounder of Random House, Bennett Cerf, commented that the applause Sheen received was "the most solid round of applause I have heard in a long time." Sheen attempted to conceal his identity by answering questions only in French and with some misdirection, to the point of forcing Daly to interpret for the panelists. For instance, when another panelist, Arlene Francis, asked if Sheen was a famous television personality, Sheen responded, *"Je ne sais pas,"* with Daly intervening to say that, indeed, Sheen was quite famous for appearing on television. However, for his second question, Cerf inquired, "Have you ever participated in the political arena?" to which Sheen responded, *"Non."* Daly did not intervene, and the audience did not respond. Sheen meant what he said, and everyone there believed him. Despite Sheen's efforts, the panelists only took nine questions to determine who he was. As he left the stage, Sheen greeted the panelists, who in addition to Cerf and Francis included David Niven and Dorothy Kilgallen. When Sheen greeted Kilgallen, a Catholic, she took his hand, knelt, and kissed his ring. The appearance was brief and lighthearted.[79]

Sheen's response to the "political arena question" illustrated how he had engaged in moral and religious concerns that directly addressed politics, but he still somehow appeared to his audience as separate from politics itself. By 1956, Sheen was at the apogee of his national popularity. He had high-profile meetings with celebrities, the vice president, the president, and the pope. He was in high demand for speaking engagements and for celebrity weddings. His sermons at St. Patrick's Cathedral in New York City brought in capacity crowds that would spill into the streets. His talks on the *Catholic Hour* provided a mass-media platform to establish common ground with a general American audience. After he ended his radio appearances, he started his television program in 1951, *Life Is Worth Living*, and received multiple awards. The published transcripts of the show had received high praise when reviewed in newspapers. During all events, except perhaps the weddings, Sheen always found a way to condemn Communism, describing how Communists infiltrated American unions, lied about wanting peace to appear more reasonable, and wanted nothing but to seize control of American rights and crush them underfoot. Sheen's efforts were not the result of a personal obsession but direct orders from Pope Pius XII.[80] Indeed, Sheen had condemned Communism for twenty-five years before appearing on *What's My Line*; his condemnation of it was a large part of why Sheen was as famous as he had become. How did no one object when he claimed not to be political?

To answer this question requires an examination of how he positioned himself as a moral and spiritual educator to the general public and elites alike. Sheen had developed strong local followings in New York City and in Washington, DC, as an advocate of Catholic patriotism. Though employed as a professor of philosophy, Sheen spent much of his time giving speeches before Catholic groups and sermons at St. Patrick's Cathedral. During these public events, Sheen preached his anti-Communist message to large audiences, often with Catholic public officials and prominent citizens in the front row. The result was a positive feedback loop. Sheen gained popularity with his increasingly popular sermons, speeches, and radio addresses agitating against Communism and calling for a return to religious commitments that unified America. He would then meet with local groups, politicians, and important people who could affiliate themselves with Sheen's message and appear as patriotic as Sheen did.

As Sheen progressed in this effort, he became one of the Catholic leaders who met in interfaith groups meant to address their common opponent found in totalitarianism. These interfaith efforts attracted even non-Catholic public officials who wanted to address the problem of totalitarianism, one that Sheen had done much to persuade the public was a problem in the first place.

By 1956, Sheen was no longer just a popular Catholic bishop but, according to a Gallup poll, the most respected man in the United States behind only Eisenhower and Sir Winston Churchill.[81] Because of Sheen's popularity, the press reported his sermons and speeches across the country. Public officials would then speak on the matters that Sheen had set as the agenda, and they would side with the position Sheen had outlined. When public figures and politicians made the political statements, Sheen appeared as the spiritual authority of the Church educating the people and public officials, and he sought to represent this position as prepolitical because of the primacy of the spiritual. The benefit was that Sheen did not appear as an agent of the Catholic Church meddling in American politics, as Protestants had traditionally worried.

Moreover, Sheen developed a reputation as a master of conversions. He was credited with the religious instruction and conversion of several prominent figures, such as Henry Ford II (grandson of Henry Ford), member of Congress and later ambassador to Italy Clare Booth Luce, former editor of the *Daily Worker* Louis Budenz, and classical composer Fritz Kreisler. These high-profile conversions demonstrated the rising spiritual power and prestige of the Catholic Church during the first half of the twentieth century and testified to how Sheen's work was primarily religious in nature. The consequence of this network of relationships was Sheen's personification of the Americanism he professed. By becoming the most famous Catholic priest in America, Sheen occupied the place he himself had set for the Church, and the prominent citizens and politicians who kept his company were acting as he prescribed. He used public speeches and mass media to influence the nation's political agenda and policy preferences according to Sheen's Americanism.

Sheen's media strategy was a twentieth-century update to the old anti-Catholic mythology of the 1920s. He demonstrated the common interests of religious liberty for churches and the salutary effects of faith on American citizens and, in turn, their government. He preached that totalitarians, especially Communists, sought to deprive Americans of that religious liberty in order to subjugate church, people, and government to a foreign, absolute arbitrary ruler. Finally, Sheen made every effort to illustrate how Catholics were patriotic, freedom-loving Americans with not merely his sermons and activities but also his conversions and political associations. How he accomplished this while appearing "above politics" was an effort so deft as to fool even scholars, who have commonly treated Sheen as a pea in the pod with the therapeutic Christianity of the 1950s typified by Norman Vincent Peale and Billy Graham.[82]

Mass Media, Antitotalitarianism,
and Catholic Patriotism

Sheen first gained popularity by giving homilies in New York City parishes and speeches to Catholic community groups. During the late 1920s and early 1930s, Sheen frequently traveled to New York City to celebrate Mass at churches like St. Patrick's Cathedral and the Church of the Sacred Heart, during which he delivered strong anti-Communist homilies. As early as 1933, the *New York Times* covered Sheen's homilies and, by 1936, began to mention how these sermons drew crowds.[83] By 1944, churches had to wire loudspeakers for audiences in the streets when the churches were too full, such as when he celebrated a Mass in honor of the 693rd anniversary of the gift of the brown scapular to a monk by the Blessed Mother.[84] The coverage illustrated how the significance of Sheen's sermons was not merely that the Church opposed Communism but that Sheen was the one giving the sermon.

Sheen's popularity became as much of a story as the anti-Communism that had made him popular. The initial reason for his popularity was without a doubt his great talent as a speaker, but his message also appealed to American Catholics. He explained to them how they could see themselves and behave as loyal Americans, while demonstrating to non-Catholics, by his preaching, the importance of Catholic loyalty to America. Much of the anti-Communism Sheen preached in sermons was about the need for sympathy for ordinary Russians and the need to pray for and support the conversion of Communists back to Christianity.[85] The church setting presented Sheen and the Catholics who flocked to him as Americans concerned about the spiritual welfare of the nation and the threat Communism posed to it. Indeed, Sheen's sermons against Communism were often as much against the failures of Christianity and the West for not fostering the necessary spiritual fortitude to resist the encroachment of Communism on the American conscience.[86] In addition to his radio program and homilies, Sheen preached anti-Communism to Catholic professional, educational, and social groups. This setting illustrated how Catholics had integrated into the mainstream of American culture and the workforce. Rather than this integration subverting the American political order, the integration had strengthened it. Sheen's visits with these groups addressed the responsibility these organizations had to furthering the Catholic fight for America against Communism.[87]

These early sermons in diverse settings presented Sheen as the moral instructor to loyal Catholics, whose spiritual and social roles were not just compatible with American practices but the greatest defense against Communism.

Sheen also used strategies other than sermons to demonstrate Catholic opposition to Communism in defense of American liberty. In one of his first mass gatherings, he called on Catholics to boycott the 1939 New York world's fair, saying no American should go "until the American flag is placed above that of communism."[88] Sheen criticized how the Soviet flag appeared higher on the horizon than the American flag, which he portrayed as a slight against America. Sheen's call for boycott became a national story, appearing in the *Chicago Daily Tribune* and *Los Angeles Times*.[89] It is important to note that he called for the boycott before a Catholic organization, the Union County Federation of Holy Name Societies. After Sheen drew attention to the issue of flag height, the *New York Times* covered how other Catholic leaders echoed Sheen's call for boycott. Rev. Dr. Edward Lodge Curran of the International Catholic Truth Society called for a boycott the same day before ten thousand Catholics, and state senator John McNaboe, also Catholic, echoed the call for boycott, calling the higher flight of the Soviet flag "subtle propaganda."[90]

Sheen also criticized antipatriotic sentiments from within American borders. While he was privately no admirer of President Franklin D. Roosevelt, Sheen publicly defended him.[91] In February of 1940, the five-thousand-member American Youth Congress (AYC) attended a speech given by Roosevelt on the White House lawn. During the speech, Roosevelt called the Soviet Union a "dictatorship as absolute as any in the world," then called the New York City Youth Council vote opposing American loans to help Finland "absolute twaddle." At this point, many in the AYC audience booed and hissed at Roosevelt.[92] At a speech before a chapter of the Knights of Columbus, Sheen used the occasion to criticize the AYC, saying, "We have had in the United States the spectacle of youths in Washington booing, [sic] the President of the United States." More important, however, was what Sheen demanded the Knights do in response: "Your duty is to preserve freedom by authority and by creating respect for it. Liberty has become doing as you please. That is not freedom. Freedom is the right to do what you ought to do. 'Oughtness' implies love and authority. And we look to you for the protection of authority."[93] Sheen showed Catholic loyalty to the president, whereas Communist sympathies among other groups made them disloyal. The AYC had increasingly gained a reputation for Communist sympathies, and it made an excellent foil for Sheen to contrast Catholic loyalty.[94]

By far the most dramatic presentations of Catholic loyalty, however, were the massive rallies of the Church leadership before tens of thousands of congregants. In October of 1940, Sheen gave a homily at a Pontifical Mass in the Los Angeles Coliseum before an audience of 110,000. During his sermon,

Sheen prayed for "peace with all classes, Jews, Catholics, and Protestants" while describing the Declaration of Independence as "not a heritage to be spent carelessly" but "an endowment like life itself, which must be purchased anew with every succeeding generation."[95] In 1941, Sheen was a speaker for the Society of the Friendly Sons of St. Patrick, which held a dinner following the St. Patrick's Day parade. Before the parade became a general kitschy celebration of things Irish, it was a demonstration of Irish and Catholic public-spiritedness, and by 1941 turned out an estimated 75,000 people. Sheen was by no means alone as a public figure in attendance; it was a who's who of New York Irish Catholic power in state and federal government, as well as in corporate boards and unions.[96] In 1947, Sheen led a "Blue Revolutionary" alternative to the "Red" May Day celebration at the Sylvan Theater beneath the Washington Monument. Before 25,000 people, he said, "We are the 'Blue Revolutionists' because we trace our origin to the Lady of the Blue," by whom he meant the Blessed Mother.[97] Sheen detailed the persecution of Catholics in Communist-controlled nations and compared those nations to imperial Rome, which had once persecuted the Church. His hope was that Russia would become a great spiritual center just as Rome had become a great spiritual center after persecuting the Church for so long. Sheen held a similar rally in Melbourne, Australia, the following year before 20,000 Catholics.[98]

In May of 1949, Sheen returned to New York City at the Polo Grounds to lead 30,000 Catholics in protest of Communism and the repression of Catholics in Eastern Europe. With him were Vice President Alben W. Barkley as well as Cardinal Spellman and the mayor of New York City, William O'Dwyer. Barkley gave a speech in which he told the audience he had seen the pope three times in eighteen months and was "one of his greatest admirers."[99] Barkley's statement represented the triumph of the Americanism Sheen had sought to establish. Though Protestant, Barkley showed respect for the pope and regarded American Catholics as equals. Catholicism was on the side of American liberty. Barkley continued: "The American trinity of values—life, liberty, and the pursuit of happiness—is being attacked by an ideology and a concept which is the utter negation of these principles. This concept has been imposed by a totalitarian system and is attempting to make inroads on our own democracy. . . . We will do well today as we enjoy our American liberties, to see to it that this wicked, crawling, creeping economic disease, this alien nostrum, shall not be permitted to invade, or get a foothold in the United States of America."[100] The "alien nostrum" was not the Church but Communism. Echoing Barkley, Sheen said at the same event: "There is not one intelligent man in the world today who believes that the state has anything to fear from the Church. Communism cannot be judged by its foreign policy. We have been on record on this from the beginning, and we say that Communism is intrinsically evil. We shall resist it despite all of its tactics and techniques. Russian foreign policy has nothing whatever to do with Communism. To keep our rights, we must keep our God."[101] Barkley and Sheen appeared together in a united front against a new wave of anti-Catholicism. At the time, the clarion call of the anti-Catholic position was Paul Blanshard's *American Freedom and Catholic Power*, published a few months before Barkley and Sheen spoke— in February of 1949.[102] Indeed, Barkley's comment about "aliens" during the 1949 Catholic loyalty parade speech appeared as a direct denial of Catholics as "aliens" in America. Sheen found in Barkley's endorsement the confirmation of Catholic patriotism, not just a common policy goal. In other words, Barkley spoke not merely of a common purpose but a common foundation for pursuing that purpose: Sheen counselled Barkley on Soviet deceit and desire to deprive Americans of their liberty, most of all religious freedom.

The 1949 and subsequent loyalty parades were in part a response to the charge by Blanshard and other anti-Catholics that the Catholic Church sought to seize control of American government to reclaim political control of Western democracies. By June of that same year, Blanshard's book appeared on the *New York Times* best seller list, where it stayed for months.[103] *American Freedom and Catholic Power*, it should be noted, was received well in high places, despite some negative reviews.[104] Poet William Carlos Williams put it on his list of "The Best Books I Read This Year" in 1949.[105] The American Library Association placed it on the "50 Notable Books of 1949."[106] Anti-Catholicism reached its peak over the appointment of an ambassador to the Vatican. In the months before Truman made the appointment, Blanshard led a meeting of high-profile members of the Protestants and Other Americans United for the Separation of Church and State (POAU) to protest the appointment. At that meeting Blanshard explained the similarities between Communism and Catholicism, saying they were "two forms of foreign imperialism that are both animated by their own type of self-interest."[107]

Indeed in October of 1951, Rev. Dr. Edward H. Pruden of First Baptist Church, and pastor to President Henry Truman, complained that he had tried and failed to stop the president from appointing an ambassador to the Vatican, a decision that pushed POAU to call for mass meetings to oppose the move.[108] In the month after Pruden revealed his efforts and the POAU protested, Sheen made several efforts to prove Catholic patriotism. He spoke at St. Patrick's Cathedral defending Catholic patriotism, saying: "If our enemies continue to attack us let them do it in the name of bigotry and intolerance, of atheism and communism, but let them not do it in the name of God or of America. . . . Are Catholics opposed to that First Amendment? Most certainly not. Without any *arrière-pensée* [mental reservation] we accept this First Amendment and the authority of the Government as duly constituted by law."[109] Sheen addressed the ninth annual congress of the Confraternity of Christian Doctrine before a crowd of 23,000 once again to proclaim Catholic loyalty to America. After the speech, choirs sang patriotic hymns and songs and were then followed by a pageant of Catholic actors from DePaul University depicting skits of Catholics serving their country.[110] Sheen attacked the POAU indirectly, saying, "Some of those who profess to be religious would do well not to stir up citizen against citizen, race against race, or religion against religion. If they would only seek to bring Americans to love God instead of accusing their neighbors of disloyalty, our country would be more blessed and prosperous."[111] Blanshard with the POAU and Sheen, both as Spellman's auxiliary bishop and as national director of the Society for Propagation of the Faith, were fighting to see who could cast more suspicion on the other.

In the end, Sheen won. In 1953, a little over a year after the public dispute between the POAU and Sheen, Methodist bishop G. Bromley Oxnam spent ten hours defending his record of connections with Communist elements in America before the House Un-American Activities Committee. Oxnam had been the founding president of POAU and served alongside Blanshard and other, left-leaning anti-Catholic clergy and allies. During the hearing, Oxnam conceded that he was on the Soviet "sucker list" but denied that his record at the POAU had weakened American opposition to Communism with anti-Catholic rhetoric. In response, committee counsel Robert L. Kunzig "immediately confronted Oxnam with an article he wrote during his service as editorial adviser [to *Protestant Digest*], entitled 'Monsignor Sheen and Clerical Fascism.' "[112] Oxnam grew visibly upset when pinned on the subject. A few months before, Sheen had also faced a national audience when he won the Emmy for Best Television Personality.[113]

Religious Conversion, Proxy Participation, and Direct Political Speech

Sheen won not merely by relying on sermons and public displays. After all, sermons could be written off as bluster or something more sinister. Public displays could be understood as a show of force against America, not a show of patriotism. To demonstrate how Catholic participation in Americanism

strengthened it against Communism, Sheen engaged in high-profile conversions and public associations. As already shown, Sheen rubbed elbows
with local Catholic and, as Sheen grew more popular, Protestant and Jewish
leaders who proclaimed the same Americanist principles that he did on the
radio and from the pulpit. First, he used conversions to show how Catholics
were both part of the American elite and proudly patriotic. Sheen converted
lapsed Catholics back to the Church and away from Communist Party activities. Second, Sheen and political elites associated with each other to demonstrate a kind of proxy participation in politics. For Sheen, his association
with political elites revealed the patriotism of American Catholics, and for
the political elites the association affirmed their opposition to totalitarianism
and favorable view of American Catholics. Third, Sheen directly intervened
in some political affairs to speak with spiritual authority.

Conversions

During the 1940s, *Time* magazine featured Sheen as a master converter to the
Catholic Church. The depiction should be no great surprise. The editor-in-
chief of *Time*, Henry Luce, was married to one of Sheen's most famous converts, Clare Boothe Luce.[114] These articles began in 1939, when Sheen was
mentioned as the instructor for journalist Heywood Broun, who was predicted
to "become the U.S. equivalent of a famed British convert—the late Gilbert
Keith Chesterton, stylist, wit, rough-and-tumble fighter for the Faith."[115] The
article showed due respect for Sheen as a public figure for the Church, calling
him "one of the ablest U.S. priests." Broun died of pneumonia several months
after conversion. When covering the funeral for Broun, however, *Time* made
Sheen the story. Before his conversion, Broun had been a staunch progressive and suspected by some of being a Communist. Sheen's funeral oration on
Broun's behalf featured stories directly answering those suspicions, depicting
Broun's conversion as a process of encountering Catholic holy places, people,
and dogma. Sheen reported Broun as saying the following during the conversion process: "I love my fellow man, and particularly, the down and out,
the socially disinherited and the economically dispossessed. . . . I want therefore a religion which has a social aspect. . . . I have never been a Communist
and never will be a Communist. . . . I have very often defended birth control.
But I would not do it now; for I have begun to see a spiritual significance of
birth."[116] As the author pointed out, Sheen's comments were not merely meant
to describe Broun's religious journey, saying the following: "They were probably intended partly as an answer to those Catholics who still viewed Heywood

Broun as an unreconstructed Red, who ought never to have been accepted by the Church. And they were undoubtedly voiced, by one of the nation's most influential Catholics, as the sincerest tribute he could make to a man who had sincerely been his friend."[117]

This coverage of Sheen was typical. Sheen appeared as the minister to the rich, the powerful, and the famous who sought to convert to the Catholic Church. Sheen was positioned well to perform this role. After leaving his post at Catholic University of America in 1950, he lived in New York City, was famous in his own right, and was by all accounts quite talented at consulting with potential converts. He was "thin, hollow-eyed," in person, spoke with "lucid confidence" with language that was "forceful but not bullying" yet also "flamboyant and shameless."[118] In short, Sheen was "the most famed proselytizer of all."[119] Sheen seemed to enjoy unprecedented success in making high-profile conversions, but neither *Time* nor anyone else at the time appreciated how Sheen's conversions were not merely about the confidence and flamboyance of Sheen. They were also about the growing confidence and flamboyance of Catholics showing their patriotism by opposing Communism. Sheen's conversions were illustrations of Catholic strength, of their penetration of the uppermost echelon of American public life.

Another one of Sheen's high-profile conversions was Henry Ford II, the son of Edsel B. Ford and grandson of Henry Ford, founder of the Ford Motor Company. Ford was already a director of the company, and his marriage and conversion to Catholicism received national coverage over a period of weeks. Coverage of Ford's conversion nearly always featured Sheen in the headline, for he as the instructor was as significant as the one who received instruction. The message was not merely that Sheen was an able priest but that he was changing the faith of the nation by changing the faith of its leaders. Sheen not only had the Fords attending a Catholic Mass and wedding, but also important Protestants, Catholics, and Jews: former assistant secretary of the navy Charles Edison, General Motors executive William Knudsen, former New York governor Alfred E. Smith, ambassador to the United Kingdom Joseph P. Kennedy, assistant secretary of the treasury Basil Harris, and Harvey Firestone Jr., who was about to take over Firestone Tire and Rubber Company. These figures (except, perhaps, Smith) were not only closely tied with Roosevelt, but Knudsen and Firestone would both later serve as industrial advisors to the manufacturing effort following the American entrance into the Second World War. Sheen's appearance before these figures to preside over the wedding of one of their own was a coming-of-age for the American Catholic Church, but it was also an illustration of the influence Catholicism wielded among those in power. Moreover, the wedding was not a national scandal but a fairy tale. That the Church was bringing another wealthy capitalist into its fold painted a picture of a thriving faith in America, not a hostile takeover. At the same time Sheen converted Ford, Dorothy Day was leading the Catholic labor movement as an alternative to secular unions who were under suspicion as Communist fronts. This larger picture gave credibility to Sheen's position that the Catholic Church was the only moral institution strong enough to confront Communists who wished America harm.[120]

In 1946, Sheen converted Clare Boothe Luce. At the time, Luce was a Republican member of the House of Representatives, serving the Fourth District of Connecticut. She had already made herself known as an anti-Communist and as progressive on issues of nonwhite immigration, specifically for Indians and Filipinos.[121] Her conversion, however, had caused her to decide not to run for reelection. Originally, when announcing her decision not to run again, she said, "My good and sufficient reasons for this decision will become abundantly clear in time."[122] After her official conversion, she released a statement explaining that her conversion was the cause: "It would be naturally asked at this time if this is related to my decision not to be a candidate for the Senate or the House. Plainly there is a relation. For the question of faith which all Americans must always wish kept out of politics might be injected by a few cynical people into campaigns in our State. Tolerant people of all faiths in our State would not wish to see such a false issue obscure the many important political issues which face our nation today."[123] In other words, Luce saw her Catholicism as the target for anti-Catholic campaigns she wished to avoid imposing on the citizens of Connecticut. Luce's conversion was the reason she chose not to run again, and her decision was news. Luce was one of the most popular and respected women in the United States. Not only was she a member of Congress but she was a member of New York high society, working as an editor for *Vanity Fair* and as a successful playwright. Her condemnation of anti-Catholicism echoed the same message Sheen himself wanted to convey about the salutary influence Catholicism could have if only America would choose it. Luce embodied that salutary influence in her conversion and then, in her refusal to run again, demonstrated the consequences of American failure to embrace the Church. By 1953, no such fears remained. During the year after Sheen won an Emmy for *Life Is Worth Living*, Eisenhower appointed Luce to be the ambassador to Italy, the second American woman to be appointed as ambassador to anywhere.[124]

In addition to Broun, Ford, and Luce, Sheen converted American Communists. By converting Communists to the same Church of the rich and famous,

Sheen was creating a united moral force loyal to America and opposed to Communism. The most important Communist convert had been baptized-Catholic. Louis Budenz was the managing editor for the *Daily Worker*, a daily newspaper run by the Communist Party. In 1938, Budenz had engaged in extended public debates with Sheen over the nature and aims of Communism.[125] Seven years later, Budenz finally decided to return to the Church after such a debate, during which he said "his soul [had] been swept by love and reverence" by a conversation about grace.[126] On the day of his official return to the Church, Budenz said, "I have resigned the managing editorship of the *Daily Worker* and have severed my associations with the communist movement. Communism, I have found, aims to establish a tyranny over the human spirit; it is in unending conflict with religion and true freedom."[127] Immediately after the service at St. Patrick's Cathedral, Sheen evidently brought members of the United States military to debrief Budenz.[128] Newspapers emphasized both Sheen's role as the one who initially pushed Budenz to convert during the 1938 debate and his role as the one who would later instruct Budenz and his family in the faith.[129] Evidently, Sheen and Budenz intended to surprise Budenz's former comrades, as he received Sheen's instruction in secret and announced his conversion and resignation on the same day. When contacted, a spokesperson for the *Daily Worker* was completely surprised and had no comment.[130] Budenz became a professor of economics at the University of Notre Dame and later Fordham University, and for the next fifteen years, he was a primary source and public witness against the Communist Party before committees of United States Congress.[131]

Budenz understood his conversion to Catholicism as also his declaration of patriotism for the United States. The statement Budenz made was covered across the nation in major newspapers, and his consultation with the US military illustrated how he was willing to protect national freedoms against those who would tyrannize America. Sheen was the instrument that transformed revolutionaries into patriots. Budenz was not the only figure to undergo this transformation. In 1948, former Soviet spy Elizabeth Bentley converted to Catholicism under Sheen's instruction. Her conversion was also a secret, and it only became known after attorneys for William Remington could not locate and serve her a suit for libel for calling him a Communist.[132] Bentley became one of the most sensational informants on Soviet spy rings and helped thrust the House Un-American Activities Committee into the limelight during the dawn of the Cold War.[133] Another convert was Bella Dodd, who returned to the Catholic Church in 1952 under Sheen's care. She had been an attorney and representative for the Teachers Union and a member of the Communist Party. One month after she returned to the Church, she attended hearings before the Senate Internal Security Sub-committee to testify about the infiltration of the Communist Party into the Teachers Union and the threat such infiltrations had on American security.[134] Dodd claimed that 1,500 teachers were Communist Party members nation-ally and that the party had infiltrated higher educational institutions.[135] As with Bentley, much of the coverage of Dodd referred to her conversion and Sheen's key role in it. Sheen always stood as the Catholic alibi for American patriotism, as if the way to repent from Communism was to join the Church. Sheen's conversion-to-Congressional-Confession pattern became so promi-nent that labor leader Michael J. Quill left the Communist Party by playing a ruse on his own staff. According to one newspaper article, "Quill knew from his own days of beatific association with the party machine that a large part of the union's clerical staff, including some of the workers in his own office, functioned as a spy network feeding information to the Communist inner circle." To tweak the nose of the party when leaving, "he arranged to have a message left in his absence that Msgr. Fulton J. Sheen had called. This indica-tion that Quill was in league with the man who had induced Louis F. Budenz to abandon the party a short while before was such a moment to the Com-munist wheelhorses in the [Transport Workers Union] that they grabbed their hats and rushed downstairs to the 'Little Kremlin' on Twelfth Street as soon the news was relayed to them."[136] Quill was not one of Sheen's converts, but he nonetheless declared war on Communists (of which he had once been the most radical for almost two decades) by pretending to side with Sheen. Sheen had become such a public anti-Communist, pro-Catholic voice that his last name was synonymous with the betrayal of the party.

Budenz, Bentley, and Dodd were Sheen's Catholic disciples fighting the moral war against Communism, which Sheen declared the most important issue facing America and the rest of the Western world. Indeed, the colorful accounts of these disciples illustrated how real this war was for both sides. It was a war of moral conversions and public declarations of loyalty, whether to the nation or the workers. Throughout the 1940s and early 1950s, Sheen won these battles and instituted in public the Americanism that placed the Church in the moral advisory role for public officials on all levels.

Association with Political Elites

Besides converting the rich and famous or Communists themselves, Sheen also increased his influence in the war against Communism by affiliating with public figures. As Sheen achieved popularity in New York City and across the nation with his radio programs and public addresses, political leaders began to congregate around him. At first, local Catholics associated with Sheen in public events meant to explain Catholic anti-Communism. Both Sheen and Catholic politicians benefited from the appearances. Sheen appeared important and influential by rubbing elbows with politicians, and the politicians appeared religiously devout and publicly patriotic.

The earliest of these politicians was former New York governor and defeated Democratic presidential candidate Al Smith. In large part because of his Catholicism and his position as a "wet," Smith lost his presidential bid against Republican Herbert Hoover, who employed Horace A. Mann from the Republican National Committee to run an anti-Catholic campaign to help boost Hoover to the election (Sheen eventually converted Mann to Catholicism).[137] Reports of contact between Sheen and Smith sometimes depicted the traditionally distant kind between priest and laity.[138] However, the close relationship between Smith and Sheen was made more obvious when Sheen served as Smith's escort to visit the pope at the Vatican. With Sheen and Smith's family were other notable public figures, such as state supreme court justice Edward McGoldrick, former Democratic National Committee chair John J. Raskob, and New York senator Robert F. Wagner.[139] Because Smith was sailing with Sheen, some speculated that the pope had, in fact, summoned Smith—essentially to tell him what to do. As one newspaper reported at the time:

> Mr. Smith, through his representatives, said he was going abroad for a holiday. Although it was true that Cardinal Pacelli, Papal Secretary of State, had invited Mr. Smith to call at the Vatican when he visited this country last Fall, the former Governor's spokesman declared, nothing was said about discussing communism or labor unrest. In Mr. Smith's party will be the Right Rev. Fulton J. Sheen, a leader in the Catholic anti-red movement in this country. Mgr. Sheen . . . is one of the best known speakers and writers of the church. He frequently has denounced the Communist philosophy on ethical and religious grounds.[140]

Sheen served as a companion facilitating the meeting with Pope Pius XI, who said of Smith "that he felt that he had known Mr. Smith all his life as he always had been an admirer of the New York leader and was acquainted with every detail of his career."[141] Sheen introduced Smith when he spoke at a luncheon at which Smith praised the pope and described how he was the first man ever to render the former governor speechless.[142]

In these early associations with Smith, Sheen was not the story. Smith was. However, Sheen helped frame some of the issues surrounding Smith. Though a Democrat, Smith was a sometimes-outspoken critic of Roosevelt and had many, like Raskob, who would have preferred him as president or, at least, that Roosevelt had not won the office.[143] In 1934, Smith joined with conservative Democrats to form the American Liberty League (ALL). In a 1936 speech before ALL, he demanded that Democrats revolt against Roosevelt drawing parallels to Theodore Roosevelt's campaign against William Howard Taft. The speech featured language condemning Socialism and Communism that Smith had evidently lifted directly from "Prodigal Son," Sheen's address to the National Eucharistic Congress.[144] His visit with the pope could have been a way to raise his stock among increasingly active Catholic voters, and his association with Sheen implied that Smith was taking a strong stance against the Soviet Union. Smith's trip to visit with the pope coincided with the high point in Benito Mussolini's reign as Fascist leader of Italy, whose Lateran Treaty and Concordat with the Vatican had, at the time, made Mussolini more palatable among American Catholics. Even so, by the time of the trip, Sheen had already criticized Mussolini, though this fact did not affect his travels.[145]

During a speech a few months following his return from Europe, Smith spoke highly of Mussolini and embraced the changes Il Duce had brought to Italian infrastructure. Ironically, Smith also used the meeting to criticize the New Deal and Roosevelt himself. Sheen gave a speech before Smith and alluded to the anti-Catholicism that Hoover had directed against him and that Smith experienced within the Democratic Party, saying, "He has had occasion for bitterness, but bitterness never entered his heart or his nature nor ever crept on his tongue."[146] Indeed, the whole affair appeared to be promoting Smith as a viable Democratic alternative to Roosevelt by drawing the Catholic vote back to him. Sheen helped give Smith that appeal. Even so, the association raised some alarm at home.[147] Sheen's close relationship with Smith also raised Sheen's stock. As Smith began to recommend anti-Communist policies on the same grounds—even, in the same words—as Sheen, Sheen himself became even more prominent as a Catholic spokesperson. By 1938, Sheen was becoming the story, as Smith's political prospects deflated. The messages in Sheen's public speeches became the focal point of the stories, and Smith's appearance was presented as a way of showing their influence and prominence among those in power. These stories ran with

Sheen's central point in the lead and with the appearance of "lay dignitaries" later in the piece.[148]

The relationship between Smith and Sheen shows the pattern in how Sheen could raise a public figure's profile while raising his own. The same pattern was part of the public relationship between Sheen and then New York City mayor Fiorello LaGuardia. The public relationship started with Sheen serving as a public defender for LaGuardia's Emergency Relief Bureau, which was created to assist those affected by the Great Depression. The charge was that the board was infiltrated by Communists, and Sheen was one among many speakers who participated in LaGuardia's defense. The setting for the event was telling, as LaGuardia confirmed anti-Communism by giving the presentation at an event put on by a Catholic group, the Ozanam Guild annual communion breakfast.[149] In 1938, LaGuardia called upon Sheen to speak out against the repression of religious groups, specifically Jews and Catholics, in Germany, Italy, and the Soviet Union. Also participating in the event were highly placed members of the Roosevelt administration, such as Henry A. Wallace, who was then the secretary of agriculture and would become in 1940 the vice president. LaGuardia's protest rally attracted a massive crowd and was designed to reflect the broad consensus against the repression of religious rights.[150]

Sheen did well enough to earn LaGuardia's appointment to speak on the same subject in 1940 for the New York City world's fair. Unlike in 1939, the Soviet flag was not higher than the American, so Sheen agreed to attend. The subject was the same as LaGuardia's protest a little over a year before—the need for a broad consensus against religious persecution. LaGuardia had built a Temple of Religion in which religious leaders would preach a common message of the compatibility and necessity of religious faith for democracy. In addition to Sheen, the fair featured speeches by Rabbi Louis Wolsey and Rev. Samuel Trexler that also stressed the need for democracy to embrace and respect religious worship. LaGuardia spoke before the guest speakers and added to the interfaith theme by introducing Herbert Lehman, the first Jewish governor of New York, to echo his sentiments and introduce the three members of clergy.[151] The next year, Lehman appeared at a Catholic fundraiser with Sheen to help with the annual push for Catholic Charities.[152]

The politics behind these appearances was the legitimation of loyal Catholic and Jewish voters as constituencies for the Democratic Party. To reach out to these voters, LaGuardia, Lehman, and Wallace appealed to their most prominent leader, and Sheen was the one who could give them rhetorical payment in return—the kind of patriotic Catholicism to which these public figures could nod their heads. To speak with Sheen became a way for political leaders to court the Catholic vote. The year after Lehman spoke to Catholic Charities, 1942, Republican Wendell Willkie spoke at the same event.[153] Willkie, the defeated 1940 Republican nominee for president, perhaps had an eye on the New York governorship when he gave his speech.[154] In 1943, New York governor Thomas Dewey, a Republican, met with Sheen on Abraham Lincoln's birthday to talk about the shortage of farm labor in New York resulting from the war. Though the coverage focused on Sheen both in presentation and in the featured picture of the two together, Dewey kept the interfaith nature of the emerging constituency at play in presidential politics, inviting Bishop Manning and Rabbi Jonah B. Wise to cover Protestant and Jewish voters.[155]

By the end of the Second World War, politicians appeared regularly with Sheen to promote Sheen's position as much as their own. What motivated this shift were Sheen's constant anti-Communism and the rise of tensions between the Soviet Union and the United States following the Second World War. Because of these tensions, Sheen's conversions, and his embodiment of Catholic patriotism, Sheen became the figure to whom politicians looked for bona fides among Catholics across the nation. On St. Patrick's Day in 1946, Secretary of State James F. Byrnes spoke alongside Sheen before an audience of Catholics about the need to maintain a strong military, saying, "Weakness invites aggression and this nation is unafraid and supremely confident of victory in an open and vigorous contest between our ideas of democracy and other political faiths."[156] Former postmaster general and Democratic National Committee chair James A. Farley spoke at a communion breakfast alongside Sheen about the need to demonstrate American moral principles in providing for the starving in postwar Europe. Such an effort would prove a contrast to the Soviets.[157] Filipino representative to the United Nations and brigadier general Carlos P. Romulo insisted America protect against Communist expansion into eastern Asia.[158] When Sheen presided over a 1947 Pan-American Mass at St. Patrick's Cathedral, chief justice of the United States Fred Vinson attended, and Truman sent White House press secretary Charles G. Ross to "represent" the administration.[159] Sheen did not waste the opportunity. During the Mass, Sheen summarized Pope Pius XII's five-point foreign policy plan for uniting the Western Hemisphere under a Catholic effort against Communism.

However, Eisenhower was the president who finally interacted directly with Sheen, inviting him to what was called a "stag party."[160] A month later, Eisenhower met with Sheen again after giving the convocation at graduation ceremonies for Sheen's former employer, Catholic University of America. Eisenhower spoke on a theme that had become a regular one for Sheen, the need to humanize the American perception of the Russian people and separate them from Soviet leaders.[161] Eisenhower invited Sheen to represent Catholics for Eisenhower's own "Back to God" appeal to the nation, which the White House produced and distributed for CBS.[162] In 1958, Eisenhower invited Sheen to speak at the Conference on Foreign Aspects of United States National Security. The conference was put together at Eisenhower's request and featured Sheen alongside former president Truman, Vice President Richard Nixon, former Illinois governor Adlai Stevenson, director of the Central Intelligence Agency Allen Dulles, Secretary of Defense Neil H. McElroy, and Secretary of State John Foster Dulles. In a little over twelve years, Sheen had transcended the provincial world of New York political street fighting and penetrated the uppermost levels of US political power—all the while pushing the same Americanism and never gaining a reputation as a political actor. At the conference, Sheen repeated the same language of the Americanism he had used in the early 1930s: "Our moral duty to aid others is because the earth and the fullness thereof were made by God for all the peoples of the earth, and not for the privileged advantage of a few. The Soviets would have the world believe there is only hunger of the belly. Our great country must recognize that 'not by bread alone doth man live.' "[163]

Direct Political Speech

The most direct political activity in which Sheen engaged was to offer his voice to a coalition of elites to oppose assistance to Communists. Sheen spoke out as a representative of the Church against Communist regimes that directly harmed the Church. The first of these efforts was Sheen's participation in a national Catholic effort to stop American support for Spanish Republicans during the Spanish Civil War. The conflict between Nationalist and Republican Spanish forces created a conflict in America between Catholics who wished to maintain an embargo on both sides and left-leaning Protestants who supported lifting the embargo for the Republicans. One hundred fifty Protestant ministers published their support for the Communists and their dismay at the practices of Fascist-backed forces on October 4, 1937, in an article, "An Open Letter in Reply to Spanish Hierarchy's Recent Views of War."[164] Ten days later, prominent American Catholics decided to increase their number to 175 clergy and laity to answer the Protestant charges and concluded, "The principles for which the Spanish Bishops stand are the principles common to all humanity. They are the principles enunciated by George Washington and the founders of the American Republic and embodied in our democratic laws and institutions."[165] Prominent Catholics like Sheen and Smith signed the letter. Sheen directly challenged Protestants to stand for the Catholics persecuted under Republican-controlled territory:

> In Spain 5,000 churches and chapels have been destroyed, 14,000 of the clergy and 300,000 non-combatant Catholics killed. If this situation should be reversed and in America we had 14,000 members of Protestant churches killed, selected from all denominations, and 21,000 of the Baptist ministers killed which would be a third of them all, as was true in Spain—and in New York they were killing 225 Episcopalians a day . . . and suppose these churches called on us for aid. If we did not help them we would be either knaves or fools, and it would be for God to decide which.[166]

Sheen referred to the Protestant behavior as a "betrayal of the intellectuals," who were "enjoying intellectual slumming . . . more than they were intended to line up against the church, against morality, against all things you and I hold most dear."[167] He mentioned by name the American League Against War and Fascism (ALAWF) and its leaders he called "betrayers," such as two nationally renowned Protestants Dr. John R. Mott of the Young Men's Christian Association (YMCA) and Dr. Harry Emerson Fosdick of Riverside Church in New York City. To respond to the betrayers, Sheen became a founding member of an interfaith organization called the Keep the Spanish Embargo Committee.[168] Sheen spoke at mass meetings the group held, and he had enough of a reputation to receive an invitation to visit Republican-controlled Spain to see the good treatment Catholics were receiving.[169] Sheen issued two conditions for visiting Spain at a Keep the Spanish Embargo Committee mass meeting. First, "that the Red Government does not pay my expenses, since Your Excellency's government paid the honeymoon expenses of an American Congressman to Red Spain he belongs to them body and soul. I prefer to remain both free and American."[170] Sheen's second condition was more gruesome. He said the following: "The second condition is that the invitation be extended by those whom Your Excellency says are enjoying religious liberties. Will you, therefore kindly ask the Bishops of Madrid, Valencia, and Barcelona to have the respective pastors of those cities invite me to their churches? I know where these clergy are, and so do you. The massacred can write no letters; the crucified can never invite; the slain can extend no hand of welcome."[171] Those conditions were not met, and the embargo remained until the end of the war.[172]

Sheen spent the years leading up to and during the Second World War engaging in direct political appeals for religious liberty, yet he kept his reputation as apolitical by grounding his appeals in a patriotic religious faith he portrayed as compatible with broader American aims. He anticipated the Molotov-Ribbentrop Pact and warned of the threat it posed to democracy.[173] Once the pact dissolved and Hitler invaded Russia, Sheen demanded that Roosevelt require the Soviet Union to establish a two-part standard: the installation of democratic elections and the establishment of freedom of religion.[174] Roosevelt's friendliness with the Soviets led Sheen to criticize the policy as hypocritical, "and are we not a bit inconsistent when we say that Hitler, who seized the left side of Poland, is an enemy, while Stalin, who seized the right, is a friend?"[175] The hypocrisy was not in condemning Hitler but giving Stalin an exception, when both had behaved in keeping with antireligious, antidemocratic ideologies.

Even after the United States entered the war allied with the Soviets, Sheen continued to denounce the relationship, equating Stalin and Hitler as both totalitarians who rejected God and, as a result, repressed human rights including religious liberty.[176] He equated the naïve trust in the Soviet promise not to expand their empire with the naïve trust in the Japanese that preceded Pearl Harbor, a point he continued to press after the war's conclusion.[177] When a Soviet state-run newspaper in 1944 accused Pope Pius XII of being pro-Fascist, Sheen interpreted the event as vindicating Catholic anti-Communism, pointing to how the Soviets could not coexist with the Church, since the latter was inherently a threat to Communist control. Sheen responded with the following: "From now on, we may expect the development of soviet Russia's policy to work out in two directions. First, we may expect a separate peace with the German army after the overthrow of Hitler. Second, we may expect an alliance between communism and naziism for the communization of Europe. The charge against the Vatican was no great surprise. Everyone who knows soviet Russia knew it was coming."[178] Newspapers across the United States covered Sheen's responses as the war of words was fought. Sheen used New Deal language to condemn the Russians, saying, "Now that Stalin attacks one of the four freedoms, we make use of the fifth freedom—the right to say thanks for showing us the serpent beneath the flower."[179]

In the early days of the Cold War, Sheen demanded an aggressive stance against Soviet expansion by highlighting the threats of infiltration of institutions at home and the ongoing persecution of priests abroad. In 1946, Sheen informed members of the Catholic Institute of the Press that "within the past week in one of the congressional committee's meetings a full-fledged

[Communist] agent was picked up."[180] Later announcements stressed that the man Sheen meant, Harold H. Buckles, was not an official Communist spy, though he was involved in exposing how Congress investigated "subversive activities."[181]

In 1949, Sheen also praised Cardinal Jozsef Mindszenty of Hungary for his "dry martyrdom" against Communist Hungary, which tortured him to give a false confession then set up for a show trial.[182] The event was a worldwide scandal that Sheen used to explain how Stalin was fighting a war with the Church in the newly acquired Soviet satellite states. Sheen said during a 1949 Lenten Mass at St. Patrick's Cathedral, "Stalin believes in the primacy of Peter far more than a few who think they have the faith and many who are outside ... he does not believe in it with charity, but he recognizes that it is the only free moral authority left in the world." Sheen added that the Catholic Church had opposed "fascism, nazism and communism when we in America believed only two were wrong."[183] The Mindszenty controversy served as Sheen's "I told you so" to the nation and became Sheen's path into accounting for the torture of Catholics in Communist nations in East Asia.[184] Sheen demonstrated that the war between Communism and the Catholic Church had real casualties for Catholics in Soviet nations. The implication in Sheen's comparison was that Americans had to oppose Communism to avoid suffering the same fate as Poland, in which religious peoples of all kinds were put to death. The pattern of Communist attacks on the clergy Sheen had condemned since the Spanish Civil War presented American Catholics as partisans for religious liberty and willing to die for religious liberty. Indeed, the contrast of Catholics dying in Communist nations was Sheen's way of shaming public officials soft on Communism, pointing out how the costs of American strategic alliances were paid in Catholic blood.

Conclusion

Sheen lived well past the height of his career, and these years were unhappy ones. By 1957, Sheen had reached the pinnacle of his influence. In addition to his rising place in the American Church hierarchy, Sheen had won an Emmy, achieved international admiration, and met regularly with the most famous and most powerful people in America. However, he remained subordinate to Spellman, and Sheen held Spellman in contempt. When in 1938 Pope Pius XII appointed Spellman archbishop of New York, Sheen complained to friend and Church historian Fr. John Tracy Ellis, saying, "It is incredible. It is

incredible. He has nothing."[185] Sheen's opinion did not change, though Spellman either did not know or did not care for as long as Sheen could be subject
to his control. In 1955, however, Sheen began to resist Spellman's authority.
Spellman requested that Sheen provide funds from the Society to pay for an
expanded effort for Catholic missionaries to distribute supplies to war-torn
parts of the world. Sheen refused. Furious, Spellman tried to bypass Sheen
through a direct appeal to the Vatican to secure the funds, but he failed. In
1957, the American government donated free of charge surplus powdered
milk to Spellman for the Church to distribute in its relief efforts. Spellman
sent the powdered milk to Sheen at the Society but then requested that
Sheen pay Spellman for the cash value of the powdered milk. Again, Sheen
refused. This time, Spellman took the matter directly to Pope Pius XII, who
was friends with both men. The pope sided with Sheen, and Spellman promised to seek revenge, pronouncing, "I will get even with you. It may take six
months or ten years, but everyone will know what you're like."[186]

Spellman spent a decade tormenting Sheen until Spellman's death in 1967.
By the end of 1957, Sheen began to recede from regular speaking engagements and walked away from *Life Is Worth Living*. He was persona non grata
in the New York Archdiocese, though he continued to make appearances to
raise Society funds. Despite his travails at home, Sheen was active during the
Second Vatican Council, making the greatest impact in the meetings of the
Commission of Missions. Between meetings, he recorded another television
series, *Quo Vadis America?* that failed to generate interest. After the end of
the Second Vatican Council in 1965, Sheen resumed his Society duties but
longed to return to television. The following year, he began *The Fulton Sheen
Show* in full color episodes but with none of the old charisma and discipline
that made Sheen famous in previous decades. The show was soon cancelled.

Pope Paul VI appointed Sheen bishop of Rochester in 1966, which Thomas
Reeves observes was "the revenge that Spellman had promised all those years
ago."[187] The move to Rochester was an unhappy time for Sheen. It began with
his public condemnation of American involvement in the Vietnam conflict.
He struggled to implement the reforms of the Second Vatican Council and
greatly displeased Rochester clergy and laity when attempting to donate an
old church building to the federal government. Sheen retired from his position at Rochester fewer than three years after accepting it. After giving away
much of his large library, he moved back to a small apartment in New York
City but resumed his role a speaker for another decade despite declining
health. By then, he had soured on the American implementation of the Second Vatican reforms, especially what he regarded as below average English

translations of the Mass and the loosening standards among priests and religious. In October of 1979, a frail Sheen met Pope John Paul II at St. Patrick's Cathedral. When the two met, Sheen fell to his knees, and the pope lifted him back up and embraced Sheen, telling him that he had "written and spoken well of the Lord Jesus" and that he "was a loyal son of the Church."[188] A few weeks later, on the day after the Feast of the Immaculate Conception, Sheen died before the Blessed Sacrament in his apartment chapel.

CHAPTER 2

The Beloved Community

Martin Luther King Jr., Civil Disobedience, and the Second Great Emancipation

[Pilate] went back into the praetorium and said to Jesus, "Where are you from?"

Jesus did not answer him. So Pilate said to him, "Do you not speak to me? Do you not know that I have power to release you and I have power to crucify you?"

Jesus answered [him], "You would have no power over me if it had not already been given from above."

—John 19:10–11

What makes the Reverend Martin Luther King Jr. different from the other civil rights leaders of his day? Why is King the one who ended up with a national holiday? Certainly, he was a successful activist for racial integration, but what elevates King above all the others is his comprehensive vision for racial reconciliation and his willingness to make the necessary sacrifices that he preached Americans of all races had to make. Specifically, King articulated a religious foundation he called the "Beloved Community." The Beloved Community was not merely a catchy slogan or a "glittering generality"; it was a theological concept reinterpreted as a national calling. King used the Beloved Community to redefine American citizenship in a way that called on all Americans—black and white—to make the individual sacrifices needed to ensure racial justice on a national scale. Moreover,

King's Beloved Community gave many the courage—and a concrete plan—to do so.

To that end, King drew on his theological training to find a common value he could offer the nation, and that value was *agape*, the sacrificial love of Jesus dying on the cross for the sins of humanity. *Agape*, King argued, was a religious value shared among denominations and an acceptable basis for human law even among religious skeptics. In politics, *agape* linked citizens in a network of mutual responsibilities to serve the needs of the community over personal interests. In contrast, segregation prevented individuals from meeting these obligations.

White Americans protected unearned racial privilege out of an irrational fear or hatred that African Americans had to confront with nonviolent direct action. Nonviolent direct action was, for King, an expression of sacrificial love for all Americans by African Americans. White Americans, on the other hand, had to relinquish their hatred and reconcile with themselves, their fellow Americans, and most of all the God of love who made such reconciliation possible. If white Americans did so, they would, under the leadership of the church, usher in the Beloved Community nearly (always nearly) achieving the Kingdom of God on earth.

The Beloved Community was a curious kind of covenant. It had few links to the Reformed tradition that had brought covenant theology to America. King called for no confession of faith, did not directly invoke Scripture as the authority for laws, and clearly had no use for the idea of an "elect." However, King preserved a covenant model of personal responsibility to community and God, as well as a sense of the church as the moral and spiritual center that denotes these responsibilities and opens individuals to grace. King still spoke of the "Kingdom of God" as the church generally, but it was separate from the Beloved Community. That separation, King believed, would slowly shrink as love worked its way through the hearts of individual Americans who then found in their daily lives the need to sacrifice their personal interests for the sake of the broader community.

King partially embraced the Social Gospel eschatology of "postmillennialism," which taught that humankind, through the church, could produce sufficient social change to usher in a new period of history prophesied in the biblical book of Revelation. This period was the millennial reign of Jesus Christ. King was enough of a Niebuhrian realist to reject the idea that humanity could usher in the Kingdom of God, but he also believed the church could ever more closely approximate it through personal and social reforms. King believed in the progressive moral character of humankind both in his reinterpretation of the Protestant covenant and in his strategy in persuading the public of it.[1]

In King's view, all political authority depended on moral authority grounded in love, and moral authority began with experiencing God as love. The church, the nascent Kingdom of God on earth, mediated God's authority. It provided spiritual nourishment and moral teaching, but King also insisted that the church had a prophetic role. Specifically, the church had to bring the state into conformity with the Beloved Community as much as possible by bearing prophetic witness to injustice. The corollary to this was that the state had political authority only as far as it obeyed the moral authority of the church.

Contemporary scholarship on King has attempted to fit him and the Beloved Community into a broader tradition of covenant theology and, alternately, into secular democratic theory. However, these scholars have too often demonstrated greater attention to covenant traditions or secular democracy than to King or his thoughts on the Beloved Community. Thus, they have distorted King's body of work to fit it more easily into their areas of study. Specifically, Barbara Allen, by way of Daniel J. Elazar, interprets King as a participant in a broader tradition of Anglo-American covenant theology stemming from the ancient Israelites of the Hebrew Scriptures to contemporary state constitutions, but the comparison depends on ignoring King's extensive departures from traditional covenant theology.[2] These departures come from his education in Boston personalism. Personalism provided the basis for King's understanding of the Beloved Community as a covenant of the heart, one that depends on personal revelation and conformity to God's love.

Yet, contrary to what Danielle Allen and George Shulman have argued, this alternative covenant was not an endorsement of secular democracy.[3] King elevated Jesus as "Lord and Master" over all nations, including the United States. The Lord and Master demonstrated authority by making the ultimate loving sacrifice, a personal yet divine *agape*, on the cross at Calvary. Therefore, King denied that democratic regimes could be sources of their own authority; only divine law had such force. Indeed, King appealed to divine law as an authority over white supremacist subversion of democratic procedures. He placed loving sacrifice, the cross, at the center of his Beloved Community and demanded political authority rest on it as much as personal or social life. Consequently, democratic politics could not be secular. It had to conform to divine law mediated by the church as expressed in what he called the "Hebraic-Christian tradition."

The Beloved Community Defined

Michael King Jr. was born to Rev. Michael King Sr. and Alberta Williams King in 1929. He was the middle child between Christine King Farris and Alfred Daniel "A. D." King. After the elder Michael King went on a pilgrimage to Germany, he changed his name to Martin Luther King Sr. and his son's name to Martin Luther King Jr. Martin Luther King Sr. was the pastor at Ebenezer Baptist Church in Atlanta, Georgia, from 1931 until 1975. Four years before taking over as pastor, he had served as co-pastor to Rev. Adam Daniel Williams, a former slave, whose daughter Alberta he would marry in 1926. Martin Luther King Jr. attended segregated schools in Atlanta and took an early admission to Morehouse College in 1944. After graduating in 1948, he attended Crozer Theological Seminary, receiving a BDiv in 1951. King continued his education at Boston University and completed his dissertation in 1955. Before completing his dissertation, King became pastor of Dexter Avenue Baptist Church in Montgomery, Alabama. The previous pastor, Rev. Vernon Johns, had agitated against segregation in the South, and church elders sought a calmer pastor who might be easier to control.[4] When Rosa Parks initiated the 1955 bus boycott, however, church leaders quickly appointed King the leader of the organization leading the boycott, the Montgomery Improvement Association (MIA). After the success of the boycott a year later, King transformed the MIA into the Southern Christian Leadership Conference (SCLC) to bring the Beloved Community to other cities the way the African American community had in Montgomery.

The Beloved Community was King's model relationship among citizens, community, and God. He deployed the term specifically in opposition to violent resistance against white supremacy. Under no circumstances did King accept violence as an appropriate response to white supremacy, since it could never usher in true peace. Instead, he insisted on organized, nonviolent resistance, explaining that "noncooperation and boycotts are not ends themselves; they are merely means to awaken a sense of moral shame in the opponent. The end is redemption and reconciliation. The aftermath of nonviolence is the creation of the beloved community, while the aftermath of violence is tragic bitterness."[5] This particular construction appears in multiple places in King's work, although he elsewhere placed emphasis on provoking the conscience of the opposition and on the dangers of succumbing to a violent response.[6] In fact, his description of the Beloved Community changed little after the Watts riots, in response to which King said, "Violence, even in self-defense, creates more problems than it solves. Only a refusal to hate or kill can put an end to the chain of violence in the world and lead us toward a community where men can live together without fear. Our goal is to create a beloved community, and this will require a qualitative change in our souls as well as a quantitative change in our lives."[7] Redemption and reconciliation—the changes "in our souls"—were on an individual as well as national and even global scale. King preached that the Beloved Community meant "the salvation of our nation and the salvation of mankind."[8]

The love in "Beloved" concerned both "our privilege and our obligation" to end segregation, and the Beloved Community involved a hierarchy of privileges and obligations.[9] Individuals sacrificed their personal needs for the sake of elevating the broader interests of the community and, in so doing, brought the nation and world ever closer to racial redemption by increasing the love Americans shared with one another. Because God was *agape*, the divine emerged in individuals through their sacrifices for others, yielding an ever-greater divine presence in the world and, with it, a greater opportunity for reconciliation. *Agape* yielded not only individual conversion but, when combined with other loving individuals, a communal redemption. As these communities came together in *agape*, so would nations and the world. Hence, King spoke of a "genuine revolution of values" and a "worldwide fellowship that lifts neighborly concern beyond one's tribe, race, class, and nation . . . for an all-embracing and unconditional love for all men."[10] He saw this as a common thread of religious faith best expressed in 1 John 4:7–21, which includes the passage, "Let us love one another, for God is love."

The Beloved Community was a covenant. Its structure of hierarchical privilege and obligation was consistent with the structure of the Protestant covenant explained by H. Richard Niebuhr. While King never studied Niebuhr's academic work on the covenant, he expressed an implicit covenant theology that Niebuhr best approximates. King needed to redefine the individual and nation in the moral universe to justify the scale and nature of the political change he preached, and Niebuhr's hierarchy of values best approximates King's redefintion. Niebuhr's account illustrated that the Protestant covenant shapes the mutual obligations among individuals, the community, and God. Such an understanding went beyond self-interest or a persuasive narrative of recent events; it explained the meaning of the individual and nation in the moral universe. Niebuhr understood the covenant as a hierarchy of human and divine relationships that he described as the "microcosmic, mesocosmic, and macrocosmic views" or, in more accessible terms, "their psychology, sociology, and metaphysics."[11] To legislate rightly required that the law correlate to the covenant made with God. Americans were God's creation before they were Americans, meaning they owed their allegiance to the state only as far as the state conformed to the covenant. God's domain encroached on every aspect of life and demanded obedience to God more than anything else and always. Human freedom meant successfully meeting the terms of the covenant.

According to Niebuhr's conception of the covenant, God reigned with eternal and rational laws. Human beings could discern these laws with their reason. These laws were not merely natural laws of gravity or geometry, such as the number of degrees in a triangle. They were also moral laws: "To be sure man was a rational being; he was a being with many interests; he was a happiness seeker; but above all his distinguishing characteristic was moral. As a moral man he was a being who could be trusted or ought to be trustworthy because he had given his word, pledged himself to be faithful to the cause and the fellow-servants of the cause."[12] According to Niebuhr, the basis for citizenship was the human capacity to make and keep promises. The covenant was a type of promise, the kind one made to God and to a community to meet one's obligations to both. Covenants, therefore, differed profoundly from legal contracts. Contracts rested on terms rooted in mutual gain for all parties and the specific rights of signers to that gain. Under a covenant, signers found equality not in their shared enjoyment of rights but in their equal promise to meet the demands God placed on them to serve the community.[13]

For Niebuhr the community existed as a unit—what St. Paul called, in the Epistles of the Christian Scriptures, the "Body of Christ"—wherein the value of each part was equal in its contribution, forming the body of which Jesus Christ was the head.[14] What bound the parts together was a shared sense of responsibility derived from a common Christian faith. The political expression of the Body of Christ was the "Kingdom of God," which in America included three elements: belief in the covenant, requiring faith in God as author of creation; belief that God redeemed humankind with the crucifixion of his Son; and belief that this intervention introduced the church as the means for spreading news of the intervention and the possibility of redemption through grace.[15] The Kingdom of God established the legitimacy and limits for secular government.[16]

Niebuhr argued that the American covenant provided the religious basis for understanding social problems. It attested to the community's failure to adhere to God's moral laws and the need for positive actions to redeem not only individuals but society as well. For Niebuhr, the Bible revealed to Americans how events in history provided humankind salvation from sin. Salvation required learning and applying the moral law revealed in Scripture.

God set the moral law to govern how humans ought to treat each other, and failure to follow that law would lead to violence. Violence was the natural consequence of disobeying the moral law, a moral consequence sewn into the fabric of creation. To preserve the community, therefore, individuals had to agree to a covenant that cohered with the moral law revealed in the Bible or they would suffer violence.

Although the American covenant contained the conceptual schema that King needed to argue that racial injustice mattered to all Americans, it had also developed serious deficiencies by the mid-twentieth century. As Niebuhr explained, by the early twentieth century, the cycle of making and remaking covenants had become a depleted moral force for a religious foundation.[17] The cycle had, over time, emptied Protestantism of its spiritual verve and its dogmatic purpose. The church had become a cultural figurehead indifferently baptizing all the affairs of its congregants. By departing from the traditional Protestant origins of the covenant, however, King reinterpreted it in a way to appeal to Americans beyond the traditional Protestant audience.[18]

The Beloved Community as an Ecumenical Covenant

King had two impediments to making such an appeal. First, he was a Southern preacher in a black Protestant denomination, but he sought a national following in a nation composed of several faiths. Furthermore, covenant theology was broadly Protestant, and what it shared with Jewish covenant theology did not necessarily entail a corresponding appreciation among Jews for Protestant covenant theology. Second, he was himself an African American man, subject to systemic racial prejudice. To compensate, King redeployed Protestant themes commonly held across racial and denominational lines. He also represented himself as theologically superior in the application of these themes to pressing political issues by preaching the covenant foundation for racial justice, while white ministers either avoided or actively opposed it. When he had persuaded enough of his audience, King's racial status moved from a liability to a benefit, because he understood firsthand the consequences of racial injustice but nonetheless sought peaceful reconciliation for the entire nation. By persuading his audience that he was on God's side, King could undermine the racial privilege of white ministers.

King's use of ecumenical religious language was reflected in his speeches, writings, and even his sermons. He spoke of God and Jesus, of course, but in a way that united disparate faiths. When experiencing the suffering that came with death threats to his family during the Montgomery Bus Boycott, for example, he called on God for grace: "At that moment I experienced the presence of the Divine as I had never experienced Him before. It seemed as though I could hear the quiet assurance of an inner voice saying: 'Stand up for righteousness, stand up for truth; and God will be at your side forever.' Almost at once my fears began to go. My uncertainty disappeared. I was ready to face anything."[19] In this broadly published account, meant for a general audience, King was judicious in his use of theological language. He used the term "Divine" and, later in this account, appealed to a general message to love one's enemies in the face of adversity. In contrast, King's published sermons appealed to a much stronger sense of Protestant Christianity. Yet even in these sermons, King decried traditional divisions that served only to hobble the true purpose of the church. Writing an imagined letter from St. Paul to 1960s America, King said, "Such narrow sectarianism destroys the unity of the Body of Christ. God is neither Baptist, Methodist, Presbyterian, nor Episcopalian. God transcends our denominations. If you are to be true witnesses for Christ, you must come to know this, America."[20] His call for an end to racial injustice was meant to fulfill and redeem the nation's religious and constitutional obligations.[21]

King embraced the Hebraic-Christian heritage as the shared basis for a national, ecumenical, racially integrated appeal. King used references to the Hebraic-Christian heritage to assure his audience of God's role atop the hierarchy of the covenant, saying: "Let us not despair. Let us realize that as we struggle for justice and freedom, we have cosmic companionship. This is the long faith of the Hebraic-Christian tradition: that God is not some Aristotelian 'unmoved mover' who merely contemplates upon Himself. He is not merely a self-knowing God, but an other-loving God forever working through history for the establishment of his kingdom."[22] In another context, King observed that the best parts of American constitutionalism stemmed directly from the American Hebraic-Christian heritage. In a 1962 speech before the New York State Civil War Centennial Commission, King preached before Governor Nelson Rockefeller and Cardinal Francis Spellman: "In the final analysis, racial injustice must be uprooted from American society, because it is morally wrong. It must be uprooted because it stands against all of the noble precepts of our Hebraic-Christian heritage. . . . The Declaration of Independence and the Emancipation Proclamation deserve to live in sacred honor; many generations of Americans suffered, bled and died, confident that those who followed them would preserve the purity of our ideals."[23] Ending racial injustice required preserving American ideals shared across denominations. King presented himself as a prophet whose clear vision of the Hebraic-Christian heritage gave him the authority—over and above Rockefeller's and Spellman's—to call for a religious revival for moral and political reform.[24]

Driving King's ecumenism was the fact that many white Americans would dismiss his ideas simply because he was an African American. In response, King had to keep his rhetoric as open and accepting of all religious faiths as possible. Even as King would sometimes appeal to the Hebraic-Christian heritage, he would also impose no denominational commitments (outside those required by *agape*) on those who supported his movement. As shown below, he was happy enough with individuals finding, through nonviolent direct action, faith in a loving God who was personally interested in Americans achieving racial redemption.

Departures of the Beloved Community
from the Covenant Tradition

This chapter is not the first to argue that King's Beloved Community has a covenant foundation. Barbara Allen also makes this case, arguing that King's view of covenant theology stems from three sources.[25] The first is the broader covenant tradition handed down to America through a combination of Reformed Christianity and English constitutional theory. For this, she draws from the work of Daniel J. Elazar. Second, she attributes King's covenant theology to his schooling, especially among the personalists in the doctoral program at Boston University, where King received his PhD.[26] Finally, she rests King's covenant theology on his correspondence with John H. Herriford, who strengthened King's religious arguments against segregation with those from political science.[27] With respect to King's correspondence with Herriford, one cannot doubt the impression this University of Minnesota student's letter made; however, King's personalism requires him to redefine the covenant in a way that significantly departs from the Reformed tradition.

Unlike Niebuhr, Elazar is predominantly concerned with covenants as political agreements to establish a government. He describes them as "a matrix, a group of equal cells framed by common institutions" with a founding that "comes about because equal individuals or individual entities join together through a covenant or political compact as equals to unite and establish governing institutions without sacrificing their respective integrities."[28] Barbara Allen echoes Elazar by describing how, in covenants, "agreement establishes enduring relationships that cannot be exited unilaterally.

Parties cannot simply discard their relationship; those who desert their commitments are absent, but still obligated, and those who have been abandoned are, nevertheless, obligated to receive the returning prodigal—at least until the covenant can be dissolved mutually."[29] Elazar contrasts the covenant with "hierarchical" polities that are "generally founded by conquest in some form . . . and are organized as power pyramids more or less in the manner of military formations" with a ruler who sits "at the apex of the pyramid commanding those below, who are organized into 'levels' of authority and power, each level subordinate to the one above it."[30] The covenant tradition, according to Allen's reading of Elazar, stems from ancient Israel, where God made direct promises to the patriarchs and, as with the Exodus covenant, Israel made promises in return. God and Israel—through a patriarch or prophet—wrote these promises down and promulgated them among the people with the understanding that they would prosper if everyone kept the promise made to God. There was no question that God would keep the covenant.

The Reformed tradition reinterpreted Jewish covenants considering Christian Scripture and in opposition to traditional Catholic theology. Reformed communities required members to compose and proclaim their commitment to the covenant.[31] While the communities would write the covenants themselves—since they were the ones individually consenting to form the community—they did so with close attention to the Bible as the basis for the principles and rules the covenant enumerated. Secular covenants included the founding documents of British colonies in America, some of which were directly informed by Reformed theology and others more by English constitutional theory (which was itself influenced by Reformed covenant theology). These documents and their subsequent replacements are, for Allen, the remnants of a diminished and still diminishing covenant theology that Elazar hoped his work would help recover.[32]

Allen is right to celebrate Elazar's scholarship but errs in applying it to King. Personalism does not square with the kind of covenant theology Elazar sees as continuous over millennia. In addition, personalism did not draw directly from the covenant tradition Elazar traced. Indeed, King rarely used the word "covenant," and when he did it was to describe what was wrong with precisely the kind of covenant that Elazar examined. During his doctoral studies King learned personalism from L. Harold DeWolf and Edgar S. Brightman at Boston University.[33] It no surprise, then, that King would so diverge from Reformed concepts of covenant, as personalism was a liberal Christian theology emerging from predominantly American Methodists. Even so, King had his own view of personalism. As Patrick Parr has documented, even during his earliest divinity education, King took issue with the problem of evil in personalism while a student at Crozer Theological Seminary. Parr describes the personalism King learned at Crozer as, "there is God, or the Supreme Personality, a parental figure who invisibly invests human beings with favor factors [Spirit, Mind, Will, and] the most vital of which are Love and Reason. Possessing these factors, then, connects us to the Supreme Personality. Simply by being human, we are fundamentally tied to God."[34] When reviewing King's student work on the subject, he notes that King disapproved of how poorly he thought personalism reckoned with the problem of evil. This problem drove King to debate with one of King's favorite Crozer professors, Kenneth "Snuffy" Smith, the merits of political activism recommended by Walter Rauschenbusch against the realism of Reinhold Niebuhr.[35] The problem of evil would remain one of the most important themes to King's ministry and civil rights activism.

King's covenant is one repurposed with personalist theology. Among King's papers from his theological training is a note card interpreting Jeremiah 31:33. On it, King wrote that the new covenant was "written in the heart, rather than on an external stone."[36] The covenant did not begin with writing down laws for the people, as it had with Moses at Sinai and Bulliger in Switzerland. Rather, King's covenant began with conversion and only afterwards adopted the laws God required humankind to suffer to continue in loving sacrifice. King certainly believed in divine law, but he thought a person first experienced God in personal loving actions.[37] Exposure to love turned a person's heart toward the source of the love, or God, and with such a turn came a subsequent understanding and acceptance of the divine law grounded in God's love. According to King's Beloved Community, the covenant did not begin with the consent of individuals, as Elazar described. King believed that a covenant began with a personal relationship with God, one in which God stood atop a hierarchy as a conqueror not of humankind but of sin and death on behalf of humankind.

King referred to Jesus as "our Lord and Master" because Jesus had borne the cross, and through that sacrifice achieved human salvation.[38] Americans, as individual persons and as a covenanted people, had to follow the same path. In the sermon "Transformed Nonconformist," King said, "Christianity has always insisted that the cross we bear precedes the crown we wear."[39] Divine suffering and divine authority were directly linked. If Americans were to govern themselves—to wear the crown as the Lord and Master does—they also had to suffer the crosses of desegregation. The covenant model

Allen describes simply does not fit with King's blending of covenant with the inverted hierarchy of Christianity's "first shall be last; last shall be first."[40] Allen presumes that individuals are capable of freely signing onto a covenant, but King believed that no person could ever avoid it, because it was universal, and that each person had to experience a personal conversion that drove him or her to embrace the covenant.[41]

The Reformed tradition required a confession of faith as a covenant of the individual to the community and of both to God, but King demanded no such confession for belonging to the Beloved Community.[42] Being a personalist, King preached the "covenant of the heart" from Jeremiah 33:31 as an emergent phenomenon rooted in the redemptive power of love. In other words, unlike the Reformed tradition, King believed the covenant was a consequence of loving action rather than a cause.[43] For King, human persons could choose what God had intended for them to choose, making them both free to choose God and destined to live a life embracing God's love. As with Niebuhr, King believed in a "thus-and-so-ness" of God's love as law, but with a strong emphasis on personal freedom to make choosing love possible.[44] "Freedom" meant moral freedom, oriented toward choosing God's love and ordered toward this love. Therefore, King prioritized liberating human beings from social injustice as well as personal sin to make choosing God's plan possible, or, given the right conditions, even likely.

What was the source of suffering? King saw it as individual and institutional failures in love, and the only way to redeem individuals and institutions was to make suffering "redemptive." Redemptive suffering depended on restoring love within individuals and institutions. Hence, the Beloved Community rested American politics on the human capacity to sacrifice willingly individual interests for the sake of others, the broader community, and their commitment to a personal God. Drawing from Harry Emerson Fosdick and the personalists, King defined "love" as *agape*, sacrificial love.[45] He preached: "*Agape* is understanding, creative, redemptive, good will to all men. It is an overflowing love which seeks nothing in return. Theologians would say that it is the love of God operating in the human heart. So that when one rises to love on this level, he ... rises to the point of loving the person who does an evil deed while hating the deed that the person does. I think this is what Jesus meant when he said 'love your enemies.'"[46] King intended for *agape* to define the religious foundation of the American nation—and, ultimately, of every nation.[47] He applied *agape* to the individual and social levels in the first definition, but extended it to lay the only legitimate foundation for "all the world," saying:

Love is the most durable power in the world. This creative force, so beautifully exemplified in the life of our Christ, is the most potent instrument available in mankind's quest for peace and security. . . . The great military leaders of the past have gone, and their empires have crumbled and burned to ashes. But the empire of Jesus, built solidly and majestically on the foundation of love, is still growing. It started with a small group of dedicated men, who, through the inspiration of their Lord, were able to shake the hinges from the gates of the Roman Empire, and carry the Gospel into all of the world.[48]

In performing acts of *agape*, Americans would serve as citizens in the "empire of Jesus" started in the early church. Notably, that empire of Jesus did not stop at American borders; the empire was the church, not the state.

A "foundation of love" established moral equality in the capacity for individuals to sacrifice their interests for the interests of others and the community at large, and to reunite themselves with God.[49] Refusal to love was to elevate oneself above the needs of the community, thus putting the good of the community at risk for the gain of one mere individual.[50] To motivate reluctant individuals required an appeal to a good beyond the individual and rooted in the community, such as the end of racism. *Agape* would also give Americans the capacity to find meaning in suffering the sacrifices needed to end racial injustice, because the result of individual acts of personal sacrifice for the community would be personal salvation. King testified to the experience: "As my sufferings mounted I soon realized that there were two ways that I could respond to my situation: either react with bitterness or seek to transform the suffering into a creative force. I decided to follow the latter course. . . . If only to save myself from bitterness, I have attempted to see my personal ordeals as an opportunity to transform myself and heal the people involved in the tragic situation which now obtains. I have lived these last few years with the conviction that unearned suffering is redemptive."[51] The redemption that suffering brought King was both personal and social. However, it only came when the suffering was part of the effort to expand love as a force for personal and social reform.

Redemption, for King, started with spiritual conversion. *Agape* was the defining feature of God as revealed in the Christian Scriptures and, as such, was the moral law that governed human affairs.[52] In this respect, King understood God as affirming a constant law open to human understanding but requiring a spiritual conversion to follow.[53] *Agape* called persons to sacrifice narrow self-interest to liberate other persons from social injustice and personal sin. Personal sacrifice generated its own saving momentum that introduced persons to a social world composed of individuals freely serving each other in loving devotion to God.⁵⁴ *Agape* was the proper response to the divine essence human beings shared with each other when creating a community of free and equal persons flourishing materially and spiritually.

Once a person, through love, formed these bonds, only then could the Beloved Community have political significance.⁵⁵ King believed that to act with *agape* was to suffer. Suffering out of love redeemed individuals by bringing them closer to God. Over time, suffering could even redeem those who caused the suffering. For King, this redemption was for white supremacists who violated the covenant with an ideology of hatred. Nonviolent demonstrations revealed white supremacy to the public, yet also revealed to white supremacists the error of their ways. Much depended on the demonstrators.⁵⁶ They had to protest with love for those who persecuted them, hence King's extensive efforts to train activists and to respect those who thought they could not suffer persecution nonviolently.

King demanded demonstrators sign pledges confirming their commitment to nonviolent direct action in service to ushering in the Beloved Community. It is in these pledges that King implemented his covenant foundation in love, but demonstrators signed these pledges only after enduring rigorous moral and spiritual development.⁵⁷ They were the vanguard of "the marvelous new militancy" that must make "the pledge that we shall always march ahead" because "we can never be satisfied as long as the Negro is the victim of the unspeakable horrors of police brutality" among other injustices.⁵⁸ The pledges were personal constitutions, covenants of the heart, which would then spread the message of God's love to the segregationists, who needed it as badly as the segregated. Once the segregationists repented and served, however imperfectly at first, their fellow persons in loving sacrifice to the broader community, they would themselves develop personal constitutions. After signing covenants of the heart, nonviolent demonstrators then sought to change political covenants by demanding moral reform of white racists and political reform of segregation laws.

Good laws, those conforming to divine law, were an effect and not a cause of the Beloved Community. They were an outward expression of an inward conversion toward God's love. Once persons lovingly served each other and their community, they could then pass just laws. These laws were grants for coercive state power to preserve the public good, but they were also declarations of community respect for persons. This latter purpose was just as important to King as the more conventional purpose of laws, because this recognition freed individuals from a sense of racial shame or "bitterness" such as the kind he feared his own children were developing.[59] Laws also promulgated ideas of individual and community obligation to each other, hence King's simultaneous respect for and frustration with the failings of the American founders and Abraham Lincoln. King interpreted the "American Dream" as one of free and equal citizens united in love, and the founders— King most frequently invoked Jefferson—were imperfect examples, because of their inability to end slavery.[60] The American Constitution, by King's reading, rested on the Hebraic-Christian heritage that empowered persons to love one another and rest that love in their laws. Americans, however, had done this imperfectly thus far on matters of race. Hence, King referred to the Constitution as a "promissory note," a check that civil rights activists were going to "cash" to ensure that all citizens obtained "the riches of freedom and the security of justice."[61] Before every improvement in the Constitution, Americans had suffered, as they suffered for civil rights during his time.[62]

In the nonviolent pledges, King's covenant model was on full display. Individuals, as persons, had obligations to themselves, their communities, and to God; yet these obligations were written on the human heart rather than in the Westminster Confession of Faith or the Plymouth Compact. For this reason, Elazar's work, as Allen uses it, is not as illuminating as Allen hopes, since Elazar's understanding of covenant follows the continuities across ancient Jewish covenant theology through its permutations in Christianity and into the development of American political covenants. King's covenant theology operates mostly outside of those continuities, because, with its emphasis on personal conversion and the Passion, it is most discontinuous with the covenant's Jewish origins and its secularization after the founding.

Agape and Racial Reconciliation

Recent political theorists have sought to filter out King's strong Christian assumptions about covenants and subsequently regard his position as a "theistic" option for democratic thought on race in America. George Shulman has attempted to demote the importance of King's reliance on revealed authority to prioritize King's commitment to democratic norms. His effort relies on the position taken by Danielle S. Allen. In *Talking to Strangers*, Allen identifies democratic citizens as individuals who form a covenant. Democratic citizens agree to a definition of the good and sacrifice their individual priorities to this higher, democratic consensus of the good. In so doing, democratic citizens preserve democracy, wherein the people are sovereign, and earn respect and honor among their fellow citizens for doing so. The product of a constant unfolding of individual sacrifice is friendship among equals, a "brotherhood" wherein citizens regard each other as sisters and brothers.[63]

Leaving aside the merit of the theory itself, Allen is wrong to think King could support it. For white Southerners, a century of white supremacy had relied on its own peculiar ideas of democratic citizenship, personal sacrifice, and respect—for each other and to the violent exclusion of African Americans. The entire mythology of the Dunning School treated white citizens as a suffering race whose sons gave their final measure to defend the sovereignty of the Southern states only to suffer defeat and, afterwards, humiliation at the hands of their conquerors.[64] Only through the political exertion of racist historians, Democratic bosses, and the rhetorical flair of those like Joel Chandler Harris, had white Southerners constructed a white supremacist regime they deceptively re-described in democratic language, and they policed that regime with lethal efficiency.

It is no wonder, then, that at the center of King's covenant was not a celebration of democracy, since democracy could be either good or bad. King also did not celebrate Aristotelian "friendship" as Allen describes it. Indeed, King celebrated divine monarchy and dismissed friendship, at least friendship on its own. King was no fan of human kings, but he was a preacher in the church, or the Kingdom of God. God, for King, was a king—the king over all creation. His law was love, and that love set the terms of the covenant. These terms were not up for democratic debate, nor would King want them to be, since divine law both sanctioned democratic debate and forbade the violence and hatred white supremacists embraced. God demanded equal dignity and respect under the law, and white supremacists had to suffer the end of segregation to create a more just regime. Hence, King said in "Loving Your Enemies," that "Democracy is the greatest form of government to my mind that man has ever conceived, but the weakness is that we never practiced it."[65] The practice of democracy rested on *agape*, which was utterly lacking in the mythology of Southern white supremacist regimes.

"Loving Your Enemies" reflected on the Sermon on the Mount, specifically Matthew 5:43–45. The final line of the biblical passage King quoted explains why he regarded friendship as secondary to *agape*, "that ye may be the children of your Father which is in heaven."[66] The reason for the demotion of friendship came from the very Sermon on the Mount from which King preaches, which says shortly after the passage King quoted, "And if ye salute your brethren only, what do ye more than others? do not even the publicans so?" (5:47).

In other words, friendship without *agape* drew a boundary between friend and enemy. King understood that white supremacists were his enemies, but God demanded that King and his church love their enemies. A love for white supremacists that was grounded in friendship alone was impossible.

King referred to friendship as *philia*, as "a sort of intimate affection between personal friends" or a "reciprocal love . . . [in which] you like a person because that person likes you."[67] The white supremacists declared themselves enemies to those seeking racial redemption. The only alternative was *agape*, the love Jesus revealed on the cross. To convert enemies into friends required sacrifice of individual goods, as Danielle Allen surmises, but only according to the divine " 'oughtness' that forever confronts us."[68] King identified the "oughtness" as " 'the image of God,' " within an enemy, and "no matter what he does . . . there is an element of goodness that he can never slough off."[69] Sacrifice, for King, must conform to the covenant God set for humankind, and its purpose was to redeem enemies who had violated that covenant. King's enemies were capable of friendship among themselves, but they premised that friendship on a moral evil. Their capacity for friendship, however, illustrated that the image of God was within them. The loving sacrifice of King and his demonstrators could provoke the consciences of white Southerners, but the love of loving sacrifice was not friendship.

For King, *agape* was the only love one could have for enemies, but the sacrifice grounded in *agape* produced love between friends and enemies. On a personal scale, King believed love could create a new sense of dignity found in shared responsibility. On a national scale, however, King also believed love could create the Kingdom of God by restoring and fulfilling the covenant. In a nation where all citizens acted with *agape*, citizens would share with each other the responsibility of giving freely from their possessions, as King imagined the early church doing.[70] The church was the Body of Christ and the "empire of Jesus" separate from the secular world. A national commitment to *agape*, however, would fully install the church as the American conscience.[71] The reunion, for King, would be the final realization of the Kingdom of God on earth that would contain and preserve Beloved Communities equally subject to God as equal citizens. The church was the primary institution for ushering in this change, and King understood "church" to mean Catholic and even Jewish as well as Protestant congregations. The church, in short, was the moral force behind establishing the Beloved Community, but the church, with God at its head, was not democratic. As Richard Lischer has observed, the phrase "Kingdom of God" denotes the church as explicitly nondemocratic.[72] Church authority rests in Christ the King, crowned in thorns.

For King, the church was separate from the state in an institutional capacity, but the state depended on the church to serve as its conscience and thereby ensure that only moral laws govern citizens. He explained:

> The church must be reminded that it is not the master or the servant of the state, but rather the conscience of the state. It must be the guide and the critic of the state, and never its tool. If the church does not recapture its prophetic zeal, it will become an irrelevant social club without moral or spiritual authority. If the church does not participate actively in the struggle for peace and for economic and racial justice, it will forfeit the loyalty of millions and cause men everywhere to say that it has atrophied its will. But if the church will free itself from the shackles of a deadening status quo, and, recovering its great historic mission, will speak and act fearlessly and insistently in terms of justice and peace, it will enkindle the imagination of mankind and fire the souls of men, imbuing them with a glowing and ardent love for truth, justice, and peace. Men far and near will know the church as a great fellowship of love that provides light and bread for lonely travelers at midnight.[73]

The separation of church and state separated individual citizens into two worlds, one of conscience and one of politics, or, as King put it, "Every true Christian is a citizen of two worlds, the world of time and the world of eternity."[74] Yet, the possibility of greater harmony between the two worlds was on the horizon. To realize this potential harmony, however, required the church to cease its "immoral and unethical" practices, emerge from "behind stained-glass windows," and stop preaching "racial exclusiveness."[75] King called the church to "recapture the Gospel glow of early Christians" whose sacrifices "put an end to such barbaric evils as infanticide and bloody gladiatorial contests" and "captured the Roman Empire for Jesus Christ."[76] As Lewis V. Baldwin has explained, "the theological vision of the Kingdom of God and the ethical goal of the Beloved Community were synonymous, for both 'expressed an optimism about the future of society and historical progress.'"[77]

A morally revived church would begin founding anew the Kingdom of God in America, but King insisted that the coming of that kingdom was contingent on the efforts of nonviolence:

> True peace is not merely the absence of tension, but it is the presence of justice and brotherhood. I think this is what Jesus meant when he said, "I come not to bring peace but a sword." Now Jesus didn't mean

he came to start war, to bring a physical sword, and he didn't mean, I come not to bring positive peace. But I think what Jesus was saying in substance was this, that I come not to bring an old negative peace, which makes for stagnant passivity and deadening complacency, I come to bring something different, and whenever I come, a conflict is precipitated, between the old and the new, whenever I come a struggle takes place between the forces of light and the forces of darkness. I come not to bring a negative peace, but a positive peace, which is brotherhood, which is justice, which is the Kingdom of God.

... This movement is a revolt against a negative peace and a struggle to bring into being a positive peace, which makes for true brotherhood, true integration, true person-to-person relationships.[78]

One should notice that "true brotherhood" is friendship, but it is "true" because of its conformity to the Gospel. The "brotherhood" of democratic citizens presupposed, for King, the "fatherhood" of God mentioned in the Sermon on the Mount.[79] The home for this brotherhood, ultimately, was the church or "the Kingdom of God." King tied the ecumenical Body of Christ metaphor to *agape*, saying, "The cross is the eternal expression of the length to which God will go to restore broken community. The resurrection is a symbol of God's triumph over all the forces that seek to block community," and, therefore, the *agape* found in Jesus was "a recognition of the fact that all life is interrelated. All humanity is involved in a single process, and all men are brothers. To the degree that I harm my brother, no matter what he is doing to me, to that extent I am harming myself."[80] King regarded the church as the primary institution for promoting brotherhood or, in Danielle Allen's language, the place for "talking to strangers" who become brothers and sisters in the church. King's expectations for the church were bound up in concrete experience as a pastor and a pastor's son; Baldwin explains how the church was a "second home" for King since it was a place for "not just local autonomy and freedom but also of church conferences, family reunions, and communal feasts—experiences animated by a lot of touching, hugging, storytelling, laughter, holy kissing, and the sharing of handshakes."[81]

However, King conceded that his movement even included those wrestling with traditional notions of God as well as those of other faiths, suggesting that even those outside the Hebraic-Christian tradition could find the capacity to serve with *agape*. Those ambivalent about organized religion formed the outermost edge of the Beloved Community. At this edge were the limits of King's macroscopic view of the covenant, a view in which even an agnostic could discover the personal redemption that was so critical to the redemption of the nation. King admitted that there would be "devout believers in nonviolence who find it difficult to believe in a personal God," yet even these men and women, to engage in nonviolent direct action, had to have faith in a "creative force that works for universal wholeness."[82] Such efforts exemplified how King had to recalibrate his theological appeals in the Hebraic-Christian milieu but always with an eye toward religious conversion.[83]

King sought to use *agape* as a common value that could bridge several religious denominations to support desegregation and civil rights more broadly. He strove to illustrate ways in which figures from all religious backgrounds demonstrated the kinds of sacrifice he demanded from white and African Americans. Not coincidentally, these figures included "extremists" who struggled against the complacency of existing institutions. King grouped these figures when defending his "extremism" against the white clergy of Birmingham: "The question is not whether we will be extremists but what kind of extremists will we be. Will we be extremists for hate or will we be extremists for love? Will we be extremists for the preservation of injustice—or will we be extremists for the cause of justice?"[84] King integrated the purposes of American political figures with those of religious prophets, indicating how politicians should find the nation's moral purpose in the covenant that King preached. He embraced the charge of extremism as a way of aligning himself with the prophetic traditions among the religious groups to whom he wrote his letters, namely Catholics, Jews, and Protestants. Catholics likely did not care much for King's appeal to Martin Luther or John Bunyan. Jews, naturally, likely did not care for the comparisons with Jesus and later Christian figures. However, what all could appreciate was King's appeal to the spirit of *agape* that motivated the prophets from the several different denominations. That spirit of sacrifice, for King, was what the heterodox Lincoln and Jefferson both embraced, although both, as King considered elsewhere, did so imperfectly.[85]

To establish the Beloved Community, King had not only to persuade white Americans to support an end to racial injustice, but he also had to persuade African Americans to resist all temptation toward violence. For the latter purpose, *agape* proved equally useful. King did not hesitate to compare Elijah Muhammad's Nation of Islam to the Ku Klux Klan, for example, because the Nation came perilously close to advocating that African Americans use violence to secure civil rights in the same manner the KKK already used violence to preserve white supremacy.[86] In his "Letter from a Birmingham Jail" King wrote:

I started thinking about the fact that I stand in the middle of two opposing forces in the Negro community. One is a force of complacency made up of Negroes who, as a result of long years of oppression, have been so completely drained of self-respect and a sense of "somebodiness" that they have adjusted to segregation, and, of a few Negroes in the middle class who, because of a degree of academic and economic security, and because at points they profit by segregation, have unconsciously become insensitive to the problems of the masses. The other force is one of bitterness and hatred, and comes perilously close to advocating violence. It is expressed in various black nationalist groups that are springing up over the nation, the largest and best known being Elijah Muhammad's Muslim movement. This movement is nourished by the contemporary frustration over the continued existence of racial discrimination. It is made up of people who have lost faith in America, who have absolutely repudiated Christianity, and who have concluded that the white man is an incurable "devil."[87]

King linked faith in America with Hebraic-Christian faith, echoing his concern over how American youth are "utterly disgusted" with the church. He contrasted Muhammad and his Nation of Islam with the "seventy-two-year-old woman of Montgomery, Alabama, who rose up with a sense of dignity and with her people decided not to ride the segregated buses, and responded to one who inquired about her tiredness with profundity: 'My feet is tired, but my soul is rested.'"[88] White supremacists, combined with passive white moderates, sapped the faith of African Americans and drove them to the Nation of Islam and away from the Hebraic-Christian consensus white and African Americans shared. Therefore, even as King rejected white supremacist violence in the KKK, he showed white moderates his fidelity to common values across racial boundaries by criticizing his fellow African Americans as well. In other words, King depended on Hebraic-Christian language to bridge racial divisions. At the same time, he raised the stakes for white moderates, since the African American good will that King sought to mobilize could not last forever.

King demanded white moderates pursue racial redemption by implicating them in the violence already occurring, and the Beloved Community was central to this effort. King decried the "myth of time" as the white moderates' fig leaf for a refusal to make the needed personal sacrifices to ensure racial justice.[89] The myth of time obscured the moral responsibility of white individuals and communities for African American suffering. White moral responsibility not only involved ending direct contribution to black suffering but also demanded that white individuals suffer by delivering their black brothers and sisters from unearned suffering. The seductive logic of the myth of time tempted white moderates to avoid their own redemptive suffering and simply wait for racial redemption to come of its own accord.

The logic was particularly seductive during the economically prosperous 1950s, as well as in the context of the legal victories the National Association for the Advancement of Colored People (NAACP) had achieved in the federal courts. However, King believed no court decision alone was sufficient for ensuring that white and African Americans met their personal responsibilities required under the Beloved Community.[90] Americans of all races had to make the personal sacrifices to motivate the implementation of these decisions, but the greatest responsibility fell on those whose burden was, in fact, the lightest, as white Americans were the ones who benefited from the undeserved racial privileges bequeathed by unjust laws. A pile of legal victories meant little if white Americans refused to recognize African Americans as equal members in the covenant made with God. Without that recognition, court decisions would not be enforced or, if enforced, would merely breed resentment between white and African Americans. King denied that the existence of an African American professional class attested to improvements in the African American condition generally, pointing out that, despite their competence, African American professionals lacked the resources needed to bring about change.[91]

King tied the reluctance of white leadership to relinquish their racial privileges with their calls for African Americans to "be patient" or "wait."[92] In a speech during the 1964 presidential election, King argued, "Whites must bear the heaviest guilt for the present situation [in the ghettos]."[93] The fault among African Americans was largely that of the leadership for withholding support for "a mere handful of well-intentioned but tragically misguided young people" who protested racial injustice by spreading garbage in the streets or blocking the entrance to public buildings.[94] Yet, King insisted, "When the white power structure calls upon the Negro to reject violence but does not impose upon itself the task of creating necessary social change, it is in fact asking for submission to injustice."[95] Nevertheless, King was aware of the impact of wholesale condemnation of white Americans; hence, he pointed to the failure of white Americans as the result of extremists—both black and white—who would exploit racial tensions rather than heal them. Under the Beloved Community, moral responsibility tied Americans together across racial barriers. The covenant demanded that white Americans make sacrifices and deny the myth of time.

Political self-sacrifice was a part of redemptive suffering demanded by *agape*, the central value shared across King's understanding of the Hebraic-Christian tradition. All Americans had to seek out *agape* as part of a personal redemption that would lead to social and institutional redemption. This conversion operated through democratic norms but only because of the common obedience to the authority of the "Lord and Master" whose love commanded all humankind to follow the divine laws that grounded democracies in the covenant of the heart. Hence, Allen's interpretation of King's "dream" confuses his view of the origins of democratic authority with hers and Hobbes's.[96] She locates King's language of the dream in the discussion of Hobbes's description of trustworthiness among partners to a covenant; however, she never mentions, in the Beloved Community, that the only trustworthy partner is God. Humankind has routinely violated the covenant in one way or another, but God's love, expressed in the ultimate sacrifice on the cross, always provided a way to return to his good graces. Allen's version of the Hobbesian covenant relies on the trustworthiness of the political sovereign to enforce rules rooted in common consent, but King had no faith in such a political sovereign, since from the mayor of Montgomery to the United States Congress, they had, in one way or another, embraced white supremacy in violation of divine law. The political sovereign had to answer to the Lord and Master. The church mediated divine authority, achieved through divine suffering, and hence called for the emulation of this divine suffering to redeem the sins of a political sovereign and those covenanted to it. In short, Allen's covenant invokes the republican motto of *vox populi; vox dei*. King, on the other hand, recurred to the motto in John 14:23: *si quis diligit me, sermonem meum servabit*.

King envisioned the Beloved Community as an ecumenical covenant of religious Americans to reform the laws and hearts of the nation. He had to make his covenant appeal across religious denominations while bolstering its persuasive power with strong elements of African American Protestant religious traditions. All individuals, regardless of race, had to meet their responsibilities to community and eschew self-interest. The failure of both white and African Americans to do so would exacerbate racial tensions, threatening violence that would only worsen racial injustice. King drew from the Protestant personalist tradition to create a goal that transcended denomination: nonviolent direct action to persuade white Americans to support civil rights reform for African Americans. King's goal of political reform depended on a prophetic witness that would prompt internal conversions to love. Thus he attempted, in the public demonstrations he led against racial injustice, to shame the nation's elected officials for their inaction, which only licensed continued racial violence. He prophesied, however, not because of his commitment to the nation or to a theory of democracy but because he was "a preacher of the Gospel," which was "his first calling" and remained his "greatest commitment."[97]

Public Activism and the Second Great Emancipation

King identified the federal government as ultimately responsible for restoring African American civil rights. The "foundations" of local and state governments in the Jim Crow South rested on white supremacy. Only the federal government, grounded in the Beloved Community, could trump the states and localities. However, King did not merely want to achieve a political end. He also wanted the redemption of the nation for all its sins against African Americans, a redemption that would purge both white self-interest and African American self-hatred. To achieve a change in policy and in the very constitution of the American people, *agape* had to take hold of the nation before it was too late. King framed civil rights as a national issue and dramatized the struggle with massive protests to attract media attention. Because he lacked access to mass media, King depended on drawing attention to the injustice of segregation. Moreover, because African Americans had little political leverage, he had to persuade the broader white public and elected officials to sympathize with the plight of African Americans. Not only did King affirm the Beloved Community to achieve this result, he also explained how working toward the Beloved Community was all that stood between the redemption of the nation and its condemnation for failing to meet its obligations.

King preached the Beloved Community to pressure elected officials into passing the Civil Rights Act of 1964. King held up three powerful models who exemplified the principles by which *agape* could topple segregation: St. Paul, Mahatma Gandhi, and Abraham Lincoln. Paul provided the message. Gandhi provided the method. Lincoln provided the political example for public officials. These three figures combined to illustrate how the nation could fulfill the covenant, which would provoke a spiritual Exodus of African Americans from segregated Egypt to the integrated Promised Land. For King, when Americans drew from the Hebraic-Christian heritage and acted with nonviolent direct action, public officials of character should respond by sacrificing their own political careers, even their lives, to achieve justice. The result would be greater fusion of Hebraic-Christian covenant principles with the secular political world, advancing the emergence of the Kingdom of God in America.

King sometimes likened himself to Paul, whose leadership of the early church supplied a moral standard against which contemporary America fell short. As one of the leaders of the early church, Paul travelled from major city to major city to preach the Gospel despite ridicule and threats to his life. He ended up in prison in Rome, where the Romans eventually decapitated him. In contrast, the contemporary American church (both white and black) mostly hid within its walls, according to King, and avoided preaching the Gospel if it meant any discomfort.

Gandhi showed how ordinary Americans could confront racial prejudice and participate in their own redemption through nonviolent direct action. Gandhi was also the symbol for how people of color could resist white supremacy without violence and still succeed in achieving their political goals for the benefit of the whole nation. After all, Gandhi led the effort to push the British out of all of India, not merely Hindu India. However, King did not fully embrace Gandhi, since Gandhi was not a Christian. Instead he astutely borrowed the wisdom of Gandhi's strategy of nonviolence and informed it with Christian principles.

Finally, Lincoln represented how public officials were to act. King's Lincoln was reluctant to free slaves but ultimately made the loving sacrifice and paid with his life. Indeed, King's three models all died violent deaths, not merely foreshadowing King's own fate but reflecting the fate of so many civil rights activists by 1963. King meant to show how all three demonstrated the power of sacrificial love, or *agape*. Sacrifice could redeem and rebuild the Kingdom of God, but it would be truly sacrifice not of an afternoon or a weekend but of life and limb.

Others have shown how King both compared himself and was compared by others to Paul.[98] King used Paul as a "prophetic persona" both to lend gravitas to the Civil Rights Movement, and to appeal to a traditional mode of exhortation. In particular, King used the Pauline persona in the "Letter from Birmingham Jail" to address the nation as an unjustly imprisoned martyr, as Paul had addressed the early church in Rome. Some scholars have noticed that King used the same persona when preaching to his congregation at Dexter Baptist Church in Montgomery, Alabama, in his sermon "Paul's Letter to the Americans."[99] However, they emphasize King's Pauline persona without extending the analogy to the people King addressed. King adopted the Pauline persona to address the nation as the Body of Christ. In other words, they only read one half of the title, "Paul's letter," and ignore the other, "to the Americans." Paul's epistles criticized early congregations for their various infidelities to the Gospel, and King adopted the same style of letters as simultaneous critique, instruction, and exhortation. King adopted the Pauline persona to demand from America, especially the churches, the same *agape* that Paul demanded of the early Christians.[100] Therefore, he was condemning the contemporary church for its failure to end segregation and adopt the loving equality of the early Christians.

Paul and the early church were victims of Roman persecution. What sustained their faith was the belief in the nearness of the return of Jesus to create the new Kingdom of God. Not only did Rome not matter for early Christians but neither did any worldly affairs, which was why sharing possessions came so easily. King wanted the *agape* of the early church but not its ambivalence about politics. Indeed, those recommending ambivalence about politics and an emphasis on spiritual salvation during the Civil Rights Movement were white preachers defending the status quo. King mentioned how sitting in prison (as Paul had) served as a form of civil disobedience, a position he said he learned in college from reading Henry David Thoreau's *Civil Disobedience*, but sitting in jail was simply insufficient for King to create a sense of urgency for achieving the Beloved Community.[101]

To that end, King appealed to Mahatma Gandhi's satyagraha as the way to mobilize a Hebraic-Christian message in politics without abandoning a commitment to nonviolence. Translated from Sanskrit, satyagraha means "holding on to truth," a term Gandhi used to describe the inspiration for nonviolent direct action. As a form of political action, satyagraha required nonviolent resistance against British imperial forces. Nonviolent resistance enabled Hindus and Muslims to regard each other as allies despite their religious differences. The effort inspired King to make his own pilgrimage to India. The influence on King was profound.[102] He said in his published account of the trip, "we [King, his wife Coretta, and friend Lawrence Reddick] had one of the most concentrated and eye-opening experiences of our lives."[103] Linked to this experience was King's reinterpretation of Gandhi's central principle for nonviolent direct action. King referred to satyagraha as "soul force" or "truth force" to help describe what impact nonviolent resistance could have in the South. King borrowed from Gandhi the position that a demonstrator must achieve a certain inward maturity, which King most clearly outlined in the "Letter" as a four-step process: "In any nonviolent campaign there are four basic steps: (1) collection of the facts to determine whether injustices are alive, (2) negotiation, (3) self-purification, and (4) direct action."[104] King followed Gandhi in seeing how the dignity of the oppressed, confronting an unjust system, could prod the conscience of those in power, leading to their inward conversion to justice, and their integration into the Beloved Community.[105]

The obvious problem for King was that Gandhi had been Hindu. How did one square the Beloved Community rooted in the Hebraic-Christian heritage with the methods of a man who appealed neither to covenant nor to the Hebraic-Christian heritage? King answered both by making Gandhi a de facto Christian and by Christianizing his account of satyagraha. In *Stride Toward Freedom*, King described the basic philosophy of the Montgomery Improvement Association as "the Sermon on the Mount, rather than a doctrine of passive resistance, that initially inspired the Negroes of Montgomery to dignified social action. It was Jesus of Nazareth that stirred the Negroes to protest with the creative weapon of love."[106] However, King explained how the Sermon on the Mount became a political weapon: "I had come to see early that the Christian doctrine of love operating through the Gandhian method of nonviolence was one of the most potent weapons available to the Negro in his struggle for freedom."[107] King then described a crucial event: "About a week after the protest started, a white woman who understood and sympathized with the Negroes' efforts wrote a letter to the editor of the *Montgomery Advertiser* comparing the bus protest with the Gandhian movement in India. Miss Juliette Morgan, sensitive and frail, did not long survive the rejection and condemnation of the white community, but long before she died in the summer of 1957 the name of Mahatma Gandhi was well known in Montgomery."[108]

Juliette Morgan was emblematic of the kind of sacrifice King believed was necessary to save the nation. King prodded her conscience, and she willingly suffered the consequences of her change of heart, although differently from how activists on the street did. To explain the event, however, King baptized and canonized Gandhi, while claiming to perfect both Christian social justice and satyagraha all at once: "People who had never heard of the little brown saint of India were now saying his name with an air of familiarity. Nonviolent resistance had emerged as the technique of the movement, while love stood as the regulating ideal. In other words, Christ furnished the spirit and motivation, while Gandhi furnished the method."[109] King suggested the compatibility of satyagraha with the Hebraic-Christian heritage by treating Gandhi a saint; because Gandhi was not Christian, his greatest value was in his innovation of a "potent weapon" rather than how he informed the "spirit" or "motivation" of the movement. As Stewart Burns explains, "The born-again black and the technology of soul force would make an irresistible synthesis to change history."[110] King retained a Pauline vision of the movement's spirit and motivation, with the early church as his model for what should result from soul force. In King's account of Juliette Morgan, the result of satyagraha was first suffering then redemption, and the meaning of that redemption was rooted in the sacrificial nature of the act. Richard Lischer interprets this as an extension of satyagraha beyond what Gandhi argued. For the prodding of another conscience to succeed required the "necessity of conforming one's suffering to the twisted agony of the crucified Christ."[111] Juliette Morgan, who ultimately committed suicide in 1957, suffered alienation and ridicule akin to what the crowds heaped on African Americans for seeking racial justice and on Jesus of Nazareth while he hung on the cross. By keeping his account of satyagraha still steeped in the language of the Hebraic-Christian heritage, King publicized the Beloved Community as something compatible both with his Pauline stature and with the covenanted people he wished to shepherd into the Kingdom.

Neither Paul nor Gandhi provided King an explanation for how the Beloved Community functioned for elected officials. As a model for elected officials, King chose Abraham Lincoln. There were several "Lincolns" from which to choose in the American collective memory, and King focused his attention on Lincoln as the "Great Emancipator" with an emphasis on the sacrifices that came with Lincoln's decision to end African American slavery.[112] King focused on three characteristics of the Great Emancipator. First, Lincoln freed the slaves but only after hedging for years. By appealing to Lincoln, King allowed a space for public officials to repent their early misgiving for the Civil Rights Movement and ultimately make the right decision. Second, Lincoln freed the slaves and preserved the Union to his own political disadvantage. King referred to this kind of individual suffering as the redemption for the earlier failure to free the slaves. Finally, Lincoln freed the slaves in part because he heeded the calls of influential abolitionist preachers. King found a place for his own leadership and movement by referring to a national figure responding to highly mobilized, socially engaged religious Americans from several denominational backgrounds. Of the three characteristics, however, King directly stated this last role barely at all; rather, he used it in the posture he adopted with respect to national leaders—as the prophet and willing adviser. King linked his Pauline persona with Gandhian political action to provoke Lincolnian responses from public officials.

The network of meaning these figures created was more than simply an intellectual framework. It was a media strategy, what S. Jonathan Bass calls "the Gospel of Publicity."[113] King and his staff on the SCLC lacked direct access to mass media. To draw in mass media attention, King held demonstrations to apply local pressure and to gain national attention. As a result of King's Pauline persona, which preached a unifying message for major American religious denominations, he appeared as a moderate, traditional, and educated African American preacher, whose sense of dignity was identical, or perhaps even superior, to that of the white folks he confronted. The Gandhian methods of passive resistance staged showdowns between often violent, white, unsympathetic police and young, unarmed African Americans who would rather suffer than fight back. To a national audience, the images were horrifying, and rightly so. Because of their large scale, King's demonstrations became newsworthy, thus driving national news organizations to cover the events. Even then, however, King had to make sure to secure the Lincolnian narrative for the events. King laid the blame on political officials who failed to make the necessary sacrifices to give African Americans the rights to which all Americans were entitled. Thus, African American protests were not "riots" or "out-of-control youths" but organized, peaceful demands for justice any other American would want if so deprived and for so long.[114] King's media strategy began its decline after the Watts riots that followed the passage of the 1965 Voting Rights Act and internal divisions among competing civil rights activists, but his strategy had succeeded at critical moments since its emergence during the Montgomery Bus Boycott, a span of ten years.

One important element to the publicity campaign was the slogan the SCLC used, "Freedom Now!" King's Pauline persona gave him prophetic standing, and this standing meant King could not merely call on the nation to restore the covenant but could also predict terrible consequences for failure to restore the covenant. This alternative narrative was King's jeremiad, and it appeared as a distant, haunting possibility, while King remained optimistic with his emphasis on "hope" through the 1956–1964 period.[115] However, King referred to the jeremiad at points when he saw flagging political support for desegregation, and he labeled several groups "outside" the Hebraic-Christian heritage, such as black nationalists, the Nation of Islam, and the Ku Klux Klan. Because these organizations advocated and used violence, they could not be reconciled with the Beloved Community or mobilized with satyagraha (though they could be converted from their erroneous positions). The purpose of the jeremiad was to make integration seem immediately necessary to the Civil Rights Movement, what King famously called the "fierce urgency of now."[116] The dignity African Americans demonstrated in nonviolent direct action was the result of newfound self-respect, but also of a faith in the American institutional responses to the demonstrations. Were officials in these institutions to fail to respond in time, that faith would die out, leaving only bitterness and violence.[117] King's leadership of the Civil Rights

Movement, then, was the last, best hope for peaceful integration of African Americans, as well as the peaceful resolution of the racial problems facing the nation. Indeed, even this image drew from the Lincolnian experience, since race once again was the basis for violence that would tear the nation apart.

King wrapped these overlapping symbols in a narrative that had long been part of the American black church tradition: the Exodus.[118] As Gary S. Selby has illustrated, King deployed the Exodus as the narrative that moved from the white supremacist pharaohs of Egypt, through the Red Sea, across the desert, and concluded with King seeing, like Moses, the Promised Land from the mountaintop. The twist to King's Exodus narrative was that Egypt and the Promised Land were the same place: America. The change would come not from a geographical relocation but personal and social redemption. In the sermon "The Death of Evil on the Seashore," King provided the clearest view of the transformation, saying:

> The death of the Egyptians upon the seashore is a vivid reminder that something in the very nature of the universe assists goodness in its perennial struggle with evil. The New Testament rightly declares: "No chastening for the present seemeth to be joyous, but grievous: *nevertheless afterward* it yieldeth the peaceable fruit of righteousness." Pharaoh exploits the children of Israel—*nevertheless afterward!* Pilate yields to the crowd that crucifies Christ—*nevertheless afterward!* The early Christians are thrown to the lions and carried away to the chopping blocks—*nevertheless afterward!*[119]

King resisted the temptation to treat America's transformation as unique; rather, he pointed to the American Civil Rights Movement as part of a broader opening of the Red Sea to find "the evils of colonialism and imperialism dead upon the seashore."[120] However, he provided a vision for how he saw America proceeding. The first stage of American Exodus was the 1619 arrival of African slaves, which a century and half later introduced a "nagging conscience" for those like Thomas Jefferson and, soon after, the abolitionists. The second stage was Abraham Lincoln and the Emancipation Proclamation of 1863 that, however, faltered with the 1896 Supreme Court decision, *Plessy v. Ferguson*, which upheld state laws imposing racial segregation in public facilities. For King, the present moment was another "*nevertheless afterward*" for the Beloved Community to reach the state and federal government and thereby further establish the Kingdom of God. He preached, "And though the Kingdom of God may remain *not yet* as a universal reality in history, in the present it may exist in such isolated forms as in judgment, in personal devotion, and in some group life. 'The Kingdom of God is in the midst of you.' "[121] The church delivered the faith that "will sustain us in our struggle to escape from the bondage of every evil Egypt" though without "such faith, man's highest dreams will pass silently to the dust."[122]

It is important to note how King's religious foundation led him to avoid making claims of American exceptionalism. The elements in the American founding and afterwards were good only as far as they were true for all people. On the contrary, King's Exodus narrative universalized the narrative for a Chosen people, connecting the segregation and slavery in America to the struggles among people of color across the globe.[123] In his 1957 reflections on the independence of Ghana, King said, "Ghana reminds us that whenever you break out of Egypt, you better get ready for stiff backs. You better get ready for some homes to be bombed," and later, "Before you get to Canaan you've got a Red Sea to confront. You have a hardened heart of a pharaoh to confront."[124] However, King continued: "God grants that we will get on board and start marching with God because we got orders now to break down the bondage and the walls of colonialism, exploitation, and imperialism. To break them down to the point that no man will trample over another man, but that all men will respect the dignity and worth of all human personality. And then we will be in Canaan's freedom land."[125] He grounded this universalization in his Christian faith in its manifestation of divine law, which, when followed, inspired a desire for freedom no matter the place or time.[126]

White Southern Protestants mobilized counternarratives to resist King's efforts to persuade the national public to favor desegregation. These counternarratives were themselves religiously inspired. As Charles Marsh has detailed, two major white supremacist Christians, Sam Bowers and Douglas Hudgins, sought to inspire local resistance to civil rights activists. Bowers founded a white terrorist organization, the White Knights of the Ku Klux Klan, who broke off from the regular KKK to stage random acts of violence to frighten organizers out of the state of Mississippi. Bowers was the son of a Methodist family, but he became a born-again Baptist who anointed his acts of terrorism with a comparison to the biblical Elijah, who slew the heretical priests of Baal. Just as Elijah refused to spare the Baalite priests, so would Bowers refuse to spare those who would bring about a latter-day Baalism in the form of racial integration and intermarriage. Bowers raged against African Americans to Catholics and Jews, but he especially hated Jews because he believed them to be agents of Communism.[127] It was Bowers who orchestrated the deaths of Congress of Racial Equality (CORE) field workers Mickey

Schwerner, Andrew Goodman, and James Chaney (Schwerner and Goodman were Jewish and Chaney African American) out of his belief that "If a black man stands up and demands his constitutional rights, I must support that man as strongly as I wish him to do for me; but if he permits himself to be deluded by socialism, he's become devoid of grace. *He must be eliminated.* God will permit his common liberty, but he will not permit Baal to come corrupt his liberty and his citizenship."[128]

More established white clergy followed the path of Rev. Douglas Hudgins, whom Marsh titles the "Theologian of the Closed Society." Hudgins preached an account of Noah's son, Ham, that was peculiar to white Southerners. After the great flood subsided, Noah became very drunk and fell asleep naked. His son Ham saw his father in such a state, and Noah cursed him: "A servant of servants shall he be unto his brother." Many white Southerners, and most white Southern Baptists, interpreted the cursed Ham to be the original ancestor of Africans.[129] Moreover, Hudgins offered a highly personal account of Christian salvation. The only path to salvation came through an individual relationship with God. Sacraments offered no grace. Moral actions were without merit. The church lacked any authority to correct members, and parachurch organizations lacked authority to correct individual churches. [130] With a deeply Tocquevillian insight, Marsh notes, "This kind of autonomy put extraordinary pressure on Baptist ministers throughout the South to maintain the status quo; if a minister rubbed the congregation the wrong way on the race issue, or any other matter, he would be dismissed. The polity structure that promised maximum individual freedom ironically proved to suffocate individual freedom by group consensus."[131] The effect, if not the intention, of Hudgins's approach was to deny any form of public dogma, which provides the only kind of moral conviction on which a democratic consensus can act.

As Marsh observes, Rev. Jerry Falwell echoed Hudgins's hostility toward black church leaders for civil rights. In a 1965 sermon titled, "Ministers and Marches," Falwell preached: "We have a message of redeeming grace through a crucified and risen Lord. This message is designed to go right to the heart of man and there meet his deep spiritual need. Nowhere are we commissioned to reform the externals. We are not to wage wars against bootleggers, liquor stores, gamblers, murderers, prostitutes, racketeers, prejudiced persons or institutions, or any other ex-prejudiced persons or institutions, or any other existing evil as such."[132] Falwell mentioned King by name to express his doubt over King's Christian "sincerity and non-violent intentions," linking him to Communism.[133] Often overlooked, however, is that Falwell took on King's treatment of the Exodus, saying, "Some, who are not acquainted with the Bible, will lift out such instances as Moses and his leading the Jews out of Egyptian bondage, and thereby try to prove that Christians today are supposed to lead people out of bondage in situations where they are being discriminated against."[134] In an unsettling passage, Falwell mocked the comparison by insisting that those imitating Moses should tell their would-be Chosen people "that they are going to lead them into 40 years of wandering in which everyone [sic] of them except two will die."[135] Instead, Falwell insisted, the "Promised Land is a parallel to the victorious Christian life on the earthly level, and our eventual Heaven on eternal plane."[136] The task of preachers was to win souls for Christ. If they put their efforts where they should be, "America would be turned upside down for God. Hate and prejudice would certainly be in a great measure overcome."[137]

The counternarratives from Bowers, Hudgins, and Falwell provided white Southern churches a kind of biblical justification for violence or indifference in response to King's claim to religious authority.[138] In addition, Hudgins and Falwell argued for a kind of separation of church and state in which Christians and churches separated from public affairs to preserve their souls.[139] If saving souls automatically improved race relations, then King's agitation was a distraction that disrupted daily affairs and deprived King's audience of a true encounter with Christ. Furthermore, deep down, Falwell fought King not merely on racial grounds but on theological ones, pitting his dispensational premillennialism against King's Niebuhr-chastened postmillennial Social Gospel. As we shall see in the next chapter, Falwell changed his mind on politics but not on his theology. When Falwell entered politics, he did so on very different theological terms from King's.

The Public Redemption of Elected Officials

After the success of the Montgomery Bus Boycott in 1956, King became a national figure and organized public demonstrations to end Jim Crow across the South. John F. Kennedy became president in 1961 and promised greater federal action on civil rights for African Americans.[140] The Kennedy campaign assisted King and exploited its assistance among African American voters; King, however, refused to endorse Kennedy, despite pressure from his own father.[141] After Kennedy's election, King was dissatisfied with what he saw as foot-dragging from the Kennedy administration. In response, King began to call upon Kennedy to commemorate the centennial of the Emancipation Proclamation with his own executive action to end segregation. King called it the "Second Emancipation Proclamation," an executive action that would desegregate all areas that fell within federal control.[142] Despite agreeing to meet with King in person, Kennedy moved slowly in response. When Kennedy adjusted policies to be fairer to minorities, King drew attention to the change both to thank Kennedy and to criticize him for not going far enough; the minor policy adjustments demonstrated Kennedy's understanding of the covenant but, more importantly, also his refusal to make the necessary sacrifice to redeem the nation.[143] In fact, Kennedy's attempts at placation became opportunities for King to make newsworthy statements demanding more comprehensive action that required Kennedy to make the sacrifice that Lincoln made, meaning Kennedy's half measures only made matters worse for the president. King contrasted the willingness of activists to sacrifice their bodily safety with Kennedy's unwillingness to do much of anything, perhaps out of fear of losing his reelection.[144]

During the period from Kennedy's inauguration until King's meeting over the Second Emancipation Proclamation, civil rights activists had started moving without King's leadership, including James Farmer of the Congress of Racial Equality (CORE) and John Lewis and Diane Nash from the Student Nonviolent Coordinating Committee (SNCC). The two organizations had led Freedom Rides in 1961 to force Southern compliance with *Boynton v. Virginia*, a 1960 Supreme Court case that outlawed the racial segregation of buses and accompanying facilities if those buses crossed state lines. During the Freedom Rides, King had more of a political role behind the scenes, thus conceding the public leadership role to the student activists. The following year, King intervened during the flagging Albany Movement, which sought to force general desegregation in a wealthy enclave in southwest Georgia. There, the allied civil rights groups encountered a canny sheriff who sought to avoid a national sensation and to fatigue activists with false promises. He succeeded. The Civil Rights Movement was stalled, and student activists mocked King as "De Lawd" as a challenge to his leadership.[145] Kennedy failed to make a significant statement on the centennial of the Emancipation Proclamation, and Robert Kennedy, the president's younger brother and attorney general, became increasingly agitated with his own failure to use the Department of Justice to solve the president's problem for him. King's middle position between segregation and an increasingly militant student movement placed the Beloved Community in danger.

In the spring of 1963, Walter Abernathy, Fred Shuttlesworth, and King led the Birmingham Campaign to highlight the extent of racism in the South and the violence local and state governments used to enforce it. The demonstrations received international coverage as white police officers clubbed and hosed with water cannons the mostly African American nonviolent demonstrators. When local officials arrested King for violating a recently passed law requiring him to secure a permit for demonstrations, he used the opportunity to distribute a public letter meant to define the purpose and ends of the Birmingham Campaign. That was the "Letter from Birmingham Jail." The influence of the letter was not immediate but slowly spread to the public.[146] The Birmingham Campaign placed increased pressure on the Kennedy administration to act on promises made to improve civil rights for African Americans. The effect of the letter was important, as King's imprisonment had provoked little outcry.[147] Also important was the violent response of Birmingham commissioner for public safety, Theophilus Eugene "Bull" Connor. National press photographed scenes from the "children's crusade" which depicted how Connor deployed high-pressure water hoses and police dogs on African American youths. Overnight, civil rights jumped to a national priority among the American public.[148] However, as Nicholas Bryant describes, "The Birmingham protests had been a watershed moment for the country, but not the president."[149] When three bombs detonated in the place where African American activists organized, civil rights went from a national priority to a crisis, as Birmingham and other cities began to experience African American unrest. It was clear to the White House that King had been right: either the federal government would restore civil rights now or the violence would come in earnest.[150]

In the summer of 1963, John F. Kennedy sent the Civil Rights Act to Congress. When Congress was about to consider the bill, Vice President Lyndon B. Johnson took his cue from King and used the context of the Civil War to campaign for the bill. Johnson gave his 1963 Memorial Day Address on the Gettysburg battleground, the place where the Union repelled a Confederate invasion and turned the tide of the war, and where Lincoln had given his famous address. The battleground steeped the Civil Rights Movement in Lincolnian imagery even as the text drew from King's Pauline message. Johnson used language resembling the sermons and speeches King had been making for years to echo the theme of sacrifice Lincoln had offered. Johnson sounded notes similar to King's Beloved Community, saying, "On this hallowed ground, heroic deeds were performed and eloquent words were spoken a century ago. . . . We are called to honor our own words of reverent prayer with resolution in the deeds we must perform to preserve peace and the hope of freedom."[151] Johnson started with a prayer to gain the strength to endure the suffering required to pursue peace and freedom. This effort stood in contrast to the contemporary inaction recommended by those who saw racial progress as a slow evolution. Johnson restated King's demand for "freedom now" as what every American citizen was due:

> The Negro today asks for justice. We do not answer him—we do not answer those who lie beneath this soil—when we reply to the Negro by asking for, "Patience." It is empty to plead that the solution to the dilemmas of the present rests on the hands of the clock. The solution is in our hands. Unless we are willing to yield up our destiny of greatness among the civilizations of history, Americans—white and Negro together—must be about the business of resolving the challenge which confronts us now. Our nation found its soul in honor on these fields of Gettysburg one hundred years ago. We must not lose that soul in dishonor now on the fields of hate.[152]

Moreover, if African Americans did not receive the freedom that was rightfully theirs, America would lose its "greatness" by sowing "hate," a warning that recalled King's prophecy for what would befall America if the country failed to keep the covenant. At the end of the speech, Johnson accepted King's comparison to Lincoln as a way of declaring presidential commitment to civil rights: "Until justice is blind to color, until education is unaware of race, until opportunity is unconcerned with the color of men's skins, emancipation will be a proclamation but not a fact. To the extent that the proclamation of emancipation is not fulfilled in fact, to that extent we shall have fallen short of assuring freedom to the free."[153] The Civil Rights Act was Kennedy's answer to King's call for the Second Emancipation Proclamation. That Johnson was the first to give that answer is significant because of Johnson's 1957 conversion from a segregationist to a civil rights supporter, which was precisely the kind of conversion King called for.[154]

On June 11, 1963, Kennedy gave his own speech after submitting the Civil Rights Act to Congress, yet his speech echoed King's only as much as it echoed his own frustrations with King's criticism.[155] While Johnson embraced King's language, Kennedy used his own while agreeing to King's interpretation of events. Kennedy said that achieving racial justice was not merely a state issue or an issue of political party: "This is not even a legal or legislative issue alone. It is better to settle these matters in the courts than on the streets, and new laws are needed at every level, but law alone cannot make men see right. We are confronted primarily with a moral issue. It is as old as the scriptures and is as clear as the American Constitution."[156] Kennedy conceded that

desegregation was more than a matter of policy but of the religious foundation on which America rested, but he conceded the position only when also
stating that the passage of the law meant the end to demonstrations "on the
streets" by civil rights groups. Kennedy repeated his desire to end demonstrations: "We face, therefore, a moral crisis as a country and as a people.
It cannot be met by repressive police action. It cannot be left to increased
demonstrations in the streets. It cannot be quieted by token moves or talk.
It is time to act in the Congress, in your State and local legislative body and,
above all, in our daily lives."[157] Congressional action required the taking up of
personal responsibility, which King also preached as the *agape* from which
one drew when confronting racial justice. Kennedy demanded the Lincolnian response of elected officials that King had demanded, but he did so at
the rhetorical expense of the Gandhian demonstrators, as if the former were
possible without pressure from the latter.

Kennedy accepted the comparison to Lincoln and framed the need
for relevant bodies to pass legislation, and for citizens to assume personal
responsibility, with a comparison to the sacrifices made during the Civil War:
"One hundred years of delay have passed since President Lincoln freed the
slaves, yet their heirs, their grandsons, are not fully free. They are not yet
freed from the bonds of injustice. They are not yet freed from social and economic oppression. And this Nation, for all its hopes and all its boasts, will
not be fully free until all its citizens are free."[158] By accepting the Lincolnian
mantle, Kennedy also accepted King's description of segregation. Segregation
had enslaved both white and African American citizens to the same injustice: white citizens were enslaved to the false notion of white supremacy and
African American citizens to the political and economic manifestation of
those false ideas. Kennedy said, "A great change is at hand, and our task, our
obligation, is to make that revolution, that change, peaceful and construc-
tive for all."[159] Kennedy's speech was much more grudging than Johnson's at
Gettysburg. Certainly, because he delivered it on a national broadcast, Kennedy needed to represent the frustrations of white citizens more sympatheti-
cally than King treated them. After all, Kennedy had a reelection to think
about; however, Kennedy conceded the most important claims King made
for the Beloved Community—that racial injustice was a moral problem, that
it required a nonviolent "revolution," and that immediate action was necessary to avoid any greater potential for violence.

On the heels of these public concessions, King's close friend and ally in
the SCLC, Bayard Rustin, organized the March on Washington for Jobs and
Freedom. The march featured a massive, racially integrated rally of citizens

that Rustin originally planned to take place before the Capitol, but that he later moved in front of the Lincoln Memorial for security reasons. The event took place on August 28, 1963, where King delivered his famous "I Have a Dream" speech. During the speech, he made direct reference, again, to Lincoln's example of *agape* as the core foundation for the American covenant. The memorial formed the backdrop for the speakers, providing the moral authority of a martyred president to those who were willing to suffer in the same way and for the same cause as Lincoln's. Of course, Rustin had wanted the march to end at the Capitol building, since the demonstration directly challenged Congress to pass the civil rights legislation, but the Lincoln Memorial alternative helped establish the moral comparison between the Reluctant Emancipator and the reluctant elected officials whom the speeches from the event were supposed to address.

The press did not miss the symbolism and presented the March on Washington as a racially integrated event driven by principles of religious faith and national purpose.[160] A *Los Angeles Times* reporter described the event as having "speaker after speaker—Negro and white—in the shadow of the towering statue of Abraham Lincoln who freed the slaves 100 years ago."[161] In the presence of Lincoln and integrated speakers were "pleas for divine help for the cause from the clergy—a Catholic, a Jew, a Protestant."[162] On August 29, 1963, journalist E. W. Kenworthy wrote a feature for the *New York Times* describing King as a dramatic figure.[163] First, Kenworthy described the speakers as members of clergy, contrasting for the reader the prophetic role the church played in instructing government. Especially important was how religion gave King, and other religious speakers who used the prophetic role, the appearance of transcending parochial interests in the name of a common, religious purpose: "The other leaders, except for the three clergymen among the 10, concentrated on the struggle ahead, and spoke in tough, even harsh, language."[164] Kenworthy equated King's sacrifice to Lincoln's, and framed the audience response as respect for that same level of sacrifice: "paradoxically it was Dr. King—who had suffered perhaps most of all—who ignited the crowd with words that might have been written by the sad, brooding man enshrined within. As he arose, a great roar welled up from the crowd. When he started to speak, a hush fell."[165] By equating King and Lincoln, Kenworthy echoed King's criticism of the Kennedy administration but also added a key component. When King compared Kennedy to Lincoln and found Kennedy wanting, King was also comparing himself to Lincoln and found deserving. Implied in King's invocation of Lincoln, then, was King's moral superiority to Kennedy. King was doing all he could for racial justice, while Kennedy, according to King, was not.

On the same day, the *New York Times* ran a story detailing the breadth of Hebraic-Christian support for the March on Washington, which emphasized King's Beloved Community. In the article, several members of the clergy articulated views King had largely already expressed. For instance, Reverend Carson Black of the United Presbyterian Church appealed to Lincoln, saying, "After 100 years of the Emancipation Proclamation, 175 years after the adoption of the Constitution, 173 years after the Bill of Rights, the United States still faces a racial crisis."[166] Irving Spiegel then quoted a Catholic leader, Matthew Ahmann from the National Catholic Conference for Interracial Justice: "Who can call himself a man and take part in a system of segregation which frightens the white man into denying what he knows to be right, into denying the law of his God?"[167] Spiegel finally quoted Rabbi Joachim Prinz, who survived Nazi persecution, equating the struggle for civil rights with the same struggle Jews had faced in Europe. The thrust of the story was to present the Hebraic-Christian heritage as united in its support for integration, as summarized in the slogan on the placards carried by many in the ecumenical group: "We march together—Catholics, Jews, Protestants—for dignity and brotherhood of all men under God. Now!"[168]

The *New York Times* also ran an editorial titled "Equality Is Their Right" that focused on the image of Lincoln and the standing of the "new Negro." The editorial said of the March: "They massed, 200,000 strong, at the Lincoln Memorial beside the seated figure of the President who signed the Emancipation Proclamation a century ago. Their declarations of resolve to make that freedom real—in jobs, voting rights, schools, housing and access to places of public accommodation—echoed Lincoln's own warning: 'Those who deny freedom to others deserve it not for themselves; and, under a just God, cannot long retain it.' "[169] The editorial also conveyed the Gandhian sense of dignity, saying of the March, "The discipline maintained by the civil rights pilgrims was as impressive as their dedication. That so vast a movement could be carried out with such decorum is a tribute to the responsibility of both leaders and followers."[170] The article made special mention of A. Philip Randolph, the leader of the Brotherhood of Sleeping Car Porters, as having a "massive dignity that has always been his armor against the walls of racial exclusion."[171] Even in an article that made no direct mention of King, he was still present. The image of the "armor against the walls of racial exclusion" bore King's imprint. As Richard Lischer explains, King made constant use of the rhetorical technique called "metonymy," which Lischer defines as "a predictable metaphor ... [that] is beautiful and makes sense, both of which attributes are crucial to the orator's success. ... [I]n metonymy the relationship between the image and the idea is *logical* and suitable for mass reception."[172] King's most famous metonyms are "the iron feet of oppression" and "the tranquilizing drug of gradualism." It appeared that the author or authors of the *New York Times* editorial could not help but borrow from the rhetoric of the March on Washington's final speaker. Indeed, King had been so successful in persuading the national press that they could escape neither the frame of the Beloved Community nor the very language King used to preach it.

When Congress finally began considering the bill, Kennedy had only then begun to answer the call King had already heeded, and Kennedy still had to ensure the bill's passage to measure up to Lincoln's *agape*. Not only was Kennedy lagging behind King, he was lagging behind ordinary African American activists. In his feature, Kenworthy told the reader of a couple he saw the night before the speech: "There, while carpenters nailed the last planks on the television platforms for the next day . . . a middle-aged Negro couple, the man's arm around the shoulders of his plump wife, stood and read with their lips: 'If we shall suppose that American slavery is one of the offenses which in the providence of God must needs come but which having continued through His appointed time, He now wills remove.'"[173] The two encapsulated the image King had created in his Beloved Community: on the evening before the march, a married African American couple read the words of Lincoln, who, in turn, was quoting the Bible. King's emphasis on the link between Hebraic-Christian support for the Beloved Community and American racial reform had reached the press, and the press reported the Civil Rights Movement as comporting with the efforts of the Civil War to end slavery and Lincoln's religious language. Johnson's speech at Gettysburg had echoed King's call. Now, journalists were looking at the march with the same perspective that King and the SCLC publicity advocated.

Immediately following the March on Washington, Kennedy appeared to answer King's call for a Second Emancipation Proclamation. First, he observed the legitimacy of civil rights claimed at the March, saying, "The cause of 20,000,000 Negroes has been advanced by the program conducted as appropriately before the nation's shrine to the great Emancipator, but even more significant is the contribution to all mankind." Moreover, Kennedy embraced Lincoln's sacrifice in the Labor Day statement he published on the same day:

We must accelerate our effort to achieve equal rights for all our citizens—in employment, in education, in voting and in all sectors of national activity. This year, I believe, will go down as one of the turning points in the history of American labor. Foremost among the rights of labor is the right to equality of opportunity; and these recent months, 100 years after the Emancipation Proclamation, have seen the decisive recognition by the major part of our society that all our citizens are entitled to full membership in the national community. The gains of 1963 will never be reversed. They lay a solid foundation for the progress we must continue to make in the months and years to come.[174]

The *New York Times* article published the transcript of the speech and featured a large picture of Kennedy standing with civil rights and labor leaders, as if he had finally taken a decisive stance on the issue and could be photographed in public with African American opponents of segregation. The *Chicago Tribune* ran a story illustrating the combined efforts of African American preachers, civil rights activists, labor, and progressive bodies to forge a consensus in Congress to ensure passage of the Civil Rights Act.[175] One should note, however, Kennedy's distance from the religious nature of the foundation he saw laid in 1963. He avoided using any of the religious language that King or other political officials later would, perhaps because of the discomfort many Americans still had with having a Catholic president. Regardless, Kennedy's obedience to King reflected the prophetic model King had adopted, exhorting American officials to embrace the values of the Hebraic-Christian heritage in the nation's Exodus to racial justice.

Of course, Kennedy would have paid electoral consequences for civil rights, which is arguably one reason he took his autumn campaign stop in Texas. There, Kennedy became all too much a Lincolnian figure: he was assassinated by Lee Harvey Oswald on November 22, 1963. On November 27 of that year, Johnson addressed a joint session of Congress to present a peaceful transition of power and to reassert the Kennedy agenda in earnest, since the assassination had led to a new groundswell of sympathy for Kennedy which could translate into political support for specific policies. Johnson interpreted the Civil Rights Bill as a way for Congress to honor Kennedy, saying: "no memorial oration or eulogy could more eloquently honor President Kennedy's memory than the earliest possible passage of the civil rights bill for which he fought so long. We have talked long enough in this country about equal rights. We have talked for one hundred years or more. It is time now to write the next chapter, and to write it in the books of law."[176] Once again, the invocation of Lincoln as the emancipator of "one hundred years or more" ago, and Kennedy's sacrifice demanded the act's passage to complete the mission Lincoln had started. Ironically, the Kennedy that King found wanting became in Johnson's speech the modern martyr most reminiscent of Lincoln's own sacrifice, and this reinterpretation of Kennedy helped connect national mourning for the fallen president with a man who was one of Kennedy's most earnest, sympathetic critics.

Johnson spoke in language reminiscent of King's, especially his use of metonyms. For Johnson, it was time for "all races and creeds" to "understand and respect one another" and a time to turn away "from the apostles of bitterness and bigotry."[177] He ended the speech with lines from "American the Beautiful," saying, "America, America / God shed His grace on thee, / And crown thy good / With brotherhood, / From sea to shining sea."[178] This language resonated with King's use of the term "brotherhood" in terms of reconciliation under divine law as it emerged among those practicing sacrificial love. In short, Johnson endorsed King's view of America and sought to use the climax of a critical speech before Congress—days after Kennedy's death—to do so.

Dueling Religious Foundations on the Senate Floor

During the Senate floor debate over the Civil Rights Act, senators deployed religious language that drew either from King's broad vision of the American Exodus or the opposing white Southern Protestant vision that deferred to state powers to determine voting rights. The floor debate revealed how King's invocation of the Hebraic-Christian consensus had moved some senators to treat the dominant religious consensus as a template for forming a new racial consensus. If Protestants, Catholics, and Jews could put aside their differences to form a consensus, then so could white and African Americans. Hence, the language of the bill that forbade religious discrimination and racial discrimination was part of a broader effort to unite the nation. Southern senators used white Southern counternarratives during their debate. The Civil Rights Act, in their view, amounted to the unjust federal seizure of state right to define the franchise.

The House passed the legislation in January of 1964. In March, Minnesota Senator Hubert Humphrey introduced the Civil Rights Act on the Senate floor with a speech describing how the Constitution, especially the Fourteenth Amendment, provided the basis for racial equality that the bill meant finally to establish; however, Humphrey did not only wish to introduce the procedural basis and constitutional legitimacy for passing the bill. Rather, he echoed King's Beloved Community as the basis for the bill, first stating the constitutional account of political equality and then its religious foundation. He said of the Constitution:

> I cannot help but marvel at the impact, the directness, and the sense of destiny captured in these 52 words. I cannot help but marvel at their relevance to the responsibility which now confronts the Senate of the United States. The preamble to the Constitution might very well have been written as the preamble to the Civil Rights Act of 1964. "We the people of the United States." Not white people, colored people, short people, or tall people, but simply: We the people. "In order to form a more perfect Union." We know that until racial justice and freedom is a reality in this land, our Union will remain profoundly imperfect. That is why we are debating this bill. That is why the bill must become law.[179]

Humphrey did not ground his interpretation of the Constitution in the historical precedents from British common law or the immanent trajectory of human progress. He looked to the same Hebraic-Christian tradition King offered as the foundation for creating racial justice in America. Humphrey immediately followed his account of constitutional equality by invoking Christian Scripture:

> Mr. President, I cannot overemphasize the historic importance of the debate we are beginning. We are participants in one of the most crucial eras in the long and proud history of the United States and, yes, in mankind's struggle for justice and freedom which has gone forward since the dawn of history. If freedom becomes a full reality in America, we can dare to believe that it will become a reality everywhere. If freedom fails here—in America, the land of the free—what hope can we have for it surviving elsewhere?
>
> That is why we must debate this legislation with courage, determination, frankness, honesty, and—above all—with the sense of the obligation and destiny that has come to us at this time in this place . . .
>
> Mr. President, as I prepared to speak today, I went to the Scriptures to find the Golden Rule in the Gospel of St. Matthew. The Golden Rule exemplifies what we are attempting to do in this civil rights legislation.
>
> Chapter 7, verse 12 of Matthew reads as follows:

"All things therefore, whatsoever ye would that men should do unto you, even so also do ye unto them: for this is the law and the prophets."

This has been paraphrased in the common language that we use so often as:

Do unto others as you would have them do unto you.

If I were to encapsulate what we are trying to do in this legislation, it is to fulfill this great admonition which is the guiding rule of human relations if we are to have justice, tranquility, peace, and freedom.[180]

Humphrey chose to frame the introduction of the civil rights bill in religious terms of obeying divine law as expressed in the "Golden Rule" taught in the Gospel.

Senators Kenneth Keating of New York and Sam Ervin of North Carolina debated the religious foundation of the Civil Rights Act. Ervin questioned Keating on whether the New York senator believed a Southern jury was incapable of rendering a just verdict. Keating answered that he "was not impugning the honesty of any jury" but merely argued "that the statutes which have been on the books for 100 years are completely outworn" and required remedy by the bill on the floor.[181] Ervin, seeking to speak for eternal truths, responded, "Those statutes are much newer than the Constitution, or the Declaration of Independence, or the Ten Commandments. I know the Ten Commandments are not outworn. However, when I see the bills of the character of the one here proposed, I sometimes think that some people believe the Constitution is."[182] Keating seized on the biblical reference and responded, "This bill is based on the Ten Commandments. I did not mention that in my original remarks, because the Ten Commandments are not a part of the basic statutory law of this country. . . . But the provisions of the bill are in the spirit of the Ten Commandments and the Beatitudes."[183] In making this claim, Keating appeared to speak from the Hebraic-Christian consensus and spoke for eternal truths by which to measure whether existing statutes were outworn.

Sensing his error, Ervin pulled back, arguing, "I would say this bill would come nearer to being based on the Beatitudes than on the Constitution of the United States. But we are not supposed to be legislating on the basis of the Beatitudes, no matter how beautiful they may be."[184] Ervin, in other words, wanted a greater separation of church and state in the legal code, essentially implying that the Constitution lacked any relationship to Christianity.

Keating responded, "That is why I did not refer to them or base my case on them, because I was afraid the Senator would challenge it if we put the bill on the basis of the Beatitudes or the Ten Commandments. But they are completely relevant."[185] The Jewish and Christian Scriptures informed the Constitution that empowered senators like Keating to push for statutes that would remedy present injustice. Sensing he was losing the exchange, Ervin harrumphed about the Preamble and concluded that "this bill would destroy the blessings of liberty" before quickly changing the subject.[186] The back-and-forth revealed Keating's reluctant admission that the Civil Rights Act rested on a religious foundation that he joined to the American Constitution.

This and other parts of the exchange between Keating and Ervin inspired Louisiana senator Allen Ellender to rise in defense of the state right to regulate the franchise. He stressed that "the right to vote has been zealously guarded, not only by the framers of our Constitution, but also during colonial times when our country was first settled."[187] Ellender then listed the voting requirements for colonial territories, which typically included a minimum property requirement. More important to Ellender, however, were requirements either that a voter be Protestant or, alternately, prohibitions on Catholic and Jewish voting rights. When arriving at Keating's state of New York, Ellender joked, "In 1701, 21 years of age and 40 pounds of realty was necessary [to vote in New York], and papists and Jews were barred. Imagine if anyone tried to do that now" and then repeated, "Papists and Jews were barred from voting in New York."[188] Ellender intended to push the issue that states, when colonies, had once thought it necessary to discriminate based on religion—a state power that the Civil Rights Act would prohibit—and that Article 1, Section 2, of the Constitution preserved this arrangement in the Constitution. States, in his view, could use voter discrimination for "varying reasons . . . , keeping in mind . . . the very fact that they have varied in each State, with the particular conditions of growth and existing population."[189] For this reason, Ellender sought to defend state voter discrimination against "unqualified Negroes" who, during Reconstruction, became "incompetents in the administration of affairs of the county and municipal governments" typical of "Negro rule."[190] In short, Ellender argued the party line of the white Southern religious defense of segregation, noting that once Americans in the colonial North thought Jews and Catholics were as incompetent to vote as African Americans.

Other senators rose to affirm Humphrey's interpretation of the moral and religious foundations for civil rights. Oregon Senator Wayne Morse expressed his support for the bill in strongly religious terms. Once a Republican, Morse switched to the Democratic Party in 1955 with the encouragement of then Democratic minority leader Lyndon B. Johnson. Morse peppered his speech with quotations of Thomas Jefferson expressing support for civil rights, yet he observed in a somewhat mangled sentence, "The great evil in the discrimination against Negroes in this country ever since the Emancipation Proclamation by reason of our failure to ever deliver the Constitution to them is discrimination that cannot be squared with the Golden Rule."[191] Morse followed King's periodization of the American exodus from Jefferson to the Emancipation Proclamation to the present. He followed this periodization with an appeal to the universally knowable religious faith that supported the civil rights cause, saying, "We are seeking to keep faith with the principle of religious teaching that runs through all the religions of the world, based upon a belief in one God. Bring to me any of the great religious books which form the foundation teaching of all the major religions in the world . . . and I will point out the Golden Rule."[192] Morse saw in the Fourteenth Amendment a "spiritual teaching" that the Senate had "denied and ignored, insofar as the Negroes are concerned, ever since the 14th amendment was adopted."[193] Those who had fought for civil rights, especially African Americans, were "imbued with the spirit of martyrdom" and remained "ready to die for their constitutional rights."[194]

Pennsylvania senator Joseph S. Clark described his support for Title VII of the Civil Rights Act, which prohibited discrimination based on sex, race, color, national origin, and religion, as a "vitally important moral issue."[195] He presented a joint statement from Catholic, Protestant, and Jewish leaders given in testimony before the Senate Subcommittee on Employment and Manpower, which read in part: "The religious conscience of America condemns racism as blasphemy against God. It recognizes that the racial segregation and discrimination that flow from it are a denial of the worth which God has given to all persons. We hold that God is the Father of all men. Consequently in every person there is an innate dignity which is the basis of human rights. These rights constitute a moral claim which must be honored both by all persons and by the state. Denial of such rights is immoral."[196] Clark then quoted a rabbi who said, "This kind of [racial] discrimination is blasphemous, it is an affront to our religious commitment and to our religious convictions, believing as we do that man is created in the image of God, and this is an affront not only to man, but certainly to God as the creator of all mankind."[197] To this, Clark added his own view that, "If I opposed this bill, I would find it very difficult indeed at the next public meeting I attended to pledge allegiance to the flag of the United States of America and to the

Republic for which it stands, one nation under God, indivisible, with liberty and justice for all."[198] Clark linked the Hebraic-Christian tradition and the republic in the same way that King had spent years preaching.

Another speech brought the subtext of many speeches to the surface. Only months after his brother's assassination, then freshman senator from Massachusetts Edward M. Kennedy rose on April 9, 1964, to give his maiden address to the Senate on the Civil Rights Act.[199] Kennedy reflected on the same theme of sacrifice found in Johnson's and in his late older brother's speeches; however, Kennedy also emphasized the religious consensus that operated out of the Hebraic-Christian tradition on which King founded his Beloved Community. The religious groups Kennedy presented were the redeemed versions of the ones King condemned in the "Letter from a Birmingham Jail," yet who later demonstrated on behalf of civil rights at the March on Washington. Kennedy introduced his speech with the theme of sacrifice, reflecting how he was putting the immediate needs of his constituents behind the good of the nation: "I had planned about this time in the session to make my maiden speech in the Senate on issues affecting industry and employment in my home State. I still hope to discuss these questions at some later date. But I could not follow this debate for the last four weeks— I could not see this issue envelop the emotions and the conscience of the Nation—without changing my mind. To limit myself in the face of this great national question would be to demean the seat in which I sit."[200] Kennedy retained King's sense of racial suffering with discrimination against religious minorities that had, by Kennedy's time, entered the political mainstream as part of the Hebraic-Christian heritage: "In 1780, a Catholic in Massachusetts was not allowed to vote or hold public office. In 1840, an Irishman could not get a job above that of common laborer. In 1910, a Jew could not stay in places of public accommodation in the Berkshire Mountains."[201] Irish Catholics and Jews suffered because of their religious beliefs, and these beliefs were primarily held in ethnically defined groups, to which Kennedy was a credible witness as an Irish Catholic himself. Kennedy echoed King's belief in the Hebraic-Christian tradition as the basis for resolving racial differences. Moreover, the combined religious bases and experiences of repression gave Catholics and Jews the insight into the need for sacrifice of privilege for the sake of American justice, though this time requiring them to make the sacrifice rather than be those for whom sacrifices were made.

Kennedy quoted local churches to cobble together a real sense of the Hebraic-Christian heritage operating against racial injustice. He directly referred to the words of Boston's cardinal Richard Cushing and Episcopal bishop Anson Stokes, and he had letters from Quakers, Jews, Unitarians, Congregationalists, and the Cape Cod Council of Churches, to name only a few. Kennedy pointed to how Massachusetts already had an active community of Hebraic-Christian religious groups in favor of desegregation: "In January of last year, there gathered in Chicago a National Conference on Religion and Race. Representatives of 67 national religious bodies, Protestants, Catholic, and Jewish, representing all of the denominations said at that time: Our appeal to the American people is this: Seek a reign of justice in which voting rights and equal protection of the law will everywhere be enjoyed."[202] Finally, Kennedy affirmed the prophetic role religion had played leading up to the Civil Rights Act: "Mr. President, when religious leaders call on us to urge passage of this bill, they are not mixing religion and politics. This is not a political issue. It is a moral issue, to be resolved through political means. Religious leaders can preach, they can advise, they can lead movements of social action. But there comes a point when persuasion must be backed up by law to be effective."[203] Kennedy harked back to Johnson's and his fallen brother's description of racial justice as a moral question with a political answer, and he affirmed the role King believed religious groups had in offering moral guidance. Kennedy had received numerous letters from Christian and Jewish groups he later read into the record. Because of those letters, according to his speech, he suspended his and his constituents' provincial needs for the sake of a moral, national good. In one case, Kennedy was so obviously taken with King's language that he borrowed a line from King's speech at the March on Washington not even a year after King had given it, saying, "As a young man I want to see an America where everyone can make his contribution, where a man will be measured not by the color of his skin but the content of his character."[204]

The bill eventually passed. In his signing statement, Johnson fully embraced the covenant language King had been using for years. He said segregation could not continue because "our Constitution, the foundation of our Republic, forbids it. The principles of our freedom forbid it. Morality forbids it. And the law I will sign tonight forbids it."[205] The effect of the law was to make "those who are equal before God . . . also be equal in the polling booths, in the classrooms, in the factories, and in the hotels, restaurants, movie theaters, and other places that provide service to the public."[206] The closing portion of the speech echoed King's demand for individuals to appeal to God as a way of eliminating racism and restoring the Kingdom of God: "Let us close the springs of racial poison. Let us pray for wise and understanding hearts. Let us lay aside irrelevant differences and make our Nation whole. Let us hasten that day when our unmeasured strength and unbounded spirit will be free to do the great works ordained for this Nation by the just and wise God who is the Father of us all."[207] Johnson invited King to stand with him during the signing ceremony for the bill, and photographs from the event showed King standing over Johnson. King had spent the time leading up to the passage and signature of the act demonstrating in St. Augustine, Florida, to continue pressuring the federal government to act. Once Johnson signed the law, King coordinated his response with other civil rights leaders to "test" the law across the South.[208]

Johnson's inaugural address in January of that year illustrated the extent to which King's covenant had framed American foundational thinking. Johnson interpreted American history as a covenant composed of the American belief in justice, liberty, and union. He saw that these values included those of exiles and strangers who came here "to find a place where a man could be his own man. They made a covenant with this land. Conceived in justice, written in liberty, bound in union, it was meant one day to inspire the hopes of all mankind; and it binds us still."[209] For Johnson, God oversaw American attempts to keep the covenant: "Under this covenant of justice, liberty, and union we have become a nation—prosperous, great, and mighty. And we have kept our freedom. But we have no promise from God that our greatness will endure. We have been allowed by Him to seek greatness with the sweat of our hands and the strength of our spirit."[210] The covenant with the land, then, was possible only by the grace of God. Johnson said that God created the moral space for acting on the beliefs that defined America, and acting on those beliefs was the only way Americans could achieve the destiny God established when the exiles and strangers originally arrived here and made the covenant with the land: "If we succeed, it will not be because of what we have, but it will be because of what we are; not because of what we own, but rather because of what we believe. For we are a nation of believers. Underneath the clamor of building and the rush of our day's pursuits, we are believers in justice and liberty and union, and in our own Union. We believe that every man must someday be free. And we believe in ourselves."[211]

Conclusion

By the time Johnson made his inaugural address, King had successfully made the Beloved Community the foundation for racial reform. While he was certainly not alone in pursuing civil rights, he had determined how proponents of the movement should explain why the reforms were of the greatest importance, and made plain how to understand civil rights as something that could bind Americans together religiously rather than separate them racially. He did so by defining the Beloved Community more broadly than white clergy had in the past, thus demarcating religious space for Jews who strongly backed the movement and for those members of the Catholic Church who did as well. Moreover, he knitted the tradition of the Beloved Community, affirmed by a latter-day Paul, to satyagraha as a way of making the foundation more immediately political. In post-Protestant America, the Beloved Community could no longer easily take hold of the American imagination but rather had to compete with alternatives, especially the separatism of white Protestant churches that dominated the South. Most important for King was to make this foundation something that could generate political influence, and his extensive use of Lincoln as the premier American example of *agape* in public office helped frame the entire effort to pass the Civil Rights Act—helped by invoking the anniversaries of the American Civil War and the Emancipation Proclamation and the use of the Lincoln Memorial. Because King and the SCLC had to work so much harder to secure press attention, his Beloved Community was the most dramatic of the foundational ideas treated in this book, thus highlighting how foundational ideas, once successfully mediated by the press, are the bridge between political theory and public policy.

After the 1965 Watts riots, King experienced increased competition for leading the Civil Rights Movement. By 1966, SNCC had openly broken with the SCLC and advocated "Black Power" as a superior approach to King's "Freedom Now." In the autumn of 1967, King publicly broke with Johnson over the Vietnam War even as white moderates had already moved on to protesting American participation in the conflict. In 1967, King published *Where Do We Go from Here: Chaos or Community?* in which he outlined a detailed plan for deploying African American economic and voting strength. The book, especially the chapter "Where We Are Going," illustrated how King was moving into a more directly partisan approach in coalition building with traditional pillars of the Democratic Party.[212] Launching this program was the SCLC's Poor People's Campaign, which sought to unite working whites and African Americans in a broader integration of labor unions and open up economic assistance to the economically marginalized. James Earl Ray assassinated King on April 4, 1968, before King could begin what he thought would be the second stage of the Civil Rights Movement, and one wonders whether, had King lived, the campaign would have achieved its results. The end of 1960s brought with it the rapid decline of the moderate and liberal mainline white Protestants who most sympathized with King even as King's own political influence had waned. Meanwhile, King's old white Southern Baptist adversaries continued to grow their churches and, as they grew, so did their anxiety about the direction the nation was headed.

CHAPTER 3

The American Dispensation

Jerry Falwell, the Nehemiad,
and the Signs of the Times

> Behold, I am sending you like sheep in the midst of
> wolves; so be shrewd as serpents and simple as doves.
> When they hand you over [to their rulers], do not
> worry about how you are to speak or what you are to say.
> You will be given at that moment what you are to say.
> For it will not be you who speak but the Spirit of your
> Father speaking through you.
>
> —Matthew 10:16–20

On May 13, 2007, the Reverend Jerry Falwell died in his Lynchburg, Virginia, office, leaving behind a national American politics he had helped shape. He had reconciled the once separatist Protestant Fundamentalist and Evangelical churches with massive, direct, and conventional participation in American politics. The participation was massive in that it covered broad regions of the nation. It was direct in that these newly mobilized Christians engaged in local political decision-making. It was conventional in that they entered into the traditional two-party system in American politics, specifically the New Conservative Movement that had seized the Republican Party. It is hard for some to admit Falwell's significant contribution to American politics. In fact, a reader may wince at calling Falwell's legacy a "contribution" at all. Even scholars friendly to the Religious Right reject Falwell as an important influence, perhaps afraid that recognizing Falwell's influence undermines the attempt to make conservative Christianity respectable.[1] Falwell was, however, less concerned with making Fundamentalist and Evangelical Protestants respectable than he was with making them relevant. Falwell appealed to an American dispensation as his foundation for persuading these Christians to participate in politics, to ally themselves with the remainder of the Judeo-Christian consensus to form the Religious Right, and ultimately to establish themselves as a core constituency of the Republican Party.

Early scholarly treatment of Falwell lumped him in with the larger Religious Right without taking seriously his dogmatic or political statements. Instead, the larger movement had become the focal point, resulting in the mischaracterization of Falwell as emulating a generic televangelism-gone-conservative-politics. The attention, therefore, has been on finding his audience and combining it with other televangelist audiences to learn the nature of the Religious Right, on examining its institutions like Falwell's own Moral Majority, and on determining how effective they were, as a constituency, in achieving short-term political goals.[2] Perhaps the cause for such inattention to Falwell himself has been the frame with which many scholars approached the Religious Right, as a thumb in the eye of the secularization hypothesis. In that case, Falwell's religious foundation was less important than the fact that he existed at all. Whereas Europe by the 1970s experienced a real decline in religiosity, America only appeared to, since Fundamentalist and Evangelical Christians had abandoned mainstream American culture.[3] During their self-exile, Fundamentalist churches established a network of parallel educational, social, and cultural institutions—ranging from huge church buildings to even larger mass media ministries—under the radar of scholars of religion. Because these Christians never meant to encounter the American mainstream, their change of heart in the 1970s felt to those within the mainstream like a sudden upheaval rather than what it was for those Christians—a triumphant and final return from exile.

The American Dispensation Defined

Jerry Lamon Falwell Sr. was born in 1933 to Carey Hezekiah Falwell and Helen Virginia Falwell of Lynchburg, Virginia. His mother was a devout Protestant, but his father was indifferent to religion for most of his life. Carey Falwell had a younger brother, Garland, who had run-ins with police, served time in prison, and eventually became an alcoholic. In a 1931 altercation, Carey shot Garland in the chest and killed him; at his trial, Carey Falwell was found not guilty. Carey Falwell spent much of the Depression as a bootlegger but also engaged in legitimate businesses that provided a good life for Jerry, his twin brother Gene, and their younger sister Jeannie. Carey Falwell struggled with alcoholism and died in 1948 shortly after a deathbed conversion to Protestant Christianity. Jerry Falwell attended Lynchburg College and studied engineering until, in 1952, he had a religious experience while listening to Charles Fuller's *Old Fashioned Revival Hour* on the radio in his mother's kitchen. He began attending Park Avenue Baptist Church but left Lynchburg to complete his studies at Baptist Bible College in Springfield, Missouri. He graduated in 1956, returned home, married Macel Pate, and began Thomas Road Baptist Church in an old factory, but the church quickly expanded into one of the largest church ministries in America.

Before explaining the American dispensation, there is an issue of nomenclature. Falwell liked to speak of "Bible-believing Christians." While this term may seem vague, Falwell had a specific meaning for it. Falwell was a Fundamentalist Protestant, meaning he held to the traditional Protestant view of biblical inerrancy, as well as some of the later doctrinal developments described below. Being "Bible-believing" was a contrast to the liberal Protestants who, in his view, had ceased to believe in real Christianity. Though Falwell spoke of himself as a Fundamentalist, he reached out to Evangelical Protestants who sometimes placed less emphasis on biblical inerrancy or differed over the age and manner of baptism but could make common religious cause with him. Falwell sought such an alliance and, to make and preserve it, spoke of them, united, as "Bible-believing Christians."[4] Falwell preserved denominational distinctions, especially Roman Catholicism, in most other cases. Hereafter, this chapter adopts Falwell's term, but such an adoption should not be misunderstood as an endorsement of Falwell's interpretation of which Christians truly believe in the Bible.

Falwell understood the American dispensation to be the proper religious foundation for America. The American dispensation began, according to Falwell, with the founding of America as a Christian nation, but the purpose of the nation would only become clear as Europe began its religious decline and left America as the last remaining political and religious leader standing between the current "Church Age" and the coming Tribulation. Hence, America faced a choice; the nation could either restore and preserve its Christian foundations and remain the last Christian mission, or continue "to stray from our original foundations" and usher in the Tribulation.[5] The aim of preserving American religious foundations, therefore, was to preserve the American state for as long as possible, thus bringing as many souls as possible to Christ before the End Times.

This foundation broke with the decades-long separatism of Fundamentalists, which Falwell had once himself advocated as an independent Baptist preacher at Thomas Road Baptist Church. Though disputing complete
separatism, Falwell still subscribed to the doctrine of biblical literalism
and the eschatology of "dispensational premillennialism." Biblical literalism treated the Bible as a source for human knowledge about both heaven
and earth that came prior to any "scientific" discovery that humanity might
apply to the world. Dispensational premillennialism, popularized during
the late nineteenth century by the "Scofield Bible" or the reference Bible
distributed by C. I. Scofield, described Christian eschatology as beginning
with the ascent of Christians (known as the "Rapture") preceding the war
between heaven and hell on earth (the "Tribulation") and a subsequent one-
thousand-year reign of Christ ("Millennium"). Falwell also insisted on the
traditional Fundamentalist doctrine that God was ultimately in charge of
the fate of nations. Unlike Dr. Martin Luther King Jr., Falwell believed that
no amount of justice or love would provoke God to establish the Kingdom
of God. The Kingdom of God only came at the End Times, and humanity
had no control over the hour of its coming. This truncated sense of human
volition was the distinction between the premillennial and the postmillennial. Nothing Americans did—Fundamentalists or otherwise—could found
the Kingdom. Only God could.[6]

As one might suspect, dispensational premillennialism carved out little
room for human action within the broader divine plan, and Falwell retained
that sense in his political preaching. He described the depravity of the human
soul and the corresponding need for immediate, personal salvation found
in Christ. God required Bible-believing Christians to proselytize to save as
many of God's children as possible. However, the church had failed to spread
the Gospel, which was the primary reason so much sin affected Americans.
Indeed, Falwell did not blame America's "sinfulness" in the late 1970s on
Communists, feminists, or hippies, but rather on the failure of Bible-believing
Christians to evangelize, and it was that failure that had given the chance for
enemies of religion to prosper. This fateful concession provided enemies the
opportunity to prevent Christian evangelization by eliminating it from public
settings. For Falwell, the greatest political issue for the church was to defend
its freedom to evangelize. He tied religious freedom in America directly to
American religious foundations. Americans were politically free because of
the religious freedom Christian settlers sought in the New World. That freedom made America the best place for world evangelization, something Falwell claimed God had ordained.

Falwell believed that God's judgment appeared as "signs of the times." Moral failures had provoked God's anger in the 1970s, and God's anger could only lead to the end of America. These signs, such as natural disasters and the decline of American power and influence, were meant to warn Americans to restore the rightful place of the Gospel at the American foundation and stage a revival of religion. Falwell based his view of national sin and punishment on his biblical interpretation. The Bible set the standard for understanding God as blessing and cursing nations. His favorite scriptural passage to illustrate this point was Proverbs 14:34: "A verse of Scripture that's come alive in my life in the past several years is Proverbs 14:34 which says in the King James Version 'Righteousness exalteth a nation, but sin is a reproach to any people.' To give you a little translation of that, that is my own, a paraphrase: living by God's principles promotes a nation to greatness. Violating God's principles brings a nation to shame. What has happened to America in the last thirty years? We have begun nationally to defy and to disobey the principles that God has set down for this nation."[7] It is important to notice that Falwell's use of this passage placed all nations on an equal footing. Righteousness and sin affected all nations and peoples and in the same ways. America was no exception for Falwell, even though America had received great blessings for two hundred years.[8] However, Falwell wanted to provoke a sense of urgency in his audience, since there was no other nation on earth that could serve as a bulwark for political liberty and the Christian faith. Without America, the church would fail. For that reason, Bible-believing Christians had to understand their citizenship responsibilities as coextensive with their spiritual responsibilities. They must pray, and they must vote.

The difficulty in Falwell's American dispensation was marking the points where God's sovereignty began and human freedom ended. The small area of human influence was in the preservation of freedom that enabled America to be the staging ground for world evangelization. According to Falwell, it was up to Bible-believing Christians to insist on protecting that freedom. Falwell defined freedom as the capacity to preach the Gospel without government interference. In one sermon, he defined American freedom as simply a means to a religious end, saying, "I think that God brought us into being in these last days for the purpose in an environment of freedom for evangelizing the world," and "I'm simply fighting to get this country a few more years of freedom so we can do what the ultimate goal of the Gospel is. That is out of freedom to give the Gospel to the world."[9] Falwell found this freedom endangered by atheistic Communism, the mass murder of children in legalized abortion, the continued secularization of public life, and the violation of the biblically sanctioned family. The threat of Communism became more real as American power and influence, for Falwell, appeared to decline, and that decline was the result of sin. Communism, as well as terrorism and economic despair, were God's warnings for repentance. By entering the political process, Bible-believing Christians could reverse the harm done by legalized abortion, secularization, divorce, and the affording of rights to LGBT groups. Indeed, Falwell believed that Bible-believing Christians were best situated to explain the need for revival. The best evidence of this religious outcome came as a somewhat self-conscious form of boasting Falwell made about the growth of Fundamentalism at the apparent expense of mainline denominations, who had conceded all the moral ground to the "secular humanism" of opposing progressive groups.[10]

The issue of "secular humanism" points to another cause for Falwell's turn to politics: the influence of Francis Schaeffer. Schaeffer was an eccentric American Fundamentalist preacher who founded a religious center called L'Abri, or "the shelter," in the Swiss Alps. L'Abri was an odd place. Young Fundamentalist Christians from America would interact with diverse groups of spiritual seekers and casual drug use, while Schaeffer preached on the Bible in one breath and pop culture in the next. As he gained popularity during the 1960s and 1970s, Schaeffer sought to dispel the notion that American Christians continued to live a religious culture; instead, Western populations had crossed "the line of despair" past which increasing numbers of Americans and Europeans no longer shared the same Christian presuppositions. Instead, they adopted a secular "humanism" he defined as "the system whereby man, beginning absolutely by himself, tries rationally to build out from himself, having only man as his integration point, to find all knowledge, meaning, and value."[11] When this humanism emerged at the end of the nineteenth century, churches confronted it with the assumption that humanism shared a concept of absolute truth beyond what a person may construct. They were wrong, and they discovered this too late, as church efforts failed to stem secular humanism as it engulfed much of the West. According to Schaeffer, the church had to stop the flood of humanism and send it back but only after recalibrating evangelism to suit the new challenge in humanism as well as the cultural changes it has wrought. Schaeffer's work influenced Falwell, persuading him to condemn abortion and to reach outside of his own independent, Fundamentalist Baptist milieu to form alliances with people of different faiths.[12]

One final cause for Falwell's turn to politics was the continued racial politics of the South. Randall Balmer has argued that, after the federal government began pursuing desegregation of public schools, Falwell and other white Southern clergy quickly established private religious schools as whites-only alternatives.[13] The conventional story of the Religious Right starts with outrage in response to the 1973 Supreme Court decision *Roe v. Wade*, which declared abortion a constitutional right, and to the 1971 Supreme Court decision *Lemon v. Kurtzman*, which struck down state funding for religious education and applied a general test to enforce secularism in public institutions. In response, Balmer argues that the true federal court decision that mobilized Southern Fundamentalist and Evangelical Protestants was the 1971 Supreme Court decision *Green v. Connally*, which upheld the Internal Revenue Service policy that revoked federal tax exemption from segregated private educational institutions. This decision motivated them to take a renewed interest in politics, which only afterwards they would disguise in concern about abortion and religious liberty. At the start, Balmer believes, it was a racist movement.[14]

As discussed in the previous chapter, Falwell had once defended segregation and condemned Dr. Martin Luther King Jr. for his efforts to mix religion and politics. In 1997, Falwell wrote an autobiography reflecting on his reversals. On his reversal about religion and politics, he cited the influence of his education, elders in his family, and a concern about pastors participating in matters for which they were not prepared.[15] As for desegregation, he described beginning the process for Thomas Road Baptist Church in 1963 and completing it by 1968. He admitted his first African American students to the Lynchburg Christian Academy, which was affiliated with Thomas Road, in 1969.[16] Falwell's depiction of these events can seem self-serving, but even he admitted that church members often withdrew support and joined different churches when he began integration. Even when painting himself in the best light, Falwell was willing to admit that his former church members placed segregation ahead of fellowship. It is fair to conclude that not all of Falwell's original audience proceeded purely from theological grounds.

The American Dispensation and the American Nehemiad

Much about Falwell seems, on the surface, to confirm that his was yet another expression of the American jeremiad. Falwell so far has appeared to present America as a Christian nation that has sinned and must repent to fulfill its divine destiny. This much about Falwell is true; however, it is not a complete picture of Falwell's American dispensation. Falwell invoked the jeremiad most of all in Moral Majority material. The Moral Majority was a political nonprofit intended to mobilize conservative Christians and Jews for the Republican Party. Because these groups differed on matters of religious doctrine, these publications often stressed a sense of common policy goals and a sense of impending doom if they were not addressed soon. As Michael Sean Winters observes, "The Moral Majority's literature did not intend to mimic the 'civic religion' of America" but nonetheless "had to distinguish dogma from morals, and the morality needed to be accessible to those who did not share a Baptist's concerns about dancing and drinking."[17] To that end, much of the Moral Majority platform concerned consensus positions on the traditional family, especially in opposition to LGBT issues,[18] as well as a strong national defense and low taxation.[19] Even so, Falwell did not deploy a jeremiad as the sole or primary narrative to persuade the American public of the American dispensation. As we saw above, Falwell denied that America was exceptional. This claim runs contrary to the prevailing view of Falwell and his political position, but scholars taking this view have neglected Falwell's sermons as counterpoints to the sharply political statements taken from his paperback books and newspaper interviews.[20] Even as Falwell published these texts, he cautioned his audience that he did not want to confuse America with the Kingdom of God.

Falwell remained fundamentally ambivalent about America, since America was not the Kingdom dispensational premillennialists were waiting for. Rather than seeing America as a nation set apart from unsaved infidels worthy only of scorn and fear, Falwell saw the unsaved peoples of the world as the responsibility the church had left unmet. Merged with Falwell's message of political engagement to protect political freedom was his message that American freedom was a means to the most important end God set forth for his church:

> God so loved the world that He gave His Son Jesus. Right now I'd like to challenge all of my friends watching by television and all of you here in this auditorium to do something for God and country. I want you to become a flag-waving American . . . freedom is everybody's business. It's important. It's good to respect your flag. A good Christian makes a good citizen. We do not believe that America is more important to God than any other nation. We do not believe that, but we do believe that America is important to God because to whom much is given, much shall be required.[21]

Elsewhere, Falwell said: "You see, Jesus didn't die for America alone. For God so loved the world, every nation in this world, every nationality, every person, that He gave His only begotten Son. Jesus died for the Russians and the Chinese and the Europeans and the Asians and on and on. He died for everybody. He died for every African. And he loved them enough to shed His own blood. Then we have an obligation to tell them. And it's only in the environment of freedom that we can do that. Christians hold the key to the destiny of this nation."[22] God chose America, according to Falwell, but God did not choose it to be the Kingdom, only the home of the church's final push to convert as many souls as possible before the Rapture.[23] Falwell believed that those souls not saved were a judgment upon the church's failure, and if the church could not even save America—despite all the freedom to save it—then the church would be at fault for the billions of souls left without salvation. Because no nation could become the Kingdom of God, the true purpose for a nation, whether America or any other, was to provide the staging ground for world evangelization. Falwell insisted in a passage that sums up the American dispensation:

> We don't believe that America is in any way approximating the millennial reign of Christ. This is not the kingdom of God on this earth, and when you see me with a flag and a Bible and all the rest, I'm not trying to say this is the kingdom of heaven. It is not. America has as much sin in it as any nation on earth. But God has blessed the principles that have been espoused here, and God does have a purpose for America, and I do feel that if the Lord is willing to give us a few more years of freedom that we in America who pastor the thousands of Bible-believing churches and the millions of Americans who love Christ in this nation can do a little better job of telling four and a half billion souls in other lands of the death, burial, and resurrection of Christ.[24]

Falwell sustained a strong distinction between the national and the sacred. The ideal of the Kingdom of God provided a measure for the United States as for all other nations, and the Bible explained world events as God's wrath for the sins of every nation. Falwell reserved his triumphant vision not for American destiny but for the destiny of the church, whose victory would come not in empire but in heavenly glory.[25]

Because Falwell insisted on the separation of church and state, his political appeals diverged from the ordinary jeremiad.[26] America faced oblivion because of sin, but so did any nation, just as any nation experienced exaltation in righteousness. The cause of American decline was primarily the failure of the church, which had gone into exile. The church must return from exile, just as Nehemiah had in the Bible. Hence, Falwell's account for restoring America was not only jeremiad but primarily a nehemiad, one in which America, like the pious and patriotic Nehemiah, would rebuild the earthly kingdom while waiting for God to establish the coming heavenly kingdom. In this way, Falwell remained true to his Baptist roots. Baptists have always remained skeptical of postmillennialist equations of the church covenant with the secular, even before the development of dispensational premillennial eschatology.[27]

At the same time the Bible-believing Christians returned from their self-imposed political exile, scholars renewed their interest in the role the jeremiad had played in influencing American political culture and institutions. Originally, only a handful of historians studied the subject, in particular how the Puritans established the jeremiad as one of their religious practices in speech that held together the community.[28] As mentioned in the introduction of this book, the jeremiad has recently become a primary interpretive frame for American religion and politics, and scholarly treatment of Falwell is no exception. The jeremiad does not sufficiently capture all of Falwell's religious foundation, yet scholars often frame Falwell's work strictly on its use. One example is Susan Friend Harding's work, in which she describes the "Moral Majority Jeremiad" yet quotes a sermon from Falwell in which he preaches primarily on the example of Nehemiah.[29] There was more to Falwell than a simple redeployment of the old Puritan standard.

The jeremiad, for Falwell, only provided the diagnosis for the problem. The continued moral decay of the nation would lead God to strike the nation down, but God wanted to bless America with prosperity because of the special role America would have in evangelizing the world. Falwell was hopeful this would happen, but he never shied from stoking the fears of national turmoil. After the 1960s and 1970s, it was especially easy for both his congregants and a broader audience to suppose that the apparently multiplying national tragedies might have something more than a material explanation. The jeremiad called people of faith back to first principles, to the original basis of religious practice. For Bible-believing Christians, this also meant a return to the social conservatism. The Fundamentalist affiliation with conservative politics was, by the rise of Falwell, nearly a century old.[30] Dispensational premillennialism was part of the broader nineteenth-century intellectual fascination with the philosophy of history; however, unlike secular trends like Hegelianism, Marxism, or Darwinism, dispensational premillennialism took a decidedly more pessimistic reading of history.[31] Dispensational premillennialists located the Kingdom of God beyond the reach of mere mortals and in the hands of God alone. No secular or religious forces on earth were capable of radical change in the human condition. That power remained in God's hands, and what defined the Church Age was the eager anticipation of the Rapture that would bring about the final passage of creation.

For dispensational premillennialists such as Falwell, the Church Age or "ecclesiastical dispensation" was the present age, defined by the need for the church to evangelize the unsaved in preparation for the coming ages of Rapture, Tribulation, and the final victory of Christ on earth in the Second Coming. Ages began and ended with God's decision. Prior ages, such as Innocence in the Garden of Eden and the formation of human government in the covenant with Israel, all started with God contacting chosen human actors, who then acted out (or failed to act out) God's commandments. Historical change, then, had nothing to do with human activity except as far as human failures determined how God would respond, but not whether God would. In short, dispensational premillennialism resisted the nineteenth-century urge to abstract God as a notion of "Providence" acting through human choices—thus harmonizing and legitimating them—but rather presented God as acting directly on earth either because of or despite human failures.[32]

By the start of the twentieth century in America, Protestants of diverse denominations had adherents to dispensational premillennialism, and they kept the same theological company as holiness preachers and revivalists. These several groups overlapped sufficiently to form their own cross-denominational camps that revolted against the attempts of liberal theologians to "modernize" Protestantism. Originally, dispensational premillennialists saw no problem with state cooperation with efforts to improve national morality through social welfare to the poor and with Prohibition, since the state was serving as a proxy for enforcing religious commitments revealed in Scripture and preached by the Church. However, modernist theologians began to prioritize the reforms themselves over the religious commitment those reforms were supposed to serve, leading to the split within denominations. The publication of *The Fundamentals: A Testimony to the Truth* from 1910 to 1915 became a defining moment for burgeoning conservative reactions against a perceived secularization of the Church.[33] *The Fundamentals*, a twelve-volume statement of Protestant orthodoxy, repudiated scholarly efforts to reduce the Bible to historical texts of human origin. Preachers like Dwight L. Moody led the exodus of Fundamentalists from their traditional Presbyterian, Baptist, and other Protestant parachurch organizations and into their own set of parallel institutions meant to preserve fundamental doctrine to which all Fundamentalists adhered. In fact, the Moody Bible Institute became a core teaching institution that provided continuity across Bible-believing churches. After embarrassments at the Scopes Trial in

1925 and the repeal of Prohibition in 1933, Bible-believing Christians understood the state not as a partner for evangelization but as a threat. As a result,
they avoided any unnecessary involvement in politics, since politics carried
with it the apostasy of modernists, to say nothing of the increased risks of
papal influence or that of the rich. By the 1940s, most of these congregations
abandoned national politics for spiritual concerns.[34] Of course, many Fundamentalist and Evangelical Protestants remained national figures, as discussed
later, but the sense of exile nevertheless settled into the imaginations of many
ordinary churchgoers who felt as if they had lost a spiritual battle.[35]

Nearly forty years later, they returned, but remained nonetheless committed to the same principles they had espoused when leaving their old
denominations. They opposed church modernization, maintained traditional doctrine on issues like human depravity and the Trinity, looked to
Scripture as the basis for public life, and adhered to a dispensational premillennial eschatology.[36] Indeed, this last feature shaped the reason for their
return. As D. G. Hart has argued, one reason for the return of Fundamentalists into politics was not the legalization of abortion, but Supreme Court
rulings against religious practices in public schools, such as school prayer
and Bible reading: "Evangelicals only took to the political arena once their
culture was threatened—a culture that may be described in ethnic categories
as WASP. Before 1970, they did not need to be active politically because most
of their social and cultural concerns, which revolved around the sanctity of
the home and the ability of the parents to reproduce their ways, were safe in
the hands of the Protestant establishment."[37] Bible-believing Christians had
essentially been free riders on the political and cultural influence of mainline
denominations during their forty-year exile. So long as mainline Protestants
maintained the status quo for all Protestants, namely the vestiges of Protestant hegemony, then Bible-believing Christians could safely abdicate politics.
However, the establishment of mainline Protestants lost influence because
of both an internal theological crisis and the rapid depletion of members.[38]
That their decline led to the elimination of Protestant religious practices in
public schools was a blow to the most important purpose of a Bible-believing
Protestant—to evangelize the public about the birth, death, and resurrection
of Christ.[39] Francis Schaeffer's opposition to abortion came soon after, but
Falwell framed the legalization of abortion as a black mark not on America
but on the church for its failure to evangelize against the procedure. Indeed,
according to Falwell, the modernists were not prodigal sons; there was no
hope for them if they rejected the literal truth of revelation in Scripture. On
the contrary, Bible-believing Christians were the prodigal sons, and their

return to politics in the 1970s was the last, best hope for the United States to avoid God's ire and, thus, to transform the nation into the starting point for the greatest world evangelization effort in earth's six-thousand-year existence.

Falwell chose to interpret the purpose of Bible-believing Christians as part of the nehemiad, in which they made alliances with gentiles to protect the holy city as a center for evangelization. Indeed, the biblical story of Nehemiah demanded that the people of Jerusalem adhere to all Jewish law out of fear that God would punish Israel for failure.[40] Falwell feared the same for America and for the Christian religion. Also, the biblical Nehemiah told the story of Jews leaving the Babylonian exile, just as the nehemiad, for Falwell, was about Bible-believing Christians returning to national politics, that is, the New Conservative Movement within the Republican Party. Like the Jews under Ezra and Nehemiah returning to Jerusalem from the Babylonian exile, Falwell understood the return of Bible-believing Christians to American politics as a return from exile.[41] While the jeremiad served as the diagnosis of America's problems, the nehemiad offered the biblical example of political participation that would redeem America and set the world on the path for salvation.

The nehemiad is the application of the narrative from the biblical book of Nehemiah to contemporary religious and political life. Like the jeremiad, the nehemiad is as old as the Puritan colonies in America, and by using it Falwell put himself, perhaps unwittingly, in the same company as Cotton Mather, Ezra Stiles, and Nathanael Emmons, as well as later evangelists of the Second Great Awakening including Charles G. Finney.[42] Nehemiah was a Jewish servant of the Babylonian king, Artaxerxes. When he heard of the disrepair into which Jerusalem had fallen, he mourned for the Hebrew ancestral capital and asked to go back and restore it. The king granted Nehemiah's request, and Nehemiah helped the already-arrived Ezra to rebuild Jerusalem and to purify the Jewish community of its foreign rituals and customs, and of intermarriage with gentiles. While Nehemiah attempted to rebuild the walls of Jerusalem, he was opposed by gentiles in the provincial government there—namely Sanballat, Tobiah, and Geshem—who hoped to discourage Nehemiah from the proper course for Israel. Falwell saw Bible-believing Christians as in the same situation as the Jews returning to their ancestral homeland. During his *Old-Time Gospel Hour* sermon, "America Needs a Spiritual Awakening," Falwell gave a typical account of this analogy:

> Today the United States . . . is in desperate need of spiritual awakening. I look on our country much like the parallel to the Jewish people who were in Babylonian captivity. They were driven out of their own

land and humiliated because of their sin and their unbelief. They
went to Babylon under coercion to a foreign land, became slaves, but
then they began to prosper and things began to happen for them. The
majority of the people never intended to go back to Israel after they'd
been in exile for a number of years because they had become content
and complacent and apathetic in their present spiritual condition.
Many Americans today are not aware that our country is in a spiritual
distress but in reality we are.... Now Christians, born again believers have an obligation, a first priority to see to it that our children are
taught the Word of God and that we are not, we are not in exile, content in Babylon as were the Jews in Nehemiah's Day.[43]

Falwell believed that the Jews were in exile because of their sins; just so,
Bible-believing Christians were in self-exile because of their sin. They had
long failed in doing the things they were on earth to do, to bear witness to the
truth of the Gospel. Bible-believing Christians had to evangelize America to
restore its religious foundations. Once evangelized, for Falwell, a redeemed
America would be once again in good standing with God.

The return from exile, as a narrative, expressed a set of principles Falwell
used to call Bible-believing Christians back to political life. First, America
in the 1970s, like Israel during the Babylonian exile, was in a state of disrepair morally and institutionally. Falwell linked the American moral decline
with the failures of American institutions at home and of American influence abroad. Second, Falwell blamed Bible-believing Christians for this state
of disrepair, since they were the ones God chose to evangelize the world.
Had Bible-believing Christians not abandoned America, the nation would
have been in better shape; therefore, Falwell placed the responsibility for
restoring American greatness specifically at the feet of the church, like the
faithful Jews returning to Jerusalem. Third, he warned that the Church, like
the returning Jews, would suffer ridicule when entering the public square,
and this ridicule would only affirm the righteousness of the path the church
would take. Finally, the restored America would require the formation of
alliances with groups who shared the goals of Bible-believing Christians but
not their basis for achieving those goals, such as when Nehemiah depended
on the Babylonian king Artaxerxes to grant his return to the homeland.
Falwell preached that the morally restored America, though once again a
Christian nation, was not the Kingdom of God, just as the restored Israel of
Nehemiah was not the coming of the messiah.

Falwell argued that America was a Christian nation. He based his position on a traditional reading of the American founding, one that first began with the establishment of Protestant settlements in New England. Falwell said, "The Massachusetts Constitution, the oldest in existence, Robert Winthrop said, in 1836 was very clearly and obviously an attempt by its framers and those who adopted it, an effort to establish a Christian state. And the same can be said of the Constitution. This is a Christian nation."[44] Elsewhere, he preached: "the Pilgrims and the Puritans left an indelible imprint upon the minds and hearts of the early Americans, the early colonists, so that when they wrote the Declaration of Independence, the Constitution, the Bill of Rights, and the various states' charters and Constitutions, you can find the philosophies of the Pilgrims and the Puritans in line after line of this very important, these very important documents. America is a nation under God . . . it is not difficult to prove that we have erred, we have strayed from our original foundations."[45] The Protestant faith that inspired and directed these colonies formed the religious foundation that inspired the second founding after the American Revolution. Even though the framers of the Constitution were not entirely Christian, Falwell believed that those who were not still appreciated the truth found in the Bible concerning how best to govern and to live. Falwell said of the second founding: "I don't believe [that the Constitution] was written under divine inspiration like the Bible, but I indeed believe it was inspired. That these men who gathered in those early days, the embryonic days of our nation, were led of God as they prayed and sought His face, to pen a document that is founded upon the Ten Commandments and its principles are the teachings of Christ as you can find them in the Sermon on the Mount. It is unreal how they parallel. And there's no question about it, this nation was intended to be a Christian nation by our founding fathers."[46] According to Falwell, the continued reliance on biblical principles provided America the needed guidance to overcome political problems and inspired the best course of action into the twentieth century, that is, until America abandoned biblical principles.

Abandoning biblical principles precipitated the decline America had faced when confronted with the greatest existential threat on earth, nuclear annihilation. Falwell listed the several disasters and failures America had suffered as a result, and he preached that God was calling for revival by humbling American "greatness" just as he had raised America up. The Iran hostage crisis, the attack on Marines in Beirut, Watergate, Stagflation—all of them were signs of the times. Falwell said in 1984:

Yes, America is under judgment clouds right now. Groups like militant homosexuals, feminists, the American Civil Liberties Union,
the National Organization of Women, the National Abortion Rights
Action League, the Nazis, the Communists, Planned Parenthood, the
National Education Association and many others. When you look at
them and look at the work they're trying to do—many of them in
my opinion to lower the dignity and value of human life in the abortion area and the euthanasia and infanticide area. As we look at them
attempting to secularize society, purging society of God and religious
heritage and others trying to eliminate all moral absolutes. When you
begin to realize what is happening in this country of ours, America is
in serious trouble and the time is very, very late.[47]

The signs of the times were dire. Falwell responded with a call for revival,
which he saw as the responsibility of Bible-believing Christians to rehabili-
tate Christian America by the use of mass media. He called this method "saturation evangelization."[48]

Upon their return, Bible-believing Christians had to proselytize and
behave according to biblical standards, but the meaning of this witness was
not merely living a decent life. It required political action that would improve
the moral state of the nation, whether directly or indirectly. The content of
that political action was the American dispensation, and Falwell outlined how
a Bible-believing Christian must act to preserve it. The least a Bible-believing
Christian could do was to pray. Falwell described prayer as the way anyone
could supplicate God for mercy and blessing. Falwell looked to Scripture to
find examples and explanations for how God responded to prayer, and he
interpreted these examples to mean that God heard the call of his people and
directed world affairs to bless them. However, the appearance of this blessing was not a bolt out of the sky but rather direct intervention in the political
actions of world leaders. Like Nehemiah with Artaxerxes: "In Nehemiah 1 he
said, 'O Lord God of Heaven, I pray before thee now day and night for the
children of Israel thy servants and confess the sins of the children of Israel
which we have sinned against thee. Both I and my father's house have sinned.'
Nehemiah had not committed those sins, but he identified with the sins of the
nation. Jesus did that for us on the cross. He who knew no sin became sin for
us. So we must pray. You see, the moral condition of America is a direct reflection of the spiritual condition of the church in America."[49] As understood in
Falwell's interpretation of Proverbs 14:34, to sin was to endanger the entire
nation, but righteous citizens would rebuild America. In other words, Falwell's

jeremiad was tied to the nehemiad. In another sermon, Falwell blamed the church not for the sins of homosexuality, abortion, and the like but for not preventing the sins he believed afflicted the nation: "Let me give you what Nehemiah's cure was, and it worked. . . . The real problem in America happens to be the churches in America. If we had not gone to sleep for the last thirty years, there could never have been a climate that would have allowed the existence of a Supreme Court that could legalize murder on demand. There could not have been legislation to allow pornography as it exists today. The drug scene could not be. The homes would not have disintegrated. There would not be all this homosexual explosion today. The problem is that we have been silent too long."[50] Again, he appeals to Nehemiah's prayer:

> I was reading this prayer early this morning, Nehemiah 1, and verse 6 he said, "Let Thine ear be attentive and Thine eyes open that Thou mayest hear the prayer of Thy servant which I pray before Thee now day and night for the children of Israel Thy servants,"—Listen, he's praying for Israel—"And confess the sins of the children of Israel." You mean I'm supposed to confess the sins of the nation? I'm supposed to confess Hugh Hefner's sins? The abortion clinic owner's sin? Yes. Because the spiritual apathy allowed that to be. This is God's judgment of the nation, and only the people of God can repent for the sins of a nation. . . . You say I haven't done all those things. Yes, but we're a part of a passive church that's allowed it to happen.[51]

However, prayer was only one, indirect form of political participation, and Falwell wanted Christians to count on more than God's decision to influence national leaders.

Falwell demanded Bible-believing Christians register to vote, and vote for candidates who adhered to moral standards found in the Bible. Falwell demanded that Bible-believing Christians "share in authority" by voting, thus claiming their "citizenship rights." He equated Christian spiritual citizenship with American political citizenship, urging his followers to become "first class citizens" in both respects.[52] Elsewhere, Falwell preached: "every American citizen who loves God ought to be a registered voter. Jesus said render unto Caesar that which is Caesar's and unto God that which is God's. Caesar is government. What is my responsibility to government? To be a registered, practicing voter. I have no right to complain about Washington or the statehouse if I am not exercising my first citizenship responsibility. Beyond that I have an obligation to get involved, to be informed about the issues."[53]

Falwell did not insist on the election of Christians to office so much as officials who would pursue a Christian agenda and focus on proper morals and
values, as the heathen Artaxerxes had served the needs of Israel. Certainly,
Christians would be best at this job, but his relative indifference to the religious faith of the elected officials reflected greater ambivalence about how
much of a difference the state itself could make in world evangelization. For
Falwell, the church remained the priority because it alone was capable of that
evangelization. The state only needed to get out of the way and stop endorsing policies that contradicted biblical principles. Indeed, Falwell outlined the
position very clearly: "We will select leaders this year at every level from the
White House to the county supervisors who believe in traditional and moral
values or we'll elect the opposite and ruin the country. No question in my
mind. We cannot have another four-year extension. It's now or never. We do
it right this time or we lose it. I believe that at every level, we lose it."[54] Considering the rigorous standards for belief within Falwell's church, the standard he sets for elected officials was surprising low, but it accommodated the
heterodox founders as well as heterodox allies that Bible-believing Christians
would need to save the nation.[55]

There is an apparent contradiction in Falwell's view of how Bible-believing
Christians should engage politically, and he answered the contradiction by
responding to a challenge put to him by an elderly woman in his congregation. She argued that Falwell showed a lack of faith that God would protect his
people from harm by demanding that Christians become politically involved.
After all, if God was with us, who could stand against us? The image of the
elderly Bible-believing Christian woman was as important as the position she
took: indeed, for Falwell, they were integrally linked. The woman took the old
view, the one Bible-believing Christians took in exile. Falwell gave this sermon
in 1980, and if the woman were seventy or eighty years old, then she had lived
through the early Fundamentalist efforts at social engagement as evangelization, the ensuing divisions between modernist and Fundamentalist congregations and clergy, the bitter public disgrace and disappointment Fundamentalists
had suffered, the rise of independent denominations and religious institutions,
and the growth of the born-again movement. Once in exile, it would seem, the
Bible-believing Christians finally found the success and peace they had sought,
and these were achieved only after Christians stopped trying to change a fallen
world that would, in the end, suffer in the coming Tribulation regardless of
even the most urgent and widespread evangelization efforts. Falwell's response
was critical, as it had to square the circle of prayer requesting divine action and
faithful Christian political action. He answered that Scripture enjoined both

prayer and action and that to confuse the two was the mistake of the unbe-
liever. Falwell explained:

> And she said, "Well don't you believe we can just forget our defense
> budget and trust God to take care of us . . . ?" God isn't stupid. We
> pray and we praise and we worship and we ask, but then we go out
> and use our hands and our gray matter, the talents that God has given
> us to cooperate with Him in the effecting of it. And a man who doesn't
> fight for his freedom is not worthy of his freedom. If somebody ever
> crawls in my house and comes after my wife and children, it's going to
> be him or me. And I won't even pray about it. If I think he's out to hurt
> my family—the Bible says a man who will not take care of his family
> is worse than an infidel.[56]

If an intruder invaded a home, then the man of the house must protect his
family, not pray that God will, since God commanded in Scripture that the
man protect the family. The implication was that the home was a small space
of human agency, hence the responsibility of those charged for its protection. One individual could not protect the entire nation from harm, hence
the need to pray earnestly to God for protection; however, many Christians
registered to vote could elect those officials of moral fortitude to protect the
nation as they would their homes:

> God could save everybody without preaching, but He's chosen, by
> the foolishness of preaching to save them that believe, and I'm glad
> He has, I'm glad He uses people to accomplish His design and His
> purpose for this age. And I am saying that defense is right and we
> need a strong defense budget. . . . If we're going to stand against the
> onslaught of the communists who are out for world conquest, we've
> got to be stronger than they are. And we cannot pussyfoot around
> about this and we need to cut out some of the welfare programs to
> finance a stronger defense budget to protect the freedom we have.
> You say, how important is freedom? Freedom is so important that you
> couldn't be in this church building today if we didn't have it.[57]

God gave Americans political freedom to protect the Church and the family.
While "only God can give ultimate victory," Americans could demonstrate
their worthiness of that victory by showing their willingness to fight for that
freedom rather than tempt God, like the infidel would.[58]

Opponents of Falwell's revival criticized him for his efforts, and Falwell interpreted these criticisms as the gentile ridicule of Nehemiah and the Jews rebuilding the walls of Jerusalem. Falwell defined the ridicule Bible-believing Christians experienced as confirmation that they were doing God's work to save America. As Falwell recounted, first alluding to Nehemiah's language about "the great work" of rebuilding Jerusalem:

> I believe a great work is going to be done. I believe we're going to see it done and it's my conviction that we can not [sic] be fighting one another. We must be joined together and so Nehemiah and a few good men looked at the situation, said let us rise up and build and they strengthened their hands for this good work and the work began. But hardly had the work began, begun when verse nineteen and verse twenty chapter two, Sanballat the Hornoite, Tobiah the servant, the Ammonite and Geshem the Arabian heard it. They laughed at us to scorn and despised us and said what is this thing that ye do.[59]

Nehemiah and the Jews in Jerusalem had suffered the ridicule of the gentiles who had taken up residence in a land not promised to them. Falwell drew a parallel between the gentiles and several un-Christian critics who found, in America, a home that they wished not to see rebuilt:

> Notice verse 10, [Nehemiah] arrived at the city and as soon as he arrived, opposition, there was Sanballat, Tobiah, they don't mention him here, but they mention him later, Geshem. Opposition. Why was the opposition upset? Because somebody had come to help the children. To seek the welfare of the children. To stop the abortions. That's why the ACLU is upset. Our Sanballat and Tobiah and Geshems today are the ACLU, People for the American Way, Norman Lear, the National Education Accusation, NARAL, NOW, the National Organization of Women, the World Council of Churches, Planned Parenthood, the Abortionists, the pornographers, the liberal politicians. Those are the persons who are against what we're doing and the liberal clergymen cursing us for doing it. Why? Because somebody has now come to seek the welfare of the children. That isn't legislating morality, that is responsible and sincere recovery of a nation. Revival.[60]

Falwell established an analogy comparing the gentiles ridiculing the Jews to the reproductive rights advocacy groups, LGBT rights groups, and civil liberty groups ridiculing Bible-believing Christians. Of course, these groups treated Falwell's religious pronouncements as attacks; however, he experienced the advocacy of these groups as the attacks, and his condemnations were meant to defend Bible-believing Christians from wrong, un-Christian points of view. The secular points of view were not mere speech for Falwell. They were attempts to justify dismantling the institutions God put into place in America to ensure its survival as the staging ground for world evangelization. According to the nehemiad, had the gentiles ridiculing the Jews succeeded in pushing the Jews back into exile, Jerusalem would never have been rebuilt, and Israel would never have been restored to glory. Bible-believing Christians must similarly persevere in withstanding ridicule to achieve victory for Christ in America. This victory, however, required Falwell to preach the correct vision for America, understood by biblical precedent. It meant rhetorical self-defense. The result, strangely enough, was a battle in which both sides saw themselves as victims of unwarranted aggression, and the response of those groups attacking Falwell helped him conform his presentation of his foundation to the very biblical precedent he was defending.[61]

It is worth noting that Falwell overstated the nature and extent of Fundamentalist and Evangelical exile from American public life. After all, by 1980, America had witnessed the incredible revivalism of Reverend William "Billy" Franklin Graham Jr. since 1947. The National Association of Evangelicals, as a body, had served as a national body engaging in national issues since 1942. During the late 1940s, Rev. Carl McIntire had operated his own separatist media dedicated to opposing liberal Protestantism at the same time Rev. Carl Henry published *Christianity Today*, as an alternative to the mainline Protestant *Christian Century*.[62] While Graham was typically welcoming of a variety of faithful, more orthodox McIntire and Henry did their best to fight the good fight—and at best preserved the status quo. Falwell's nehemiad, therefore, is not so much factual, since aspects of Bible-believing Christianity had for decades remained part of American public life, as it was felt to be a failure among his frustrated congregants.[63] Ordinary Bible-believing Christians had kept to their churches even as their allies in leaders like Graham or Henry had not done enough. With the decline of the mainline during the 1960s and 1970s, Falwell saw that the hour of the Fundamentalist was at hand. His church must restore the true faith as dogma, and it would use conventional politics to serve that end.

Falwell invited his listeners to see for themselves. The issues of greatest moral and social concern were, in Falwell's view, the breakdown of the traditional structures of the family, the church, and the state, which he believed were the three biblically sanctioned human organizations in creation. The successes of the three were interrelated.[64] The family had to conform to the standards God set out in the Bible, of one man and one woman bearing children. The church had to hold true to biblical principles to preach to its members to conform to this biblical standard and apply it to the state.

Repudiating Sanballat: Provocation and Persecution

During the late 1970s and early 1980s, Falwell tied the American dispensation directly to the success and failure of conservative Republicans to win elections, especially the presidency. Falwell engaged in direct partisan politics meant to elect state and national officials who would work to end policies Falwell saw as hostile to American principles. His strategy followed the order of events told in the nehemiad. According to Falwell, Bible-believing Christians would return from political self-exile and bring with them the faith and principles God favored for America. They would then rebuild American politics according to those principles both as a way of atoning for their own failure to steward American moral principles and to avoid the final destruction of the nation. While restoring America's religious foundation, Falwell claimed, these Bible-believing Christians would suffer ridicule and criticism, as the Jews had from gentiles upon returning to the holy city to rebuild its walls. However, the final victory would come with the election of candidates who would represent America and the principles that had made the nation great—or the final ruin of America at the hands of pornographers, LGBT advocates, and abortion providers. To that end, Bible-believing Christians had to return from exile and participate in politics, as well as form political alliances with like-minded conservatives. To succeed required working with allies, outside of Bible-believing Christian communities, on which this recovery depended, just as Nehemiah had to depend on the Babylonian king to bring the Jews back home to rebuild the walls of Jerusalem.

Falwell used his own separate mass media apparatus to communicate his American dispensation and to affiliate publicly with a political party and its candidates to establish the American dispensation. He had developed his own mass media for delivering sermons and other Christian programming across the nation. During the 1960s and 1970s, he bought up cheap television time slots or radio wavelengths on local affiliates in areas where he wanted to "win souls for Christ," then used the money raised from those audiences to buy even more spots in new areas. The strategy followed the same separatism that guided Bible-believing Christians to create their own schools, colleges, and periodicals. Falwell created alternative mass media programming for families, and promoted publishing houses like Sword of the Lord and later his own based at Liberty University. He and others involved in Falwell's Thomas Road Baptist Church or the various Liberty endeavors generated content that drew congregants away from conventional mass media, which Falwell condemned as a corrupting influence, not to mention as competition for his own material. Falwell said at one point, speaking of both Americans in general and Bible-believing Americans in particular, that "we alone possess the raw material, the young people, the churches, the Bible, the printing presses, the money, the schools—we alone, humanly speaking, possess all the necessary raw materials to carry out the Great Commission."[65]

In addition to having his own mass media to promulgate the American dispensation, Falwell directly affiliated with conservatives in the Republican Party. He met with elected officials to endorse their political conservatism and campaign for their elections. Except for Senator Harry Byrd Jr., Falwell associated entirely with conservative Republicans, and given Byrd's voting record, it is hard to call him an exception. When Falwell suffered criticism for directly mixing religion and politics, he affirmed that he did so for the salvation of the nation and rebuked his critics for their lack of faith. Indeed, for Falwell, the critics revealed their own corruption by criticizing the efforts to rebuild Jerusalem, as Sanballat had when mocking Nehemiah.

Falwell rolled out the communications strategy following the order the nehemiad took. He began with a return from political exile, starting with his opposition to the Equal Rights Amendment and his support for the Briggs Initiative (or Proposition 6) in California, which would have banned LGBT Californians from teaching in California public schools. In 1979, Falwell picked up speed with the formation of the Moral Majority and the publication of mass-marketed texts he advertised on his *Old-Time Gospel Hour* as the "Christian Survival Kit," such as Francis Schaeffer's *The Christian Manifesto*, Falwell's own *Listen, America!*, and the edited volume of Moral Majority backers in *How You Can Help Clean Up America*. These texts outlined how the moral state of affairs in the United States was leading to the slow destruction of the Christian principles that, according to Falwell, had kept America free and prosperous. These texts also contained a muted sense of the coming Tribulation, about which Falwell was much more aggressive in preaching in his sermons, but these texts were meant to have a greater initial reach than even Falwell's extensive evangelical mass media had.

In addition to the books, Falwell promoted rallies like the I Love America tour and Washington for Jesus. Falwell himself led a rally at the Capitol for Bible-believing parochial school students. He taped and broadcast events in Washington, DC, on *Old-Time Gospel Hour* episodes. The purpose of these events was to demonstrate that Bible-believing Christians could love the United States and that their nonparticipation in politics had produced the poor moral state in which they found it. Falwell and his Moral Majority had explained in print, over the radio, and on television exactly how to reestablish these moral principles, restore American greatness, and avert divine retribution. The message was simple: Bible-believing Christians helped make the mess the nation was in, and it was up to them to clean it up.

The next step was to find and back candidates who adhered to these moral principles, and conservative Republicans were those candidates. Behind the formation of the Moral Majority were conservative activists Paul Weyrich, Richard Viguerie, and Howard Phillips, who in late 1978 through early 1979, discussed its formation with Falwell. Falwell worked with them to form the Moral Majority as a way of supporting conservative Republicans who held to policy positions that Falwell and Bible-believing Christians prioritized: the reinstatement of prayer in public schools, opposition to abortion, resistance to LGBT rights, and support of Israel.[66] Conservative Republicans answered the call. Ronald Reagan, Robert Dornan, and Paul Laxalt became some of the first leading conservative Republicans to appear with Falwell and support his efforts to reform the Republican Party into something more socially conservative. With the election of Moral Majority conservatives, Falwell claimed that the nation was on the slow return to sound moral principles, but that progress was beset, Falwell also claimed, by an organized opposition that criticized and ridiculed the faithful for their efforts. Falwell had two strategies for handling criticism. First, he continued to reject his critics in the national press as part of the organized resistance to American moral principles. Second, he continued to offer alternatives to the national press in his own programming.

The American Dispensation in Parallel Institutions

Fundamentalist Protestantism had been a separatist faith for two generations by the time Falwell began to enter national politics. Separatism for these churches referred to the withdrawal of congregants from political and social life in favor of a set of parallel institutions rooted in the sect's religious values.[67] These religiously based institutions were not just substitutes for mainstream America. They formed the basis for expansion of the true Gospel into as many homes as possible. Falwell converted the separatist approach to function in the political realm. Just as Bible-believing Christians had established parallel institutions to replace traditional institutions they viewed as corrupt, so did Falwell establish alternative political sources for the Judeo-Christian heritage he sought to defend. He described these institutions as nascent, embattled, and ultimately the last hope for America.[68] In other words, he extended the specific task of Bible-believing Christians to the conservative allies who would help those Christians achieve their goals. Harvard University had succumbed to secular humanism, making its graduates and faculty unreliable. Liberty University, on the other hand, was reliable because of its biblical and conservative values.

Falwell and other Bible-believing Christians practiced a "soul-winning" revivalism that was meant to expand until it had reached everyone in the world. The ultimate vision for these institutions was that they would replace those from which the Fundamentalists had separated, making inevitable the conflict between the secular status quo and the religious alternatives these churches created. As Bible-believing churches in the 1960s began to succeed in gaining numerous adherents without notice by the mainstream, the mainstream became more secular.[69] Mainline Protestant churches increasingly abandoned traditional religious teachings, and, in key Supreme Court decisions, public schools lost their remaining elements of Protestant worship and religious education. At least at the elite level, religious disestablishment no longer meant the protection of churches from state interference; it meant the protection of the state from church interference, what Wilfred McClay calls the movement from "negative secularism" to "positive secularism."[70]

Progressive reform led to increased public secularization into the 1970s, even as Bible-believing Christians achieved their greatest number of conversions yet. At the same time, other religious denominations encountered their own political issues. The Supreme Court decision *Roe v. Wade* and its support within the Democratic Party compromised the Catholic vote, as more conservative adherents felt increasingly uncomfortable with candidates supporting a privacy right that the Vatican described as murder.[71] Secularization itself became an issue among public theologians, such as then Lutheran but later Catholic Father Richard John Neuhaus.[72] As Yasser Arafat of the Palestinian Liberation Organization came to be viewed as an equal partner with the Israeli chief executive, some Jewish Americans looked for public leaders who would defend Israeli national sovereignty against what they saw as a terrorist group funded by enemies of Israel and the United States. Moreover, Jews in the Soviet Union were under intense persecution for their continued religious practices under Communism. For some American Jewish communities, the policy of détente with the Soviet Union amounted to abandoning Soviet Jews to the Communists.[73]

This loose set of issues facing disparate religious denominations was ripe for mobilization. In 1979 New Conservative Movement leaders like Viguerie, Phillips, and Weyrich pitched Falwell's formation of the Moral Majority as the organization that would unite Fundamentalists with Evangelicals, and the two groups with conservative Catholics and Jews on a platform of aggressive opposition to abortion and secularization of public life, strong anti-Communism, and unflagging support for the state of Israel.[74] Because national elections were a game of margins in winner-take-all contests for electoral votes, the conversion of even small numbers of Jews and Catholics in the Northeast to the Republican Party and the mobilization of previously separatist Bible-believing voters could swing state outcomes in favor of a national Republican candidate who spoke to the Moral Majority platform.

The formation of Falwell's group was artificial. Falwell did not build his reputation from the ground up based on advocating a religious foundation for American public policy. He began establishing the American dispensation having already built an international Evangelical enterprise with hundreds of thousands of devotees. Those devotees were separatists and did not necessarily have any interest in one of their preachers defying a firmly established norm against political engagement. That problem was precisely why it was Falwell whom Viguerie, Phillips and Weyrich approached. Only someone of his reputation among Bible-believing Christians could reverse this rigid separatism. Falwell represented marginalized voters, but they had intentionally marginalized themselves to keep away from political corruption.[75] As we have seen, Falwell needed to explain how exile had led to the failure of their church to protect American values, thus necessitating their urgent and immediate return to the public sphere they once spurned. In addition, Falwell had to demonstrate that these returning Bible-believing Christians really were the only hope. To make the case, he highlighted and, sometimes, strategically provoked the outrage of the progressives he condemned and who condemned him. Their outrage would hold together Bible-believing Christians in pressing for the policies Falwell preached. Moreover, it could bring together these Bible-believing Christians with conservative Catholics and Jews as allies in achieving policy goals, even if for different reasons.

The strategy had some obvious limitations. First, many of Falwell's own religious persuasion were not willing to follow him into politics. For example, Rev. Bob Jones condemned Falwell for his venture.[76] As we have already seen, Falwell himself had once objected to political participation in a now infamous sermon, "Ministers and Marchers," in which he preached against the black church leadership of the 1960s Civil Rights Movement.[77] Not only did Falwell have to account for his apparent support of segregation, as he attempted to do in his autobiography, but he also had to reverse the antipolitical positions he took.[78] The Moral Majority suffered from inexperience in voter mobilization.[79] These limitations, however, often served only as salves for soothing the fears of those who opposed Falwell or conservative politics more generally. The lack of unanimity was no surprise among Falwell's supporters, as many of these churches were independent of any parachurch institution or were part of a voluntary association rather than a hierarchy. Disagreement and dissent were par for the course.[80] The failure of some Moral Majority branches to produce immediate results in elections surfaced only after the Moral Majority had achieved a high profile and was perceived as a powerful political organization.

In the immediate political context of the 1980s, national perception of the Moral Majority counted for more than its influence on the ground. First, by appearing as the leader of the Moral Majority, Falwell appeared no longer as just a Fundamentalist Baptist minister but instead as the leader of a coalition of religious conservatives united in a common goal: protecting American religious foundations. Second, insofar as Falwell led the Moral Majority, he also embodied the Moral Majority, at least in the way the press covered him. Whenever Falwell made a statement or met with a political leader, he demonstrated the influence he could wield and the importance of the Moral Majority platform to those leaders who met with Falwell. Falwell had to make the American dispensation attractive enough to political leaders for them to affiliate with it. Transferring Falwell's leadership from Thomas Road Baptist Church to the Moral Majority made it possible for those not affiliated with Bible-believing Christianity to identify with him and his view of the American dispensation. Thus, the Moral Majority established among elected officials a platform for defending socially conservative positions without necessarily belonging to a specific religious faith.

There was an obvious problem with this approach to establishing a religious foundation, and that problem was that the foundation was treated almost as a liability, one from which politicians could distance themselves.

Even as Falwell asserted a dispensational premillennial view of time and the important role of America within it, the Moral Majority dulled the foundational language in favor of sharpened policy specifics. Falwell's solution was the same as Sheen's and King's: to preach more ecumenically in some circles and more specifically theologically in others. Of course, this solution was one established in practice less than in theory, but the practical solution reflected the political nature of religious foundations. They serve not to ground democratic practices as universally understood or theoretically consistent; they serve to ground discrete political positions now, despite whatever tensions might arise. Falwell's American dispensation did not propose to reunite Christendom; it merely called Bible-believing Christians and like-minded conservatives to participate in politics and thereby forestall the coming disaster.

Falwell regarded elite institutions with suspicion. The parallel institutions that educated Bible-believing Christians stressed biblical education over scientific or liberal education. Indeed, as a biblical literalist, Falwell denied the validity of geological time and the theory of evolution. In his view, the Ivy League colleges turned their backs on conservative theologians, as Princeton Theological Seminary did with J. Gresham Machen in 1929, in favor of the "modernist" theology that had precipitated the split with Fundamentalists.[81] The primary function of an Ivy League education, for Falwell, was to give sin a different name to make it easier to sin. An ordinary person without an Ivy League education at least knew what to call sin when she saw it. It is important to point out that Sheen and King also praised the simple wisdom of everyday folk, but they did so as successful clergy with elite educations, thus able to testify to its relative value in making moral decisions or understanding American foundations.[82] Of course, the larger point was that neither Sheen nor King denied the validity of scientific discoveries in the same way or on the same scale as Falwell.

The combination of these factors and strategies explained the formation of what has become known as the "Culture War" that Falwell helped declare. By aligning conservative religious people across denominations on a short number of policy outcomes, Falwell and other conservative leaders turned what had been the "Judeo-Christian heritage" against the encroaching New Left, or "the liberal elite," that had emerged during the late 1960s and early 1970s. Rather than persuade progressive authorities embedded in elite universities or the mainstream press, Falwell offered a form of politically engaged separatism. He used separatist strategies to unite religious conservatives based on the Bible-believing Christian experience of parallel social and educational institutions, hostility for traditional authority as corrupt, and a lingering sense of embarrassment due to their political failures two generations before. While uniting religious conservatives, Falwell privileged strongly his own Fundamentalist position, one that described America as in decline directly because of its neglect of biblical commandments and as punishment from God. To prevent that punishment required aligning the interests of Jews, Catholics, and Protestants. Failure would lead to wrath and the likely destruction of the individual goals each group pursued. Together, as with Nehemiah, they were doing a great work. Why should their work cease when their enemies called them to negotiate a truce?

Falwell on the Wall in Troublesome Times

Falwell experienced early success in establishing religious conservatives in the Republican Party. Their arrival was, for him, a return from exile to rescue the nation that Bible-believing Christians desperately needed to save. These successes were his great work, the rebuilding of Jerusalem's walls. With his success, he helped demonstrate that the wariness of Bible-believing Christians to enter politics was unfounded. Not only could they have a positive influence on which issues were discussed but they could also win elections for political leadership. Their influence could reach nationally, and the salvation of a nation morally adrift was at hand.

Falwell's growing influence was credited for the shift in Republican leadership. During the 1980 Republican National Convention, Guy O. Farley Jr., a Virginia born-again Baptist, became the new RNC leader. Despite his statements to the contrary, both Republicans from within and observers from outside agreed that Farley was elected partly to serve as a liaison to the growing number of religious conservatives.[83] Falwell's influence also extended to bills presented in Congress during the campaign to demonstrate Republican support for the protection of the "traditional family." Senator Paul Laxalt of Nevada submitted the 1980 Family Protection Act in the Senate while serving as both Reagan's campaign cochair and making frequent appearances on Falwell's *Old-Time Gospel Hour* both in print and on screen.[84] Reagan himself made the traditional family his focus in his address accepting the Republican nomination for president, saying, he wanted a "new consensus with all those across the land who share a community of values embodied in these words: Family, work, neighborhood, peace and freedom."[85] As one columnist interpreted, "By naming the family first, Mr. Reagan signaled the growing importance of a cluster of issues referred to as 'traditional moral values' by those who are trying to mobilize a new constituency around them."[86]

In some of this coverage, journalists lumped Falwell together with pastors Marion "Pat" Robertson and James Robison as the "big three" preachers, but Falwell began to single himself out in his ability to secure coverage, such as in a four-part *New York Times* feature on the rise of Christian conservatives. He took credit for important increases in support for conservatives in regional elections, such as in Alaska and Iowa.[87] In that series, the American dispensation was front and center. The first two pieces covered the rise of Bible-believing voters and their integration into the Republican Party, but the third highlighted a national "moral slide" that "imperils the nation": "Evangelical Christians, growing swiftly in numbers, influence, and determination to affect the results of this election year, are working to remedy what they see as a sharp moral decline imperiling the well-being of American society . . . they say they feel like outsiders who must fight the forces of 'secular humanism,' and atheism on such issues as abortion."[88] While these articles contained interviews with several Fundamentalist theologians and preachers who articulated the same foundation as Falwell, he was the one who had begun the biggest shift from exile to public engagement in conservative politics back in 1978. The arrival appeared complete at the National Affairs Briefing in Dallas, Texas, in late August of 1980. Organized by McAteer and his Religious Roundtable, prominent activists and public figures attended, but the most important figure to attend was Reagan as the Republican Party presidential nominee.[89] During this seminar, Falwell infamously stated, "you can't be a good Christian and a liberal," a position from which Reagan only somewhat distanced himself.[90] While giving a sermon before seventeen thousand attendees, including seven thousand preachers, at the Reunion Arena, Falwell also used language from the nehemiad: "I'm sure to some people we look like fanatics. . . . But anyone involved in it realizes it is a real commitment and a positive force. I used to worry about what they think . . . but I don't anymore."[91] The Dallas event was a kind of arrival for those who heard the American dispensation and agreed—but felt ridiculed for doing so. Reagan spoke directly to that sense among the audience when he said to the preachers in the audience, "I know you can't endorse me. But I endorse you, and what you are doing."[92] With the president's endorsement, Falwell recognized that the ridicule from ideological opponents would only get worse and showed others by his own example that the criticism they would experience should not matter. For him, the ridicule of opponents only confirmed that Bible-believing Christians would be a positive force in averting the ruin of America.

One month after Dallas, surveys during the campaign revealed that Falwell was gaining among only a specific set of Bible-believing Christians. He certainly lagged among Evangelical African Americans and white Evangelicals who did not watch the national programs of Falwell, Robertson, or Robison. The conclusion at the time, however, was that "Falwell . . . may have the most political influence per viewer. People who regularly listen to him support Reagan by a nearly 2-to-1 margin."[93] Even so, Falwell and Reagan kept a rhetorical distance between each other. Falwell offered a personal endorsement of Reagan as the "lesser [sic] of three evils."[94] Reagan also lacked some authenticity as a "born-again" candidate, since he was the only candidate in the race to have been divorced, and had lived a "Hollywood lifestyle" and provided a thoroughly modern way of life for his children, a point noted by his critics.[95]

In more regional and local elections, the press featured Falwell's Moral Majority influence prominently. In Falwell's native Virginia, he was particularly noted, but not with praise, even among Republicans.[96] In one case, Falwell and new RNC chair Farley lost the effort to install a Moral Majority–aligned candidate as the Republican eastern vice chairman to the more moderate, conventional Republican Kenneth D. Smith Jr.[97] Even before forming the Moral Majority, Falwell began as a Virginia kingmaker of sorts in 1977, when he indirectly endorsed Republican John C. Dalton for Virginia governor by attending a rally he held.[98] Dalton later won the election. During the Virginia senatorial contest the following year, both the Republican candidate John W. Warner and the Democratic candidate Andrew P. Miller came to services held at Falwell's Thomas Road Baptist Church the month before the election, though one Democratic leader could not help but go on the record saying that "it's become part of the process . . . coming here to visit the guru."[99] Falwell refused to endorse, claiming Warner and Miller were equally satisfactory to him and that he did not want to deal with upsetting either campaign.[100]

By 1980, however, with the Moral Majority in place, Falwell's apparatus helped push the previously defeated Frank Wolf into office in Virginia's Tenth House District.[101] The Moral Majority also managed to seize control of the Alaska Republican organization. They defeated the incumbent Alabama congressman John H. Buchanan Jr., who also happened to be an ordained Baptist minister. In his place, the Moral Majority helped position the much more conservative Alfred L. Smith Jr. as the Republican candidate, who later won the election.[102] Buchanan was publicly furious with the Moral Majority and secured sympathetic coverage from the press after his surprise loss.[103] The Moral Majority also backed Admiral Jeremiah Denton, a former Vietnam prisoner of war, in his bid to take the Senate seat, which he later won.[104] Falwell threw his weight behind the strongly contested reelection campaign of Robert Dornan in California against Carey Peck, who had come very close to defeating Dornan in 1978, by inviting Dornan onto the *Old-Time Gospel Hour*.[105] Falwell even managed to publish an op-ed in the *Los Angeles Times* touching on the issues both he and Dornan supported, though Falwell steered clear of speaking of Dornan directly.[106]

Falwell's early success was enough to garner attention from the press during the 1980 presidential election. This coverage evolved from curiosity to suspicion and finally to open opposition. Falwell's nehemiad, however, anticipated the Sanballats, Tobiahs, and the rest of the gentiles who would condemn Bible-believing Christians for demanding their voice be heard to save a nation. Falwell had already laid the groundwork for suspecting the mainstream press, saying that they were tied up in the same organizations that spread pornography and defended Marxist ideas.[107] When the press's criticism of Falwell came, it did not fail to meet expectations. The volume of criticism Falwell received, as the nehemiad explained, was only evidence that Bible-believing Christians were making a positive difference, since such criticism was built into the nehemiad as testimony of enemy frustrations.

The Press in the Plains of Ono

Coverage of Falwell started with lumping him into the category of the "electric church" that surfaced as an enormous force—in number of congregants, annual conversions, and fundraising terms—almost from nowhere and was composed of flashy, theologically unserious white Southern men. Over time, Falwell distinguished himself from other televangelists not merely by refusing to wear the pink tuxedos Jim Bakker preferred, but by preaching American dispensation for national politics and forming the Moral Majority to put it into place, an activity that many televangelists avoided. The press covered Falwell's political efforts with skepticism and often ran columns decrying the perils of mixing religion and politics. The coverage was negative but muted, portraying Falwell as a rich, shallow, provincial minister who hid his most deeply felt, most dangerous beliefs from all but his most beloved congregants. In response, Falwell had to show that he used church money for church causes, had to maintain a personal commitment to his beliefs, had to hold his own when moving in circles hostile or indifferent to his ministry and political positions, and finally had to demonstrate that he was not a reactionary. He succeeded at the first three, but the fourth proved to be where Falwell struggled the most.

Early coverage of Falwell grouped him in with popular televangelists and large, independent Protestant churches. The particular issue was the declining support these church leaders showed to the first "born-again" presidential candidate, Jimmy Carter. In 1976, just a month before the election, Falwell commented on the disappointment he felt in Carter's decision to give an interview to *Playboy* magazine and said that his congregation appeared to have flipped from a majority approving of Carter to one disapproving of him.[108] Falwell's comment was merely one among several of those reported in what was meant as a review of important Protestant opinion leaders. Two years later, however, Falwell was increasingly becoming a central focus for press interest in the "electric" or "electronic" church. Indeed, as Falwell, as well as Pat Robertson, Jim Bakker, and Oral Roberts, became symbols for its meteoric rise in numbers and mass media outreach, major newspapers from all over the country were publishing their own features on the subject. Coverage of the electric church focused on its unprecedented reach through mass media, its tremendous fundraising power, and the fear that Falwell and those like him were responsible for the rapid decline of mainline Protestant denominations.[109] Three articles even opened in the same way, focusing on the media-savvy, high-cost nature of the religious enterprises.[110]

In 1978, Falwell began to separate from the rest of the electric church by touring state capitals in what he called the "I Love America" tour. His message during the tour was threefold: that America was a great nation, that moral and political decline were compromising that nation, and that Bible-believing Protestants had to rejoin politics to stop that decline. The title, "I Love America," communicated more than simple patriotism but a single-sentence rationale directed specifically to Bible-believing Christians for why they should register to vote and vote for conservative candidates. To make America worth loving, Falwell had to persuade his audience that America was not truly a nation that watched pornography, banned prayer in schools, and legalized abortion. These were anti-American. Instead, he had to argue that America, at its foundation, was a Christian nation, and it was that very Christian foundation that was threatened when groups defended pornography and abortion but not prayer and free exercise of religion. The culmination of the tour came with the "Clean Up America" rally that featured 8,000 students from 156 Christian schools. On hand for the rally, in addition to Falwell, were several elected officials who had appeared at some of the I Love America stops, including Representative Robert Dornan, and Senators

Gordon Humphrey, John Warner, Paul Laxalt, and Jesse Helms. While Helms was a born-again Christian, others standing with Falwell were from different backgrounds, such as Dornan's Catholicism and Warner's Episcopalianism. What brought them together was the common commitment to restoring and preserving American Christian foundations and, thus, avoiding the impending disaster toward which the recent social changes were steering the nation.[111]

After the forming of the Moral Majority, the press at first continued to use the "Elmer Gantry" image of the wealthy televangelist with its implications of hypocrisy and manipulation. Often, coverage of Falwell would point out his ownership of a private jet.[112] Televangelists at the time were under scrutiny for how they handled the tremendous sums they brought in. One particularly scandal-ridden preacher was Bakker. In one particularly well-publicized case, Bakker claimed to invest all his personal finances in expanding the ministry while putting a $3000 down payment on a houseboat. Meanwhile, his staff misappropriated funds raised for a Christian television program in South Korea to pay for other projects.[113] Falwell himself was charged with making the same kinds of exaggerations. He claimed that he had to halt construction of then-named Liberty Baptist College and had to consider pulling the *Old-Time Gospel Hour* from the air unless he could raise more money, which he eventually did though from uncertain sources. The fundraising trouble became a common complaint, and the *Los Angeles Times* ran a story meant to educate readers on the lack of transparency in how preachers raised money, listing Falwell's as one of the churches that did not report an independent audit to the Council of Better Business Bureaus.[114]

Falwell also found himself in hot water with local governments. The Commonwealth of Virginia pursued Falwell for his failure to pay $67,000 in property taxes for Liberty Baptist College. Falwell claimed he did not owe the taxes, since the property was used for religious and educational purposes exempt from taxation under the state constitution. The process took months to resolve.[115] The Fair Political Practices Commission in the state of California investigated Falwell's fundraising for Proposition 6.[116] The initiative failed, but Falwell's political advocacy marked a shift in press coverage that took him out of the ranks of the posturing televangelists and into the place of a reactionary political threat to progressive causes.

Progressive critics of Falwell surfaced once the election campaign between Carter and Reagan entered full swing. One of the earliest articles was an essay by Ellen Goodman. She focused on the desire for Christian conservatives to gain "control," an idea that "has united people here as different as Henry A. Kissinger and Jesse Helms. It is a new language that reaches out and touches all of us right now in one way or another."[117] She observed how Falwell had helped influence the preamble to the Republican platform: "They are rising up in 1980 to say that this confusion must end; this drift must end; we must pull ourselves together as a people before we slide irretrievably into the abyss."[118] Religious conservatives saw "a pattern of dissolution and chaos. Parents have lost control of children. Men have lost control of women. We have lost our leadership in the White House. . . . Their answer is to harden lines, to return to a cold war in our religious life and in our private life."[119] Goodman's editorial marked a shift in the treatment of Falwell. No longer was Falwell merely a well-heeled religious showman; Goodman presented Falwell as someone with power to reverse the recent progressive changes by mobilizing an awakened giant of moral reactionaries. As she concluded her piece: "now those who call themselves part of 'a moral majority' have moved in from the fringe, riding on the mainstream fear that 'things are out of control.' But along with my new word [control], I've also brought home a new and uncomfortable sensation: confusion isn't the only thing that frightens me."[120] Other columnists echoed the shift in perception of Falwell and the Moral Majority.[121] Meg Greenfield compared Falwell to the Golden Horde: "The evangelicals are coming. Not since Genghis Khan rode west . . . has anything so ominous been in prospect."[122] The focus of these new articles was to point out how Falwell's religious foundation required state intervention in issues perceived, at least among progressives, as private. Greenfield put it in the following way: "If those of us in the complaisant liberal middle don't want to be known (justly) in time as the wonderful folks who brought you President Jerry Falwell, then we will have to stop inviting the Feds into people's every personal decision and we will have to assert a moral sensibility of our own."[123] The "cold war" risked becoming hot, as the "liberal middle" began to divide along religious lines, as Goodman later explained when Jews and Catholics split over whom to vote for in Boston.[124] After journalist Bill Moyers aired a television special on Fundamentalist Protestants, columnist and author Anthony Lewis commented, "The scariest piece of television I have seen in a long time is not fiction. It is a report by Bill Moyers, to be shown on public stations starting this Friday, on the activities of fundamentalist Christian ministers in the 1980 election campaign."[125]

The coverage grew more intense as the presidential election loomed ever closer. The Carter administration began to echo the press outcry against Falwell. Secretary of Health and Human Services Patricia Roberts Harris equated the politics of Falwell with those of Ayatollah Ruhollah Khomeini, then spiritual leader of Iran, who adhered to a strict, reactionary interpretation of Shi'a

Islam.[126] The equation did more than equate Falwell to a backward religious leader but also condemned Falwell as a would-be tyrant who would deprive men and especially women of rights taken for granted in the United States. The *New York Times* published an op-ed that explored that comparison and derived the following distinction: "it is one thing to propagate a religious faith but quite another to use the political process to proselyte. Motive, and tone of voice, are crucial. People of faith have every right to speak as citizens, with a citizen's right to be wrong. They are wrong, and menace religious freedom, when they aim to make religious dogma binding upon others."[127] Pastor, Civil Rights Movement leader, and former Carter ambassador to the United Nations Andrew Young condemned Falwell's motives.[128] The *Times* column agreed with the assessment of Rev. William Sloane Coffin and other mainline Protestant clergy, who condemned Falwell for his conservative motives and his unpleasant tone of voice when referring to groups he saw as detrimental to American life.[129] Some columns were more sanguine about the capacity for the regime to withstand Falwell's assault, citing King and the Civil Rights Movement as precedent for the intrusion of politicized religion into American politics.[130] Even the right-leaning *Wall Street Journal* condemned Falwell's politics as shallow and pointless, shrugging its editorial shoulders: "One man or woman's morals is another man or woman's sin. It was this, and the fact that more than one person resided at America during the time when the government was originally established, that caused the founding fathers to delegate matters of morality to the individual, family, clergyman, psychiatrist or private library."[131] These final condemnations of Falwell proved ineffective, as Reagan convincingly won the election over Carter (and independent candidate John B. Anderson). Reagan won all Southern states except for Carter's home state of Georgia, showing in the eyes of experts at the time that the mobilized Christian conservative vote had changed the political landscape, as some had anticipated.[132] Falwell, as their most recognized leader, rose to national prominence among conservatives. Years later, Carter's close friend and key advisor Charles Kirbo lamented:

> One thing I couldn't figure out—and nobody else could—was how to deal with the Moral Majority. I saw that thing getting really rough on the TV hour. Falwell had a Senator on one of the stations, and talked about—the others would, too—about conservatism in government and in getting into those things. You could tell they were aimed right at Carter. I talked with him about that. Rosalynn did too. But I finally quit talking about it. There really was not a thing you could do. You

couldn't jump on the church, or jump on the preacher, or anything like that. A lot of those people were people who supported Jimmy, and if they knew the true facts, they'd still support him. That's what hurt us. It hurt him.[133]

Media Scorn as Moral Alibi

Criticism in national press had little impact on the way that Falwell spoke to his audiences on television. Because his audience participated in institutions parallel to the national press, they were insulated from the criticisms. Participation in these parallel institutions was both an endorsement of Falwell's credibility over that of his critics and the choice to hear his message over theirs. As a result, Falwell could interpret political events in a decidedly different light with little fear of contestation. As Cal Thomas explained in an edited volume that the Moral Majority helped distribute: "The press has done a horrible job in reporting the resurgence of moral values and conservative political clout. . . . Fortunately, we no longer have to rely exclusively on the commercial press to get our viewpoints across. The growth of special interest publications and the direct mail industry have given us the opportunity to speak directly to our people and to by-pass the commercial press, which is, by and large, dominated by persons who share a similar [liberal] worldview."[134] During Reagan's first term, the anxiety that critics in the press expressed concerning Falwell's desire to restore religion in public institutions was, for Falwell and his audience, a source of promise. Despite not engaging in national politics as aggressively during these years as he did in 1980, Falwell persisted in presenting the cultural politics of his ministry that would interpret the Reagan administration as the fulfillment of the American dispensation.[135] The allegiance between Bible-believing Christians and like-minded conservatives had created opportunities for them to create political conditions of which God would approve, though the critics or "gentiles" in the national press would certainly mock and oppose them every step of the way.

Early in his career as a national figure, Falwell published politically themed sermons in *America Can Be Saved*, some of which directly treat criticism according to the nehemiad. In the sermon "Wide Open Doors, Many Enemies," Falwell presented the possibility of a Christian revival as greater in the present than ever before, owing to the greater means of spreading the Gospel. However, Falwell reminded the reader that spreading the Gospel necessarily entailed conflict with critics he called "enemies" or "adversaries."[136] Despite introducing enemies as a problem for evangelization, Falwell only mentioned them in passing in this sermon except to say that the greatest enemy to one who would witness the Gospel was the feeling of discouragement.[137] However, Falwell directly treated critics as enemies in "Capture America for God." The primary method critics used to dampen the message of Bible-believing Christians, according to Falwell, was the same as in Nehemiah's day: persecution. Falwell spoke plainly:

> Persecution is simply a part of successful ministry. God is not in need of sissies and quitters. . . . I hear of this or that preacher who sold his ministry for a mess of pottage. Pressure? Perhaps. Family problems? Morals? There are lots of excuses but no reasons, for the callings of God are without repentance. God has called us to be successful. . . . This thing called the ministry is not intended for babies, it is not intended for sissies, it is not intended for anyone but soldiers—soldiers who have been through boot camp, who have met the enemy eyeball to eyeballs and who have said with Job, "Though he slay me, yet will I trust him," who have said, "I will not stop. I will not quit. All the forces of Hell cannot turn me back!"[138]

Christian soldiers were meant to defend "The Establishment," a word that Falwell used to refer to civil government, the family, and the church. He intentionally borrowed the word used by his adversaries, the left-leaning social activists of the 1960s and 1970s. The battle, though, was one of social standards. For Falwell, that put Bible-believing Christians on the hard path, one that gave the Left greater appeal: "I know the pressures of conformity are on. And I well know that for the college president or the pastor of a church these pressures will increase. From every corner there are those who would cause us fundamentalists to somewhat dilute our message and change our emphasis. But if we do, in due time we shall go the way of all flesh."[139] Falwell depicted the fight of the Bible-believing church as against the appeals of Communists seeking to exploit weakness at home and against the "hippies and yippies" responsible for that weakness. Fortunately, Falwell asserted, these hippies and yippies "have blown it and they are down the drain. This is the day of the fundamentalist. We need to re-establish our churches on soul winning, holy living and evangelism. We need to re-establish this nation. We have been second-class citizens too long. We need to elect some godly men to the legislative and executive branches of government. And we need to pray some godly men into the judiciary."[140] And in depicting persecution, Falwell also depicted the reason Fundamentalists felt like second-class citizens. Bible-believing Christians had returned from exile and naturally found themselves excluded from society. The press conspired against their success like Sanballat, Tobiah, and Geshem had against Nehemiah's. Falwell's response was the same as Nehemiah's—simply to reject criticism in the press as gentile persecution of the good work of rebuilding the walls of the nation.

By the time Reagan won the 1980 election, Falwell had developed his understanding of gentile persecution to refer to specific groups he saw as organized to oppose the alliance between conservatives and Bible-believing Christians. However, Falwell also had to demonstrate to his audience the positive influence the alliance was having on their mutual enemies. Just as Sanballat had protested and mocked Nehemiah's efforts to rebuild the walls of Jerusalem, so were critics ridiculing the Reagan efforts to rebuild the religious foundation of the nation. One of the best examples of how Falwell reinterpreted criticism through the nehemiad aired on the July 11, 1982, episode of the *Old-Time Gospel Hour* called "America's Children: Free to Pray?" Falwell opened with footage in which Reagan addressed the 250 members of clergy announcing the White House effort to amend the United States Constitution to allow prayer in public schools.[141] The opening linked Reagan and Falwell together as political allies in pursuit of the same policies.[142]

While for the reader such a relationship may seem obvious, Falwell had to show proof that the return from exile was worth the potential costs to the soul of the church. Falwell bound up Reagan's move with the spiritual salvation of the original enemy to school prayer, William J. "Bill" Murray, son of Madalyn Murray O'Hair, who had been a plaintiff whose case had been consolidated with others in the 1963 Supreme Court decision in the 1963 Supreme Court case banning prayer in school, *Abington School District v. Schempp*.[143] A few years before his interview with Falwell, Bill Murray had become a born-again Christian who had publicly renounced his mother and stated his regret over the outcome of *Abington*. Murray and Falwell both condemned the prayer ban and those behind it, with Falwell saying at one point to Murray's approval, "In the two decades of legal battling we've heard from the American Civil Liberties Union, judges, atheists and liberal clergymen, but nobody has thought to ask the children what they think about the freedom to pray in schools. After all, they are the ones who will either suffer or benefit."[144]

The program then cut to children giving the reasons they approved of prayer in schools, paralleling how Murray was a child in public schools when his mother sued before asking children what they wanted. Falwell again challenged the gentiles: "Can those who have opposed prayer in our public schools honestly look us in the eye and say that our children are better off today than they were twenty years ago?"[145] The challenge was obviously meant to refer to the successful line Reagan had used in his 1980 presidential campaign, and Falwell's invocation of Reagan provided a transition to the president's May 6, 1982, remarks at the White House Ceremony in Observance of National Day of Prayer:

> It's an inspiration for me to see all of you Protestants, Catholics, members of the Jewish faith and others who are gathered here at our national home to pay homage to the God in Whom we trust. . . . Prayer has sustained our people in crisis, strengthened us in times of challenge, and guided us through our daily lives since the first settlers came to this continent. . . . I have never believed that the oft-quoted [First] Amendment was supposed to protect us from religion. It was supposed to protect religion from government tyranny. Together let us take up the challenge to reawaken America's religious and moral heart, recognizing that a deep and abiding faith in God is the rock upon which this great nation was founded.[146]

Falwell portrayed Reagan as in line not merely with what Fundamentalists wanted but with what the American people wanted, saying:

> Well, the American Civil Liberties Union will forever be busy throwing manger scenes out of city halls and attempting to put God out of public life in this country. They do not represent the will of the people. The *Washington Post* poll of last year, an NBC poll of this year indicate that three quarters, at least, of the American people want prayer in schools. The key word being voluntary prayer, and I don't see how the A.C.L.U. or any enemy of the nation under God could possibly deny the people what they want once they have the opportunity of referendum.[147]

The word "enemy" was not meant as an exaggeration. Falwell resumed his interview of Murray (shortly after referring to the ACLU as an enemy of the nation under God) to ask Murray to talk about his mother's activity before and leading up to the *Abington* suit.

However, before returning to Murray, Falwell interviewed Senator Jesse Helms of North Carolina to explain how Reagan was keeping the terms of the American dispensation.[148] Falwell asked Helms, "What did you think of the president's speech?" to which Helms responded, "He has fulfilled the commitment that he made to himself and to his Lord and to us, and this is the beginning of what I hope will culminate in restoring the right of children to pray in schools."[149] Falwell then asked an important follow-up question to the born-again, Bible-believing Helms, "Do you think—someone asked or suggests that it was just politics."[150] Helms responded, "Not at all. Ronald Reagan, as you know—you have sat with him as I have, and he's perfectly sincere. I had hoped that maybe it would come a few weeks earlier, but this man had a plateful of problems to deal with and in any case we could not have gotten it up on the Senate floor before now."[151] The two men provided bona fides for Reagan, with Falwell asking Helms, a long-standing ally of the Moral Majority, for testimony that Helms affirmed in part on the basis of Falwell's own experience.

Falwell also used the interview with Helms to establish Murray's credibility, both by having Helms speak for the man but, just as importantly, by explaining that Murray had been ignored by the media covering Reagan's announcement. Falwell said:

Bill Murray is a Christian now, the son of Madalyn Murray O'Hair, who as a teenager was responsible with his mother for the expulsion of prayer and Bible reading from public schools in this country. All the networks have just about ignored him. I mean, he was the main story today. He was here at the Rose Garden. He was present when the president read his proclamation and nobody even asked whether he was for or against it, and yet here he is a Christian now encouraging a constitutional amendment which is necessary because of some action he and his mother took twenty years ago. Why have the networks snubbed him?[152]

Helms provided an explanation that would alarm nearly anyone in Falwell's audience:

You know I can't read minds but when a pattern develops then you can draw your own conclusions. Now the first time I ever saw Bill Murray was in Dallas after that big rally in October of 1980. You remember you were there and Ronald Reagan, Senator [William L.] Armstrong [of Colorado] and I and some others . . . and I was standing in line when up came this young man who said he was Bill Murray. . . . And then he began to explain to me what happened way back then, and he said, you know, I've been trying to tell this about how the

Marxists—and he named names of the people who came to his mother's home during the orchestration of this lawsuit—and he said I've
been trying to talk to the major media about this for literally years,
and he said every time I bring up that aspect of it they shut up their
notebooks and they cut off their lights.[153]

For Falwell and Helms, the conventional media had shown greater interest in
protecting a status quo established by Marxists than in hearing family opinions about school prayer. In showing their allegiance to a Marxist-inspired
status quo against prayer in schools, they had in the eyes of Falwell's audience
undermined their credibility. Falwell, in featuring Murray prominently, had
affirmed his own. Helms, however, noted an optimistic influence that illustrated the value of Bible-believing Christians acting in politics. He concluded
his response to Falwell by saying, "Now I raised that question [of Marxists
behind ending prayer in school] on one of the television networks this morning. Why—and I asked them that. Why don't you get Bill Murray in? And
maybe they'll do it, Jerry."[154] Falwell responded with the same optimism,
"Because of your leadership the grass roots Americans now are beginning
to stand up and say what needs to be said, and they're finding out they can
make a difference."[155] The conversation between Falwell and Helms spelled
out exactly the state of affairs Bible-believing Christians had been so late
in acting against, but they ended their interview on a note of hope. Falwell,
Helms, and the people they represented had not been too late. Indeed, they
were rebuilding the nation, even as they redeemed themselves for previously
allowing conditions to get this bad.

    Falwell interviewed Murray in part to demonstrate how anti-American
and anti-Christian the effort to end prayer in school had originally been.
Murray provided to Falwell the story that the press had refused to tell, thus
showing Falwell's positive contrast to the press who had condemned Falwell.
Murray provided details about his mother that condemned her entire enterprise.[156] He went on to explain that the Communist Party even offered its own
lawyers for O'Hair's case, but O'Hair wanted "complete control of the case,
and of course the party doesn't allow anybody to have complete control of
anything."[157] He also detailed her and his own involvement in the Students
for Democratic Society and the Young Communist League, his attempt to
run as an atheist for Congress in 1976, losing but still getting 43 percent of
the vote, becoming an alcoholic, but eventually finding God because of the
prayers and ministry of his own employees at the airline where he eventually
found work.

However, as Murray explained, he had had a conversion only three years before the interview (1979), the point at which Bible-believing Christians had fully returned from exile. His conversion was part of the story Falwell's episode was meant to tell: that the return of Bible-believing Christians to politics had stopped Marxist influences, elected a God-fearing president, challenged the control of an enthralled press, and saved souls. Only when Christians fought to reclaim the nation from the peril in which the enemy had put it could someone as lost as Murray find his way and demonstrate the blessings God would bestow on a nation. Falwell ended the program with a conversation with Cal Thomas in which the two agreed that the ACLU would not stop fighting because of these early gains; thus, Falwell's Bible-believing viewers had to continue financially supporting the Moral Majority and its political efforts to oppose the ACLU.

By no means was this episode the only one where Falwell presented the nehemiad as a reinterpretation of the criticisms and triumphs of Bible-believing Christians. Indeed, during Reagan's first term, Falwell frequently told his audience about his success in laying the American dispensation at the foundation of American life:

> During the 1960s and the 1970s, as a nation we experienced two decades of moral decadence, a falling apart, a removal from the foundation stones on which this great nation was established. And as a result of those some twenty years of moral permissiveness, as a result of those nearly twenty years of repudiation of the Judeo-Christian perspective, traditional and family values, we saw a drug epidemic begin that today has paralyzed the minds and bodies of millions of our young people and continues to do so. . . . We forgot the God Who made us and Who established us, but thank God, as I bring the message today on the subject of the healing of America. There is in process and in progress in this country today a moral and spiritual rebirth that is undeniable. I want to talk to you about the evidence of such a moral and spiritual rebirth, what the causes for that moral and spiritual rebirth are, and what you can do to be a part of the solution instead of part of the problem.[158]

Episodes of *Old-Time Gospel Hour* normally followed the same pattern. First, they offer a religious basis for political participation. Second, Falwell recommends periodicals that went into details about the problems and solutions. Finally, he then integrates these solutions into the broader religious message his sermon offers. Among the problems were organized groups who attempted to thwart Bible-believing Christians and other conservatives. While not every episode focused on political problems, the ones that did followed this format. Falwell spoke of how the universities that had contributed to the moral problems of the 1960s and 1970s were teaching a new generation of students who were less tolerant of sin and more ready to accept traditional values, and he affirmed to the audience that Bible-believing pastors and their congregations were the chief cause.[159] The victories of Bible-believing Christians were not absolute but merely battles won in the larger war. Falwell continued to warn of "The Law of Sowing and Reaping," which was a sermon on God's continued direct intervention in American national well-being rooted in adherence to the moral principles established since the Puritan founding. The sermon even featured extended endorsement of several of Falwell's periodicals and publications meant to offer the parallel interpretations to the secular mainstream.[160]

Murray's conversion gave Falwell's audience a sense of hope that their decision to abandon political self-exile was the right one. If Bible-believing Christians could increase conversions before the End Times by engaging in politics, then they had every obligation to do so. Persecution ceased to be a sign of a fallen world beyond saving; it became a sign that they were saving the fallen world to the protest of a small, mean, and still dangerous minority. America might not have been worth saving for its own sake, but if saving America meant saving souls, then America was worth saving after all. Falwell made that case and succeeded. The American dispensation burned across state lines and to the top of the national ticket in the short span from 1978 until 1984, and burned out just as quickly.

Conclusion

The 1984 elections repeated the cycle of media criticism and its reinterpretation by Falwell as persecution and proof of the nehemiad. However, by the end of the Reagan administration, Falwell had all but shut down the Moral Majority. This was just as well for him and Bible-believing Christians. The American dispensation, its nehemiad, and the formation of the Moral Majority had served their purpose—to mobilize Bible-believing Christians for conservative candidates. The transition to the Christian Coalition in the 1990s illustrated how, in the terms of the nehemiad, the once-exiled had succeeded in rebuilding the walls and repudiating the gentiles. Conditions had changed, which meant that Falwell's old way of interpreting events had lost its rhetorical force, but the sense of persecution remained latent.

For example, in January of 2017, Rev. Robert Jeffress, a Southern Baptist preacher at First Baptist Church in Dallas, Texas, gave a triumphant sermon titled "When God Chooses a Leader" in St. John's Episcopal Church.[161] His chief audience was Donald J. Trump, who was about to be sworn in as the forty-fifth president of the United States. Jeffress selected as his biblical text the book of Nehemiah. Jeffress observed the same traits in Nehemiah that he saw in Trump. Nehemiah had two "chief antagonists" who were "the mainstream media of their day" who "spread false rumors while he and the Israelites were building the wall."[162] Nehemiah also experienced "tremendous obstacles even as he attempted to rebuild the nation: an economic recession, terrorist attacks from enemies, and discouragement among the citizens."[163] What Nehemiah did to fight against his enemies and his obstacles was to turn to God, "who empowered Nehemiah nearly 2500 years ago" and remained "available to every one of us today who is willing to humble himself and ask for His help."[164] While it remains unclear whether Trump has humbled himself before God since the inauguration, what Jeffress illustrated was the continuation of the American nehemiad within a certain number of Baptists that Falwell had restored and promulgated for another unlikely presidential audience.

American Religious Foundations After the Judeo-Christian Consensus

> They cried out, "Take him away, take him away!
> Crucify him!"
> Pilate said to them, "Shall I crucify your king?"
> The chief priests answered, "We have no king
> but Caesar."
>
> —John 19:15

Summary of Cases

Ven. Fulton J. Sheen, Dr. Martin Luther King Jr., and Rev. Jerry Falwell preached very different religious foundations to ground very different policy agendas. What they shared was the appeal to religious foundations as well as their use of mass media to persuade a national audience of their truth. For each, the goal was for the foundation to serve as a kind of religious dogma, a salutary restraint on popular sovereignty. Sheen condemned popular sympathies with totalitarian states and raised up American Catholics as patriots despite lingering suspicions among Protestants. King condemned local and state segregation laws and called upon the federal government to bring them to an end. Falwell regarded sexual liberation as a violation of God's law and called the church out of exile to push for the restoration of biblically inspired political representation and norms before the coming of the End. The media strategies they deployed differed by time and circumstance, yet they always had a media strategy. Sheen sought out new technologies to reach wide audiences. Because he lacked access to mass media, King brought the mass media to him with demonstrations that made him and the issue of segregation constantly newsworthy. Falwell owned his own mass media enterprise, which he converted to a source of public advocacy that rivaled established venues.

Even as three men sought to lay foundations as a source for American dogma, they improvised on inherited narratives and traditions. Sheen spliced together Americanism from its dueling definitions, and he retold the old anti-Catholic narratives in their application to totalitarianism. King's Beloved Community drew from personalism to update traditional Protestant covenant theology, drew from new strategies of nonviolent direct action, and emphasized the traditional African American Exodus narrative with a jeremiad only in the background. Falwell preached the American dispensation by, knowingly or not, restoring the old American nehemiad tradition to recount a Bible-believing Christian return from exile. In each case, the clergy improvised, modified, or rejected what social scientists have often treated as conceptual frames to persuade new audiences.

Emerging among the cases are some additional similarities. All three disputed American exceptionalism. Sheen regarded the Catholic Church as the seat of the true "city on the hill." King located the sacred in the emerging Kingdom of God among those practicing sacrificial love for others. Falwell located it in God's will, blessing the good and reproaching the wicked. All three used the superior divine authority to set firm limits to political action. Sheen insisted on protecting religious liberty because God made every man free to pursue spiritual goods. King insisted on racial justice because God created all human persons with equal rights. Falwell insisted on his view of biblical morality because the state lacked the power to change God's will and, in attempting to do so, it put its citizens at risk of divine retribution. Even so, all three found a special purpose for the nation. Sheen saw America as the arsenal and pantry of democracy, whose leadership on religious freedom was its true calling. King saw America as a leader in the liberation of people of color from the remnants of colonialism and slavery. Falwell saw America as the last, great hope for world evangelization before the End Times began.

For each figure, however, there was a risk. Tocqueville observed that American religion was powerful because it exerted an indirect force on democracy. Religion resisted the deification of the majority. Tocqueville observed small fissures in American religious foundations. Public figures might privately doubt the truth of religion, but they agreed to its necessity and submitted to the popular consensus that held Christianity to be true. Tocqueville noted that some clergy, especially the Catholic, seemed uncomfortable or unhappy with the demotion of the clergy to mere leaders of voluntary organizations. Even so, the product of the arrangement was the alliance of the spirit of liberty and the spirit of religion. The alliance depended on the disestablishment of churches and the willingness of clergy to stay out of politics. When Sheen, King, and Falwell began their public ministries, they put this separation under stress, and Falwell finally broke the separation entirely.

Each man encountered charges that he married church with state. Sheen deflected this charge with demonstrations of Catholic patriotism. King persuaded audiences that his appeals merely fulfilled the promise of the American founding. Falwell, on the other hand, sought to integrate Bible-believing Christians into an ideological movement that had found a home in a political party. Religion thereby became a political force rather than a spiritual force, which then rested the fate of religion on the fate of the party. The party's fate was to secure a majority in public offices, thus dividing the spirit of religion from the spirit of liberty. Tocqueville would have understood this arrangement as precisely the one that had compromised French Christianity, pitting it as the spirit of religion against the antireligious spirit of liberty. Some might argue that it was the New Left that first began the changes in mores that threw religious conservatives on the defensive, thus necessitating their political mobilization. That may be true, but nothing about the social revolutions of the 1960s required the kind of political mobilization that Falwell and other religious conservatives instigated. The social revolutions of the 1960s provided a counterconsensus to the Judeo-Christian consensus. Under the religious leadership of the 1980s, the Judeo-Christian consensus doubled down on political and social control. Falwell disqualified his opponents as "Sanballats and Tobiahs," meaning that they were bad-faith political conspirators with whom he could not be bothered to engage, and pointed to short-term political success as evidence of his foundation's superiority. Indeed, even the very name, "Moral Majority," concedes the unconstrained majoritarianism Tocqueville feared could take over America.

Whither the Judeo-Christian Consensus

Since the 1990s, Americans have shown a significant decline in their religious faith and affiliation with religious denominations, and these trends follow a first drop-off from during the 1960s.[1] Scholars have used quantitative methods to demonstrate that America has endured two waves of politicized religion that have provoked two backlashes. The 1960s produced a drop-off in religious devotion among mainline Protestants as these denominations engaged in progressive politics. While the first drop-off continued, a second one among more conservative Evangelicals and Catholics began in the 1990s, and its effect has become clearer in the data as older cohorts have gone to their eternal reward. These scholars have stressed that these two declines do not herald a delayed arrival of secularization, since those disaffiliating from religious denominations do not then adopt the faith in the progress of scientific materialism. Instead, they engage in alternative forms of spiritual practice or residual devotions, such as private prayer. The evidence suggests that declining religiosity correlates with poor religious education, but poor religious education begins with the departure of Americans from politicized churches. Scholars have confirmed the observations Tocqueville made almost one hundred and eighty years ago: when religious authorities seek direct political influence, congregations split and decline. Therefore, for religious foundations to remain authoritative requires religious institutions to remove themselves from direct political activity.

Progressive religious leaders have nevertheless sought to revitalize the "Religious Left" as a force for advancing radical social change. After decades of dismissing King as too hierarchical and religious to serve as an example, activists on the Left have taken renewed interest in the later, more apparently radical language King adopted during the Poor People's Campaign of 1967. Reverend William Barber began his "Moral Mondays" campaign to draw attention to the exploitation of the poor and to discrimination against people of color. Under his leadership, progressive clergy have appeared at the tremendous rallies of progressives against the presidency of Donald J. Trump and the white nationalists emboldened by the president's campaign and eventual election. One of the most impassioned calls for engaging a renascent Religious Left was Matthew Sitman, the literary editor at *Commonweal*, who wrote in *Dissent* about the need to reclaim religious language to appeal to the consciences of people outside the ordinary, more secular constituencies for progressive political candidates.[2] Author and *Washington Post* editor Elizabeth Bruenig has already started doing this work by interpreting the theology of St. Augustine of Hippo into a social democratic vision for America.[3] However, for all the coverage that the Religious Left has received, the leading scholars remain pessimistic that these efforts could succeed. Laura R. Olson found substantial disunity among what might constitute the Religious Left, casting doubt on its revival.[4] Kimberly H. Conger has published empirical analysis indicating that the Religious Left has numerous clergy and elite backing but very little in the way of congregational support or capacity to mobilize.[5] In 2017, scholar and activist Cornel West and local progressive clergy in Charlottesville, Virginia, opposed the fascist "Unite the Right" rally, but as they linked arms no one lined up behind them. It made for a sad contrast to King and his clergy marching at the front of the protesters in Birmingham.

At the same time, conservative religious scholars and advocates have concluded that the formation of the Religious Right has not produced the kind of political and social changes that they might once have hoped for. As discussed in the Introduction, political theorist Patrick Deneen, constitutional law scholar Adrian Vermeule, public intellectual Rod Dreher, and editor-in-chief at *First Things* Russell "Rusty" Reno have called for religious people to reconsider the compatibility of liberalism with forms of orthodox Christianity. In *Why Liberalism Failed*, Deneen assaults the faulty anthropology he attributes to all liberal thought.[6] Liberalism begins with an isolated individual in the state of nature, and individuals remain similarly isolated as they consent to join civil society and constitutional governments. The preliberal institutions, such as churches, sustain a liberal democracy by preserving natural communities, but with liberalism at its heart, these regimes necessarily break down preliberal institutions with constant government interventions until individuals inhabit the unnatural isolation that liberalism demands. Moreover, the success of liberalism in America has cut citizens off from preliberal traditions that once sustained them under the intensifying pressure of liberalism. The only solution would be to begin these traditions anew by engaging in intentional community building and the inauguration of new customs of true liberty.

For these reasons, Dreher has spent the past few years persuading all religious believers to commit their congregations to the "Benedict Option," which is a conscious removal of the faithful, broadly defined, from the free-market-nanny-state complex.[7] The Benedict Option provoked a vast number of alternative "options" that sought more engagement in the culture to make it more devout, but Dreher has remained unconvinced that American culture, so long as it remains liberal, can countenance religious appeals. Instead, religious congregations should preserve and recover their traditions to resuscitate the nation after its impending social collapse. Vermeule and Reno have worked to revise the more optimistic vision of their forebears, scholars like Fr. Richard John Neuhaus and Michael Novak, considering the failure of returning religion to the public square. While Reno has focused on scaling back the possibility of marrying the Judeo-Christian consensus to free market capitalism,[8] Vermeule has suggested that a postliberal order Deneen and Dreher anticipate has something to learn from antiliberal theorists, such as the political thought of Carl Schmitt.[9] In another revealing piece, Vermeule muses that to be a devout Catholic means to be homeless in the world, since one is destined to an eternal home in the life to come.[10]

This conclusion is understandable, given the incredible decline conservative religious groups have experienced in the last decade. The conclusion is also wrong. Among them, Deneen is the one who is most surprising, since he draws so much of his criticism of contemporary liberalism from Tocqueville. Even as Deneen uses Tocqueville to elevate the preliberal traditions and institutions on which Americans depended, he condemns the American founding as liberal to the core and in need of purging. It is a very strange doctrine to find, on the one hand, that the American regime is liberal, and on the other hand, that the liberal regime was home to Tocqueville's *beau idéal* of a democracy, the New England township. When Tocqueville contemplated the end of the township, he predicted many causes, and chief among them was the direct participation of religion in politics. Missing from his list was "liberalism."

The Future of Religious Foundations

The decline of the Judeo-Christian consensus does not make the United States any less dogmatic. One should recall that Tocqueville identified the dogma of a democracy as the dogma of popular sovereignty. Its only competition was the salutary servitude of religion, which could temper but never vanquish popular sovereignty, lest it vanquish democracy itself. Once unleashed from the salutary servitude of religion, the sovereign people secure what Tocqueville regarded as a kind of divine power that governs by the "impious maxim" that "everything is permitted in the interest of society."[11] This dogma is manifest in a kind of modern revision of pantheism, which "enclos[es] God and the universe within a single whole" and "aspires to be able to link a multitude of consequences to a single cause."[12] A pantheist, by Tocqueville's view, "gets used to no longer viewing citizens so as to consider only the people; one forgets individuals so as to think only of the species."[13] In contrast, Tocqueville claims as Plato did in *The Statesman* that "God does not ponder the human race in general. At a single glance he sees separately all of the beings of which humanity is composed, and perceives each of them with the similarities that bring [each one] closer to all and the differences that isolate [each one] from [everyone else]."[14] Losing religion means losing the human person to the crowd of undifferentiated mass of faces, leaving the individual equipped only with "general ideas."

General ideas are a poor substitute for dogmas of salutary servitude. They "do not attest to the strength of human intelligence, but rather to its insufficiency, because there are no beings in nature exactly alike."[15] To compensate for the limits of human intelligence, however, an individual pretends as though humans are indistinguishable and interchangeable, which permits "the human mind to bring rapid judgments to a great number of objects at one time; but on the other hand, they never provide it with anything but incomplete notions."[16] As the number of facts concerning the human species increases, so does the need for an individual to develop general ideas that compensate for the failure to comprehend the differences of individual persons, but the sheer volume of facts is overwhelming. Tocqueville lamented that for a democratic individual, "to explain what happens in the world, one is therefore reduced to searching for a few great causes."[17] He thought that the English were less likely than the Americans or French to succumb to general ideas on account of their ancient aristocracy having the habits and leisure to discern individual differences in what, to a democratic citizen, would appear to be an undifferentiated mass. Americans were less likely to succumb to general ideas than the French, however, because of the American experience with self-government. Without experience in self-government, the French fostered a "blind . . . faith in the goodness and absolute truth of any theory" and conceived "very general ideas in matters of government."[18] The French wrongly thought to compensate for their ignorance with speculative theories of general forces operating on restless, often isolated democratic individuals. Americans, during the 1830s, had considerably more experience in local government, which dispelled any general ideas of politics. Even so, Tocqueville saw American intellectuals operate under conditions that drew them to general ideas, saying those in "intellectual careers" are "full of an ambition that is at once lively and soft; they want to obtain great success right away, but they would like to exempt themselves from great efforts. These contrary instincts lead them directly to search for general ideas, with the aid of which they flatter themselves by painting very vast objects at small cost and attracting public attention without trouble."[19]

When an individual depends on general ideas and a pantheistic worldview, she sees the world as combat among quasi-divine forces that oppress or liberate the people as a species. Hegel saw the Zeitgeist as developing the German people into the full realization of the state. Marx saw the socialist utopia emerging from the contradictions of capitalism. Schumpeter saw in his gale the forces of innovation blowing away the world of horse and buggy in favor of the combustion engine. Bakunin was even more thorough, seeing a conspiracy in all things against the individual's natural liberty. Examples in contemporary America abound. American intellectuals behave as the French did by introducing general ideas about the threats from liberalism, progressivism, socialism, capitalism, conservatism, Christian nationalism, anti-Semitism, the deep state, the media, and too many more to mention. These forces, like Gnostic demiurges, are always, at first, unnoticed but then revealed to be at work disrupting institutions and practices. An individual subject to these forces has "a model of salvation that is merely interior, closed off in its own subjectivism," while faith in one or another general idea "presumes to liberate the human person from the body and the material universe, in which traces of the provident hand of the Creator are no longer found, but only a reality deprived of meaning, foreign to the fundamental identity of the person, and easily manipulated by the interests of man."[20] Unlike the Americans of the 1830s, Americans today mostly lack the habits of self-government and, hence, lack the experience in politics that render them skeptical of general ideas. Therefore, as the salutary servitude of religion has lost influence, these general ideas have gained influence. Citizens who once shared a dogma that facilitated public participation now dispute everything because of their affiliation with opposing general ideas. At best, opponents only manage to debate but never settle on first principles; more typically, however, debates begin and end with efforts to deny the opposition the moral standing to participate in public discussion at all, since hearing the opposition is to make everyone an accomplice with the forces opposing the true will of the majority—or what is called today "no-platforming."

American religious foundations have shifted from a dogma placing limits on the people to one liberating them from those limits. With the people unleashed, they grab onto whatever beliefs provide them with access to powerful factions and then seek out allies in forming a majority to crush their opponents. An appeal to religion is of no avail, since opponents view religions as no different from several alternative general ideas combining or competing over majorities to enact their collective wills. One of the greatest contributors to this outcome was the politicized church that took on the appearances of merely another political entity—whether the defunct Religious Left or the diminished Religious Right—rather than as source for consolation, salvation, education, and community formation. Churches must resume these functions to provide the indirect influence that once preserved the republic, but these churches must ready themselves for the persecution these efforts have always provoked. The alternative is for the conditions only to worsen, as opposing ideological groups seek out majority power to build up a state that, in turn, tyrannizes everyone. Whereas Americans once regarded God as love and that love as the model relationship they should have with their families, neighbors, and even strangers, now they seek the state which, as Tocqueville warned, "in its nature is fearful [and] sees the most certain guarantee of its own duration in the isolation of men, and it ordinarily puts all its care into isolating them."[21] Indeed, this state, "readily pardons the governed for not loving him, provided that they do not love each other"[22] or, as the prophet Samuel prophesied, "On that day you will cry out because of the king whom you have chosen, but the Lord will not answer you on that day."

NOTES

Introduction

Note to epigraph: All biblical quotations are from the New American Bible unless otherwise noted.

1. Danielle S. Allen, *Our Declaration: A Reading of the Declaration of Independence in Defense of Equality* (New York: Liveright, 2014), 138, 276.

2. Patrick J. Deneen, *Why Liberalism Failed* (New Haven: Yale University Press, 2018), 7, 40–41.

3. Patrick J. Deneen, *Conserving America? Essays on Present Discontents* (South Bend: St. Augustine's Press, 2016), 11.

4. Ibid.

5. Deneen, *Why Liberalism Failed*, 196.

6. Rod Dreher, *The Benedict Option: A Strategy for Christians in a Post-Christian Nation* (New York: Sentinel, 2014).

7. Deneen, *Why Liberalism Failed*, 5.

8. James P. Byrd, *Sacred Scripture, Sacred War: The Bible and the American Revolution* (New York: Oxford University Press, 2013); Daniel L. Dreisbach, *Reading the Bible with the Founding Fathers* (New York: Oxford University Press, 2017); Thomas S. Kidd, *God of Liberty: A Religious History of the American Revolution* (Philadelphia: Basic Books, 2012); Carl J. Richard, *The Founders and the Bible* (Lanham: Rowman and Littlefield, 2016).

9. The abbreviation "Ven." is short for "Venerable." Readers familiar with Sheen but not his canonization may have been surprised not to see the title "Archbishop," since this was his title at his death. There is currently an effort to canonize Sheen as a saint in the Roman Catholic Church. He was named to "Servant of God" in 2002 once the cause for canonization began and was later given the title "Venerable" by Pope Benedict XVI in 2012. The canonization effort is currently stymied by a dispute over Sheen's final resting place, though he is likely to become beatified and given the title "Blessed" once the relevant authorities resolve the dispute.

10. Alexis de Tocqueville, *Democracy in America*, ed. and trans. Harvey C. Mansfield and Delba Winthrop (Chicago: University of Chicago Press, 2000), 278–288.

11. Ibid., 423–424.

12. Ibid., 501–503.

13. Ibid., 11.

14. Ibid., 112.

15. Ibid., 95.

16. Aristide Tessitore, "Tocqueville's American Thesis and the New Science of Politics," *The Spirit of Religion and the Spirit of Liberty: The Tocqueville Thesis Revisited*, ed. Michael P. Zuckert (Chicago: University of Chicago Press, 2017), 19–49, 27.

17. Ibid., 93. See also Aurelian Craiutu and Matthew N. Holbreich, "On Individualism, Authority, and Democracy as a New Form of Religion: A Few Tocquevillian Reflections," *The Spirit of Religion and the Spirit of Liberty: The Tocqueville Thesis Revisited*, ed. Michael P. Zuckert (Chicago: University of Chicago Press, 2017), 123–154.

18. Tocqueville, *Democracy in America*, 407.

19. Alan S. Kahan, *Tocqueville, Democracy, and Religion: Checks and Balances for Democratic Souls* (New York: Oxford University Press, 2015), 77.

20. Tocqueville, *Democracy in America*, 408.

21. Ibid., 418.

22. Ibid., 420–421.

23. Ibid., 423.

24. Ibid., 203. Beneath the surface of *Democracy in America* and more explicitly in his letters, Tocqueville was more concerned about the future of American religion, especially is Protestantism. See also Giorgi Areshidze, *Democratic Religion from Locke to Obama: Faith and the Civic Life of Democracy* (Lawrence: University Press of Kansas, 2016), 124–139.

25. Ibid., 423. See also J. Judd Owen, *Making Religion Safe for Democracy: Transformation from Hobbes to Tocqueville* (New York: Cambridge University Press, 2015), 131–133.

26. Tocqueville, *Democracy in America*, 424.

27. Ibid.

28. Alan S. Kahan says of Tocqueville's view, "Precisely because religion must appeal to unchanging dogmas about an unchanging God, too close a link with changeable political institutions is always dangerous and can be fatal." *Tocqueville, Democracy, and Religion*, 83.

29. Cited from Kahan, *Tocqueville, Democracy, and Religion*, 89.

30. Tocqueville, *Democracy in America*, 277.

31. Ibid.

32. Ibid.

33. Ibid.

34. Ibid.

35. Ibid.

36. James T. Schleifer, "Tocqueville, Religion, and *Democracy in America*: Some Essential Questions," *The Spirit of Religion and the Spirit of Liberty: The Tocqueville Thesis Revisited*, ed. Michael P. Zuckert (Chicago: University of Chicago Press, 2017), 49–67.

37. Perry Miller, *The New England Mind: From Colony to Province*, vol. 2 (Cambridge: Beacon Press, 1960), 29–39.

38. Sacvan Bercovitch, *The American Jeremiad* (Madison: University of Wisconsin Press, 1978); James A. Morone, *Hellfire Nation: The Politics of Sin in American History* (New Haven: Yale University Press, 2003); Andrew R. Murphy, *Prodigal Nation: Moral Decline and Divine Punishment from New England to 9/11* (New York: Oxford University Press, 2009).

39. Bercovitch, *American Jeremiad*, 176–210.

40. Morone, *Hellfire Nation*, 496–497; Murphy, *Prodigal Nation*, 166–171.

41. Robert N. Bellah, "Civil Religion in America," *Daedalus* 96, no. 1 (Winter 1967): 1–21, 8.

42. Peter Gardella, *American Civil Religion: What Americans Hold Sacred* (New York: Oxford University Press, 2013); Philip Gorski, *American Covenant: A History of Civil Religion from the Puritans to the Present* (Princeton: Princeton University Press, 2017).

43. Keith Bates, Liam J. Atchison, and Darin D. Lenz, eds., *Civil Religion and American Christianity* (Mountain Home: BorderStone Press, 2015).

44. John D. Wilsey, *American Exceptionalism and Civil Religion: Reassessing the History of an Idea* (Downers Grove: IVP Academic, 2015), 25.

45. The notion that the American civil religion could exist independently from revealed religion rests on theological liberalism. "Theological liberalism" refers to a belief in the sovereignty of the individual believer to decide whether to consent or not to a specific religious creed or authority. As Philip Hamburger has argued, the theological liberal treats religion as a private activity rooted in a personal concept of one's obligation—if any—to the divine. Hamburger has charted the efforts of theological liberals to push individual sovereignty throughout the development of American religious denominations, often with recourse to constitutional interpretation or statutory reform. Theological liberalism never became the presumptive foundation for American religious views. It most certainly does not monopolize how people of faith understand the relationship between church and state. Because of their emphasis on division between private faith and public politics, only theological liberals could imagine a civil religion totally divorced from revealed religion. Most religious peoples believe their faith has a strong claim on public life, both in the collective endeavors of the state and in the personal activities of citizens. Hence, they can regard patriotism and veneration for political leaders with ambivalence. Instead, preachers and congregations must evaluate the extent to which they want to incorporate commemorations not directly affiliated with their faiths. Philip Hamburger, *Separation of Church and State* (Cambridge: Harvard University Press, 2002).

46. Hugh Heclo, "Christianity and Democracy in America," *Christianity and American Democracy* (Cambridge: Harvard University Press, 2007), 1–144, 20.

47. Ibid., 31.

48. Ibid., 29.

49. Ibid., 35.

50. Donald S. Lutz, *The Origins of American Constitutionalism* (Baton Rouge: Louisiana State University Press, 1988), 11.

51. Rogers M. Smith, "What If God Was One of Us?" *Nature and History in American Political Development* (Cambridge: Harvard University Press, 2006), 141–168, 146.

52. James W. Ceaser, "Foundational Concepts and American Political Development," *Nature and History in American Political Development* (Cambridge: Harvard University Press, 2006), 1-89, 12.

53. Ibid.

54. Ibid., 13.

55. Ceaser, "Foundational Concepts and American Political Development," 5.

56. On the relationship between foundation and dogma, see Harvey C. Mansfield, "Tocqueville on Religion and Liberty," *The Spirit of Religion and the Spirit of Liberty: The Tocqueville Thesis Revisited*, ed. Michael P. Zuckert (Chicago: University of Chicago Press, 2017), 189–215.

57. The subject of the Protestant hegemony is too great to address at length in this book. For an excellent start on its rise and fall, see the following: Eldon J. Eisenach, *The Next Religious Establishment: National Identity and Political Theology in Post-Protestant America* (Lanham: Rowman and Littlefield, 2000); Roger Finke and Rodney Stark, *The Churching of America, 1776–2005: Winners and Losers in Our Religious Economy*, 6th ed. (New Brunswick: Rutgers University Press, 2014); Mark A. Noll, *America's God: From Jonathan Edwards to Abraham Lincoln* (New York: Oxford University Press, 2002). I borrow the term from D. G. Hart, "Mainstream Protestantism, 'Conservative' Religion, and Civil Society," *Religion Returns to the Public Square:*

Faith and Policy in America, ed. Hugh Heclo and Wilfred M. McClay (Baltimore: Johns Hopkins University Press, 2003), 195–225, 198.

58. Martin E. Marty, *Pilgrims in Their Own Land: 500 Years of Religion in America* (Boston: Little, Brown, 1984), 106–224, 336–372; Robert T. Handy, *A Christian America: Protestant Hopes and Historical Realities*, 2nd ed. (New York: Oxford University Press, 1984).

59. See Philip Jenkins, *The New Anti-Catholicism: The Last Acceptable Prejudice* (New York: Oxford University Press, 2004); Mark S. Massa, *Anti-Catholicism in America: The Last Acceptable Prejudice* (New York: Crossroad Publishing, 2005); Justin Nordstrom, *Danger on the Doorstep: Anti-Catholicism and American Print Culture in the Progressive Era* (South Bend: University of Notre Dame Press, 2006); John C. Pinheiro, *Missionaries of Republicanism: A Religious History of the Mexican-American War* (New York: Oxford University Press, 2014).

60. Massa, *Anti-Catholicism in America*, 7–39.

61. Matthew S. Hedstrom, *The Rise of Liberal Religion: Book Culture and American Spirituality in the Twentieth Century* (New York: Oxford University Press, 2013); Kevin M. Schultz, *Tri-Faith America: How Catholics and Jews Held Postwar America to Its Protestant Promise* (New York: Oxford University Press, 2011); Mark Silk, "Notes on the Judeo-Christian Tradition in America," *American Quarterly* 36, no. 1 (Spring 1984): 65–85. For a broader view of the subject, see Wendy L. Wall, *Inventing the "American Way": The Politics of Consensus from the New Deal to the Civil Rights Movement* (New York: Oxford University Press, 2008). Kevin M. Kruse provides a less-than-flattering account in *One Nation Under God: How Corporate America Invented Christian America* (New York: Basic Books, 2015).

62. Edward K. Kaplan, *Spiritual Radical: Abraham Joshua Heschel in America, 1940–1972* (New Haven: Yale University Press, 2009), 215–230.

63. Kathleen L. Riley, *Fulton J. Sheen: An American Catholic Response to the Twentieth Century* (Staten Island: Alba House, 2004), 91–92.

64. Mark K. Bauman and Berkley Kalen, eds., *The Quiet Voices: Southern Rabbis and Black Civil Rights, 1880s to 1990s* (Tuscaloosa: University of Alabama Press, 1997); Mark K. Bauman and Stephen Krause, eds., *To Stand Aside or Stand Alone: Southern Reform Rabbis and the Civil Rights Movement* (Tuscaloosa: University of Alabama Press, 2017); Debra L. Schultz, *Going South: Jewish Women in the Civil Rights Movement* (New York: New York University Press, 2002).

65. Merrill Simon, *Jerry Falwell and the Jews* (Middle Village: Jonathan David Publishers, 1984).

66. Yaakov Ariel, "It's All in the Bible: Evangelical Christians, Biblical Literalism, and Philosemitism in Our Times," *Philosemitism in History*, ed. Jonathan Karp and Adam Sutcliffe (Cambridge: Cambridge University Press, 2012), 257–288; Victoria Clark, *Allies for Armageddon: The Rise of Christian Zionism* (New Haven: Yale University Press, 2007); Samuel Goldman, *God's Country: Christian Zionism in America* (Philadelphia: University of Pennsylvania Press, 2018).

Chapter 1

1. Fulton J. Sheen, "The Cross and the Double-Cross," *For God and Country* (New York: P. J. Kennedy and Sons, 1941), 77–91, 83.

2. Sheen was apparently quite a difficult colleague. See Kathleen L. Riley, *Fulton J. Sheen: An American Catholic Response to the Twentieth Century* (Staten Island: Alba House, 2004), 12–19.

3. The former attacked Communism as a violent, openly hypocritical, and deadly enemy of democracy, and the latter was one of his many attempts to dismantle Freudian psychology,

a topic this paper will not cover. What matters in both cases was the tremendous success these books achieved and how they solidified his place as a popular religious figure in America.

4. Jonathan P. Herzog, *The Spiritual-Industrial Complex: America's Religious Battle Against Communism in the Early Cold War* (New York: Oxford University Press, 2011), 135–163.

5. John Higham, *Strangers in the Land: Patterns of American Nativism, 1860–1925* (New Brunswick: Rutgers University Press, 1983), 180–182.

6. Ryan P. Jordan, *Church, State, and Race: The Discourse of American Religious Liberty, 1750–1900* (Lanham: University Press of America, 2012), 105–139.

7. See Philip Jenkins, *The New Anti-Catholicism: The Last Acceptable Prejudice* (New York: Oxford University Press, 2004); Mark S. Massa, *Anti-Catholicism in America: The Last Acceptable Prejudice* (New York: Crossroad Publishing, 2005); Justin Nordstrom, *Danger on the Doorstep: Anti-Catholicism and American Print Culture in the Progressive Era* (South Bend: University of Notre Dame Press, 2006); John C. Pinheiro, *Missionaries of Republicanism: A Religious History of the Mexican-American War* (New York: Oxford University Press, 2014).

8. Tracy Fessenden, *Culture and Redemption: Religion, the Secular, and American Literature* (Princeton: Princeton University Press, 2007); Thomas S. Kidd, *God of Liberty: A Religious History of the American Revolution* (New York: Basic Books, 2010); Nathan O. Hatch, *The Democratization of American Christianity* (New Haven: Yale University Press, 1990); H. Richard Niebuhr, *The Kingdom of God in America* (New York: Harper and Row, 1937; repr., Middletown: Wesleyan University Press, 1988); Mark A. Noll, *America's God: From Jonathan Edwards to Abraham Lincoln* (New York: Oxford University Press, 2002); Jody M. Roy, *Rhetorical Campaigns of the Nineteenth Century Anti-Catholics and Catholics in America* (Lewiston: Edwin Mellen Press, 2000).

9. Fulton J. Sheen, *Communism and the Conscience of the West* (Indianapolis: Bobbs-Merrill, 1948), 46.

10. Fulton J. Sheen, *Freedom Under God* (Milwaukee: Bruce Publishing, 1940), 167.

11. Michael Breidenbach, "Conciliarism and the American Founding," *William and Mary Quarterly* 73, no. 3 (Summer 2016): 467–500; Peter Augustine Lawler, "Introduction: The Civilization of the Pluralist Society," *We Hold These Truths: Catholic Reflections on the American Proposition*, by John Courtney Murray (Lanham: Rowman and Littlefield, 2005), 1–22; Richard M. Reinsch II, "Introduction: Orestes Brownson's American Search for the Truth," *Seeking the Truth: An Orestes Brownson Anthology*, ed. Richard M. Reinsch II (Washington, DC: Catholic University of America Press, 2016), 18–23; Riley, *Fulton J. Sheen*, 94–95.

12. Fulton J. Sheen, Address before the National Council of Catholic Men, January 9, 1939, as cited in Riley, *Fulton J. Sheen*, 107–108.

13. Matthew S. Hedstrom, *The Rise of Liberal Religion: Book Culture and American Spirituality in the Twentieth Century* (New York: Oxford University Press, 2013); Will Herberg, *Protestant, Catholic, Jew: An Essay in American Religious Sociology* (Garden City: Doubleday, 1955); Kevin Michael Schultz, *Tri-Faith America: How Catholics and Jews Held Postwar America to Its Protestant Promise* (New York: Oxford University Press, 2011); Mark Silk, "Notes on the Judeo-Christian Tradition in America," *American Quarterly* 36, no. 1 (Spring 1984): 65–85.

14. A sample of those who have worked on this subject include Anita Talsma Gaul, "John Ireland, St. Eloi Parish, and the Dream of an American Catholic Church," *American Catholic Studies* 123, no. 3 (Fall 2013): 21–43; Philip Gleason, *Contending with Modernity: Catholic Higher Education in the Twentieth Century* (New York: Oxford University Press, 1995); Robert A. Herrera, "Orestes Brownson's Vision of American Life," *Modern Age* 43, no. 2 (Spring 2001): 133–145; David J. O'Brien, *American Catholics and Social Reform* (New York: Oxford University

Press, 1968); David J. O'Brien, *The Renewal of American Catholicism* (New York: Oxford University Press, 1972); David J. O'Brien, *Isaac Hecker: An American Catholic* (Mahwah: Paulist Press, 1992); William L. Portier, *Divided Friends: Portraits of the Roman Catholic Modernist Crisis in the United States* (Washington, DC: Catholic University of America Press, 2013).

15. Herzog, *Spiritual-Industrial Complex*, 137.

16. Felix Klein, *Americanism: A Phantom Heresy* (Atchison: Aquin Book Shop, 1951). See also Margaret M. Reher, "Phantom Heresy: A Twice-Told Tale," *U.S. Catholic Historian* 11, no. 3 (Summer 1993): 93–105.

17. Martin E. Marty, *Pilgrims in Their Own Land: 500 Years of Religion in America* (Boston: Little, Brown, 1984), 273–276.

18. James L. Chapman, *Americanism versus Romanism, or the Cis-Atlantic Battle Between Sam and the Pope* (Nashville: printed by the author, 1856), 169.

19. Ibid.

20. Jordan, *Church, State, and Race*, 116–127; Massa, *Anti-Catholicism in America*, 18–34; David J. O'Brien, "American Catholicism and American Religion," *Journal of the American Academy of Religion* 40, no. 1 (March 1972): 36–53; Samuel J. Thomas, "Mugwump Cartoonists, the Papacy, and Tammany Hall in America's Gilded Age," *Religion and American Culture: A Journal of Interpretation* 14, no. 2 (Summer 2004): 213–250.

21. Fulton J. Sheen, *Life Is Worth Living*, First Series (New York: McGraw-Hill, 1953), 250.

22. Ibid., 251.

23. Ibid., 250. The spy was never found. For more, see Donald F. Crosby, *God, Church, and Flag: Senator Joseph R. McCarthy and the Catholic Church, 1950–1957* (Chapel Hill: University of North Carolina Press, 1978), 15.

24. "Then Simon Peter, who had a sword, drew it, struck the high priest's slave, and cut off his right ear. The slave's name was Malchus. Jesus said to Peter, 'Put your sword into its scabbard. Shall I not drink the cup that the Father gave me?'" John 18:10.

25. "Put your sword back into its sheath, for all who take the sword will perish by the sword." Matthew 26:53. The speaker is Jesus.

26. Fulton J. Sheen, "Evil Has Its Hour," *The Catholic Hour*, originally aired March 14, 1943.

27. Sheen, *Freedom Under God*, 238.

28. Ibid., 239. The context of Sheen's story was to show why Soviet Communism would fail because it lacked the virtue of Charity found in Christianity.

29. Gleason, *Contending with Modernity*, 125.

30. Mark S. Massa, *Catholics and American Culture: Fulton Sheen, Dorothy Day, and the Notre Dame Football Team* (New York: Crossroad Publishing, 1999), 91. One might be tempted to associate Sheen's narrative with the "paranoid style" described by Richard Hofstadter in "The Paranoid Style in American Politics," *Harper's*, November 1964, 77–86. In places, the comparison is apt, but Sheen was much more careful than his contemporary Fr. Charles Coughlin to stick to verified facts concerning totalitarian executions of Catholic clergy, religious, and laity. As for Sheen's occasional rhetorical excesses, see Riley, *Fulton J. Sheen*, 144–164.

31. Fulton J. Sheen, *Moods and Truths: How to Solve the Problems of Modern Life* (New York: Century, 1932; repr., New York: Popular Library, 1956), 70. Page numbers refer to Popular Library reprint.

32. Fulton J. Sheen, *Life Is Worth Living*, Fifth Series (New York: McGraw-Hill, 1957), 137.

33. Christopher Lynch, *Selling Catholicism: Bishop Sheen and the Power of Television* (Lexington: University of Kentucky Press, 1998), 59.

34. Fulton J. Sheen, *Declaration of Dependence* (Milwaukee: Bruce Publishing, 1941), 125.

35. Sheen, *Freedom Under God*, 166.

36. Ibid., 174–175.

37. Ibid., 1–92, particularly, "False Liberties" and "True Liberty" (12–23, 24–36). As Philip Gleason has shown, Sheen held this division of labor between church and state from the beginning of his career. See Fulton J. Sheen, "Educating for a Catholic Renaissance," *National Catholic Educational Association Bulletin* 26 (1929): 45–54. Philip Gleason, *Keeping the Faith: American Catholicism Past and Present* (South Bend: University of Notre Dame Press, 1987), 144–145.

38. H. Richard Niebuhr, *Christ and Culture* (New York: Harper and Brothers, 1951), 116–148.

39. Sheen, *For God and Country*, 8–9. See also Riley, *Fulton J. Sheen*, 129–186.

40. Sheen, *Communism and the Conscience of the West*, i–ii.

41. Ibid., ii.

42. Ibid.

43. Fulton J. Sheen, *Life Is Worth Living*, Fourth Series (New York: McGraw-Hill, 1956), 76.

44. Sheen, *Communism and the Conscience of the West*, 49.

45. Ibid., 22.

46. "Historical liberalism is a parasite on Christian civilization, and once that body upon which it clings ceases to be the leaven of society, then historical liberalism itself must perish. The individual liberties which historical liberalism emphasizes are secure only when the community is religious and can give an ethical foundation to these liberties." Ibid., 21. This is a rare example of mixed metaphor for Sheen.

47. Ibid., 50.

48. Fulton J. Sheen, *Thinking Life Through* (New York: McGraw-Hill, 1955), 36–44; Sheen, *Life Is Worth Living*, Fourth Series, 78–91.

49. Sheen, *Communism and the Conscience of the West*, 58.

50. Fulton J. Sheen, "The Last of the Enemies," *Catholic Hour*, originally aired January 12, 1936.

51. Sheen, *Communism and the Conscience of the West*, 109–121.

52. Sheen, *Life Is Worth Living*, First Series, 152. The telecast was famous because Sheen prophesied God's judgment of Stalin throughout. A week after the original airing of the program, Stalin died.

53. Sheen, *Life Is Worth Living*, First Series, 268.

54. Herzog, *Spiritual-Industrial Complex*, 57–66, 157–159. See also Irvin D. S. Winsboro and Michael Epple, "Religion, Culture, and the Cold War: Bishop Fulton J. Sheen and America's Anti-Communist Crusade of the 1950s," *The Historian* 71, no. 2 (Summer 2009): 209–233.

55. Ibid., 138.

56. Massa, *Catholics and American Culture*, 97.

57. Ibid.

58. Riley, *Fulton J. Sheen*, 185.

59. Ibid., 186.

60. The Vatican, of course, sits on one of the traditional seven hills of Rome.

61. Sheen, "The Last of the Enemies."

62. Sheen, *Declaration of Dependence*, 139.

63. Sheen, *Moods and Truths*, 47.

64. Ibid., 51.

65. Ibid.

66. Ibid., 54.

67. Ibid.

68. Ibid., 55.

69. Sheen, *For God and Country*, 106–107.

70. Sheen, *Declaration of Dependence*, 140.

71. Ibid., 125–126.

72. Ibid., 32–33.

73. Slavery was the one exception to "American righteousness," but Sheen points out that this exception was also a cause for war. Room does not permit analysis of Sheen on slavery and Abraham Lincoln, but his comments on the two related strongly to Sheen's notion of Providence. One can find his efforts in Sheen, *Life Is Worth Living*, Fifth Series, 187–202.

74. Sheen, *Life Is Worth Living*, First Series, 15.

75. Sacvan Bercovitch, *The American Jeremiad* (Madison: University of Wisconsin Press, 1978); James A. Morone, *Hellfire Nation: The Politics of Sin in American History* (New Haven: Yale University Press, 2003); Andrew R. Murphy, *Prodigal Nation: Moral Decline and Divine Punishment from New England to 9/11* (New York: Oxford University Press, 2009).

76. Sheen, *Life Is Worth Living*, First Series, 15.

77. "God's purpose in giving man the moral law was to lead him *freely* to his perfection." Ibid. (emphasis added).

78. "Microphone Missionary," *Time*, April 14, 1952, 72.

79. Appearance on *What's My Line?* aired October 21, 1956, New York: Columbia Broadcasting System. Footage of the appearance, accessed August 6, 2018, is available at https://www.youtube.com/watch?v=T74qnT7WFZw.

80. "Pope Is Leader in World Drive Against Reds," *Washington Post*, December 14, 1936.

81. George Gallup, "Eisenhower Rated as Most Admired," *Los Angeles Times*, December 30, 1956.

82. Massa, *Anti-Catholicism in America*, 90–96.

83. "Bolshevism Traced to Atheism by Sheen," *New York Times*, April 3, 1933; "Catholics Urged to Convert Reds," *New York Times*, March 30, 1936; "Sees French Revolution," *New York Times*, August 24, 1937; "Views War as Judgment," *New York Times*, November 30, 1942.

84. "The celebration of the giving of the scapular to St. Simon Stock of England took place before 1000 persons in the National Shrine of Our Lady of the Scapular, 339 East Twenty-eighth Street. A loudspeaker conveyed the sermon to 400 celebrants in the street." "Mgr. Sheen Predicts Conversion of China," *New York Times*, July 17, 1944.

85. "Communist 'Faith' Defined by Sheen," *New York Times*, May 25, 1935; "Neglect of God Held Cause of Reds' Rise," *New York Times*, March 15, 1936; "Mgr. Sheen Predicts Conversion of China," *New York Times*, July 17, 1944; "Msgr. Sheen Hails Spirit of Russians," *New York Times*, April 2, 1945; "Sheen Asks Prayers to Win Communists," *New York Times*, March 24, 1947.

86. "Mgr. Sheen Warns of Godless World," *New York Times*, December 16, 1935; "Sheen Says World Robs Man of Soul," *New York Times*, May 2, 1936; "Sheen Says Man Is Being Crucified," *New York Times*, March 7, 1938; "Flight from Cross Held Trend Today," *New York Times*, March 27, 1939; "Msgr. Sheen Says 'Sense of Guilt' Oppresses U.S.," *Washington Post*, March 11, 1940; "Emphasis on Guilt Is Urged by Sheen," *New York Times*, March 11, 1940; "Sheen Finds Peril in a Static Nation," *New York Times*, March 10, 1941; "America Is Nation Falling in Decay, Says Msgr. Sheen," *Washington Post*, March 10, 1941; "Gethsemane Spirit Held Need of U.S.," *New York Times*, March 2, 1942; "War Called Knight of 'Great Surgeon,'" *New York Times*, March

23, 1942; "Peace Without Morals Can't Last, Prelate Asserts," *Washington Post*, April 12, 1943; "Worry Is Atheism, Msgr. Sheen Says," *New York Times*, February 23, 1948.

87. "Assails Einstein's Views on Religion," *New York Times*, November 16, 1930; "Dr. Sheen Scores Rise of Paganism," *New York Times*, February 5, 1934; "New Catholic Stand on Communism Urged," *New York Times*, March 9, 1936; "Mgr. Sheen Sees Man Losing Self in Materialism," *Washington Post*, October 24, 1934; "Action by Catholics Urged," *New York Times*, September 20, 1936; "Father Sheen Asks Exposure of 'Isms' in U.S. Schools," *Washington Post*, April 23, 1939; "Mgr. Sheen Assails Worldly Philosophy," *New York Times*, November 16, 1942; "Prayers for Stalin Said by Mgr. Sheen," *New York Times*, April 23, 1944. This last article actually explained how Sheen was inspired to give his talk on loving one's neighbor after reading about a speech J. Edgar Hoover had given before the Daughters of the American Revolution a few days before.

88. "Catholics Denounce Russian Fair Statue," *New York Times*, May 22, 1939.

89. "Dominant Red Symbol at Fair Hit by Prelate," *Chicago Daily Tribune*, May 22, 1939; "American Flag Display at Fair Attacked," *Los Angeles Times*, May 22, 1939.

90. "Catholics Denounce Russian Fair Statue," *New York Times*, May 22, 1939.

91. Fulton J. Sheen, *Treasure in Clay: The Autobiography of Fulton J. Sheen* (Garden City: Doubleday, 1980), 82–84; Thomas C. Reeves, *America's Bishop: The Life and Times of Fulton J. Sheen* (San Francisco: Encounter Books, 2001), 90–91.

92. "Roosevelt Condemns Russia Before 5,000 Youth Delegates," *Washington Post*, February 11, 1940.

93. "Mgr. Sheen Scores Youth Congress," *New York Times*, March 4, 1940.

94. "Youth Congress Members in Anti-War Demonstration," *New York Times*, February 5, 1940; "Mrs. Roosevelt Denies Youth Follows Reds," *Washington Post*, February 6, 1940; Frank S. Adams, "Youth Congress Moves on Turbulent Course," *New York Times*, February 11, 1940.

95. "Self-Sacrifice Call Sounded," *Los Angeles Times*, October 14, 1940.

96. "75,000 Irish Parade Here Tomorrow," *New York Times*, March 16, 1941.

97. "25,000 Rally to Pray for World Peace," *Washington Post*, May 2, 1947.

98. "Sheen in Australia, Gives Red Antidotes," *Washington Post*, May 8, 1948.

99. "30,000 Catholics Protest on Reds," *New York Times*, May 2, 1949.

100. Ibid.

101. Ibid.

102. Paul Blanshard, *American Freedom and Catholic Power* (Boston: Beacon Press, 1949; repr., Santa Barbara: Greenwood Press, 1984).

103. "The Best Sellers," *New York Times*, June 26, 1949. Ironically, Sheen's book *Peace of Soul* was at number three. Blanshard's was at number sixteen. However, by September 18, Blanshard's book was beating Sheen's—the former at fourth and the latter at fifth. Sheen eventually overtook Blanshard in October at fourth. Other books pushed Blanshard down to eighth, including, even more ironically, Norman Vincent Peale's *A Guide to Confident Living*.

104. John W. Chase, "Expanded Articles," *New York Times*, May 15, 1949. Chase opined that Blanshard's better ideas on the secular education are pushed out in favor of more paranoid depictions of Roman Catholics as "foreigners."

105. "The Best Books I Read This Year—Twelve Distinguished Opinions," *New York Times*, December 4, 1949.

106. Milton Merlin, "Books," *Los Angeles Times*, March 19, 1950.

107. "Sees Parallel in Catholic, Russian Policy," *Chicago Daily Tribune*, February 2, 1951. Blanshard published these views in *Communism, Democracy, and Catholic Power* (Boston: Beacon Press, 1951).

108. Kenneth Dole, "Truman Pastor Tried to Halt Naming of Envoy, He Revealed," *Washington Post*, October 22, 1951.

109. Kenneth Dole, "Bishop Sheen Hails Loyalty of Catholics," *Washington Post*, November 26, 1951.

110. "23,000 Vow Patriotism at Catholic Parley," *Chicago Daily Tribune*, November 12, 1951; Kenneth Dole, "Bishop Sheen Hails Loyalty of Catholics," *Washington Post*, November 26, 1951.

111. Dole, "Bishop Sheen Hails Loyalty of Catholics."

112. William Edwards, "Bishop Oxnam Defends Red Front Links," *Chicago Daily Tribune*, July 22, 1953.

113. "'I Love Lucy,' Bishop Sheen Win TV Emmies," *Chicago Daily Tribune*, February 6, 1953.

114. Some of the *Time* articles preceded Luce's conversion. Luce began to explore conversion in 1946. The first of the *Time* articles was in 1939. Three of the five were during the Luce conversion time frame.

115. "Religion: Conversion," *Time*, May 22, 1939.

116. "Religion: Biography of Sheen," *Time*, January 1, 1940.

117. Ibid.

118. "Religion: Converter on Wax," *Time*, May 6, 1946.

119. "Religion: How to Win a Convert," *Time*, July 12, 1948.

120. "Ford's Grandson May Become a Catholic; Receiving Instruction from Mgr. Sheen," *New York Times*, March 25, 1940; "Msgr. Sheen Instructs Ford Scion in Bride-to-Be's Faith," *Washington Post*, March 25, 1940; "Henry Ford's Grandson Becomes Bridegroom," *Los Angeles Times*, July 14, 1940; Bessie Phillips, "Miss Anne McDonnell Is Wd to Henry Ford 2d at Shore," *New York Times*, July 14, 1940.

121. Marco Mariano, "Fear of a Nonwhite Planet: Clare Boothe Luce, Race, and American Foreign Policy," *Prospects* 29 (October 2005): 373–394.

122. "Clare Boothe Luce Chooses Not to Run," *Decatur Daily Review*, January 30, 1946.

123. "Rep. Clare Luce Received into Catholic Church," *Los Angeles Times*, February 17, 1946.

124. Edward F. Ryan, "Mrs. Luce Appointed Ambassador to Italy," *Washington Post*, February 8, 1953.

125. Riley, *Fulton J. Sheen*, 149–154. See also Reeves, *America's Bishop*, 170–172.

126. Reeves, *America's Bishop*, 172.

127. "Red Editor Quits to Go Back to His Catholic Faith," *Chicago Daily Tribune*, October 11, 1945; "Daily Worker Editor Renounces Communism for Catholic Faith," *New York Times*, October 11, 1945.

128. "Communist Daily Head Quits, Rejoins Church," *Los Angeles Times*, October 11, 1945.

129. "Foster Calls Budenz 'Deserter' from Labor; Sheen Tells How Editor Rejoined Church," *New York Times*, October 12, 1945.

130. "Officials of the Communist party could not be reached last night for comment on the resignation. Mrs. Susan H. Woodruff, one of the three stockholders in the Freedom of the Press Company, Inc., which owns *The Daily Worker* and *The Sunday Worker* said she had not 'heard of Mr. Budenz's resignation.' She refused to comment further." "Daily Worker Editor Renounces Communism for Catholic Faith," *New York Times*, October 11, 1945.

131. Budenz was loathed as a turncoat, and his testimony nearly caused a violent outbreak during the prosecution of Communist Party leader John Santo on immigration violations.

Alexander Feinberg, "Budenz Calls Santo a Leader in Red Infiltration of Unions," *New York Times*, September 13, 1947. See also Reeves, *America's Bishop*, 172.

132. "In Retreat," *Los Angeles Times*, November 16, 1948; "Miss Bentley, Former Red Spy Ring Aid, in Catholic Retreat," *Chicago Daily Tribune*, November 16, 1948; "Miss Bentley, Ex-Spy, Becomes a Catholic," *New York Times*, November 16, 1948; "Miss Bentley, Self-Styled Spy, Becomes a Catholic," *Washington Post*, November 17, 1948; "Elizabeth Bentley, Former Soviet Spy Becomes a Catholic," *Chicago Daily Tribune*, November 17, 1948.

133. John Earl Haynes and Harvey Klehr, *Venona: Decoding Soviet Espionage in America* (New Haven: Yale University Press, 2000); Ellen Schrecker, *Many Are the Crimes: McCarthyism in America* (New York: Little, Brown, 1998); Gary May, *Un-American Activities: The Trials of William Remington* (New York: Oxford University Press, 1994).

134. "Bella Dodd Back in Catholic Fold," *New York Times*, August 6, 1952; Charles Grutzner, "Teachers Union Witnesses Assail Senate Red Inquiry," *New York Times*, September 24, 1952. Dodd wrote a somewhat melodramatic book about her experiences: see Bella V. Dodd, *School of Darkness: The Record of a Life and of a Conflict Between Two Faiths* (New York: Devine Adair, 1954).

135. Charles Grutzner, "1,500 U.S. Teachers Red, Dr. Dodd Says," *New York Times*, September 9, 1952.

136. A. H. Raskin, "Presenting the Phenomenon Called Quill," *New York Times*, March 5, 1950.

137. Riley, *Fulton J. Sheen*, 74, 80.

138. "Pontifical Mass Sung in Cathedral," *New York Times*, March 18, 1933; "Friendly Sons Hold St. Patrick's Event," *Washington Post*, March 19, 1933; "Cardinal Bestows Papal Blessing on Throng at Mass in St. Patrick's," *New York Times*, April 13, 1936.

139. "Smith Sails May 15 on First Trip Abroad," *New York Times*, April 13, 1937; "Al Smith Sails for Europe; Plan Audience with Pope," *Los Angeles Times*, May 16, 1937; "Al Smith Sets Sail in a Brown Derby," *New York Times*, May 16, 1937.

140. "Smith Denies Report of Vatican Summons," *New York Times*, May 11, 1937.

141. "Smith Is Greeted by Pope as an Old Friend; Amazed, at First Audience, by Pontiff's Vigor," *New York Times*, May 27, 1937.

142. "Words Failed Smith for the First Time in Audience with Pope, He Confesses," *New York Times*, May 29, 1937.

143. Jordan A. Schwarz, "Al Smith in the Thirties," *New York History* 45, no. 4 (October 1964): 316–330.

144. "Capital Is Divided on Smith Threat," *New York Times*, January 27, 1936.

145. Riley, *Fulton J. Sheen*, 104.

146. "Smith Reiterates Dig at New Deal," *New York Times*, August 16, 1937.

147. Riley observes "In the context of the Spanish Civil War, and the papal concordat with the government of Mussolini, some Americans perceived the Church as a friend of fascism, and the red-baiting campaign waged against communism by some Catholics lent credence to this view. The very idea of a papal directive raised the issue of the authoritarian nature of the Church and the supposed political power of the Pope. These problematic issues and nuance in interpretation escaped Sheen's attention for the most part." *Fulton J. Sheen*, 44–45.

148. "Catholic Charities Opens Conference," *New York Times*, March 14, 1938; "6,000 Attend Mass at St. Patrick's," *New York Times*, April 18, 1938.

149. "No Bias in Relief, Mayor Declares," *New York Times*, April 19, 1937.

150. "Wallace to Attend Protest Rally Here," *New York Times*, December 8, 1938; "La Guardia Rally Warns of Danger of Hatreds in U.S.," *New York Times*, December 10, 1938. Judging

from Wallace's political career after 1938, he seems to have left the rally unconvinced of Sheen's points—both religious and anti-Communist.

151. "Fair Not Courting a 'Chief Speaker,'" *New York Times*, May 7, 1940; "Temple Dedicated to True Freedom," *New York Times*, May 12, 1940.

152. "Lehman Appeals for Catholic Fund," *New York Times*, March 23, 1941.

153. "Willkie to Aid Hospital," *New York Times*, January 11, 1942.

154. Steve Neal, *Dark Horse: A Biography of Wendell Willkie* (Garden City: Doubleday, 1984), 217–230.

155. "Dewey Promises Move to End Crisis on Farms of State," *New York Times*, February 13, 1943.

156. Alexander Feinberg, "No U.S. Alliances," *New York Times*, March 17, 1946.

157. "Farley Stresses Legislative Duty," *New York Times*, May 27, 1946.

158. "Romulo Warns U.S. to Cultivate East," *New York Times*, January 27, 1947.

159. Robert Tate Allan, "U.S. Marks Holiday with Emphasis on Sharing," *Washington Post*, November 28, 1947.

160. "Eisenhower Invites 21 to Private Stag Dinner," *Los Angeles Times*, October 27, 1953; "President Gives Dinner," *New York Times*, October 27, 1953.

161. Edward T. Follard, "President Speaks at Catholic U.," *Washington Post*, November 20, 1953.

162. "U.S. Will Hear President on 'Back to God' Appeal," *New York Times*, January 28, 1954.

163. "Why Foreign Aid? What Eight Leaders Say," *New York Times*, March 2, 1958.

164. The article was published in *New York Times*.

165. "The Reply of 175 Catholic Clergy and Laymen to Protestant Letter on Spain," *New York Times*, October 14, 1937.

166. "Dr. Sheen Cites Anti-Fascists as 'Slummers,'" *Washington Post*, November 11, 1937.

167. "Catholics Fight Lifting Ban on Arms to Spain," *Washington Post*, December 31, 1938.

168. Ibid.

169. "2 Parleys Set Tomorrow on Arms Embargo," *Washington Post*, January 8, 1939; "Catholics Invited to Loyalist Spain," *New York Times*, January 9, 1939.

170. "Rival Camps Open Embargo Battles," *New York Times*, January 10, 1939.

171. Ibid.

172. While Sheen's impassioned argument defended the Church, it had the unfortunate implication of defending Fascism, which was not Sheen's real intention. See Riley, *Fulton J. Sheen*, 104–113.

173. "Fusion of Hitler and Stalin Feared," *New York Times*, May 20, 1939. Sheen credited the correct prediction to the pope: "Pope Foresaw Nazi, Red Pact, Sheen Reveals," *Washington Post*, December 11, 1939.

174. United Press, "Religious Freedom Guarantee Urged as Basis for Assistance," *Washington Post*, October 8, 1941; "Mgr. Sheen Says Nazi Paganism Menaces World Christianity," *New York Times*, November 17, 1941; "A Challenge: Msgr. Sheen Asks Backing for President," *Washington Post*, December 15, 1941.

175. "States Friendly to Soviet Scored by Sheen; Not Fighting for Kingdom of God, He Says," *New York Times*, March 3, 1941.

176. "Sheen Condemns False Tolerance," *New York Times*, February 23, 1942; "End of False War Ideas Is Urged," *Washington Post*, January 4, 1943; "Sheen Cites Three Dogmas at War Today," *Washington Post*, January 11, 1943; "Nazi and Soviet Ideologies Identical, Msgr. Sheen Asserts," *Washington Post*, October 29, 1943.

177. "Our 'Naïve Trust in Japan' Is Assailed by Sheen as 'False Optimism' of the West," *New York Times*, March 15, 1943; "Sheen Sees Better Soviet-U.S. Relations," *Washington Post*, January 23, 1949.

178. "Blast Fails—Prelate," *Chicago Daily Tribune*, February 9, 1944; "Prelate Scores New Red Charge," *Los Angeles Times*, February 9, 1944; "Sheen Assails Russia," *New York Times*, February 9, 1944.

179. "Russian Paper Says Vatican Aiding Fascism," *Los Angeles Times*, February 2, 1944; "Reds Call Pope Pro-Fascist; Fascists Say He's Red: Sheen," *Chicago Daily Tribune*, February 2, 1944; "Assails Soviet Cry of 'Fascist' Against Pope," *Chicago Daily Tribune*, February 4, 1944; "Blast Fails—Prelate," *Chicago Daily Tribune*, February 9, 1944; "Prelate Scores New Red Charge," *Los Angeles Times*, February 9, 1944; "Sheen Assails Russia," *New York Times*, February 9, 1944.

180. "Msgr. Sheen Says Soviet Agent Was 'Picked Up' in Congress," *Washington Post*, March 25, 1946.

181. "Revealed House Aid Quizzed on Smear Attack," *Chicago Daily Tribune*, March 26, 1946.

182. "Sheen Calls for Action," *New York Times*, February 7, 1949; "Religion-Red War On, Says Msgr. Sheen," *Washington Post*, February 14, 1949; "Sheen Lauds Mindszenty," *New York Times*, February 14, 1949.

183. "Stalin's Fear Held Persecution Basis," *New York Times*, March 21, 1949.

184. "Catholics Put to Red Torture, Sheen Charges," *Chicago Daily Tribune*, February 22, 1951; "Priests and Nuns Tortured in China, Says Msgr. Sheen," *Washington Post*, February 22, 1951; "Bishop Reports Torture," *New York Times*, December 6, 1951.

185. Reeves, *America's Bishop*, 118.

186. Ibid., 254.

187. Ibid., 286.

188. Sheen, *Treasure in Clay*, 355.

Chapter 2

1. The final words of King's last public address contain a postmillennial apocalyptic vision: "We've got some difficult days ahead. But it doesn't matter with me now. Because I've been to the mountaintop. And I don't mind. Like anybody, I would like to live a long life. Longevity has its place. But I'm not concerned about that now. I just want to do God's will. And He's allowed me to go up to the mountain. And I've looked over. And I've seen the promised land. I may not get there with you. But I want you to know tonight, that we, as a people, will get to the promised land. And I'm happy, tonight. I'm not worried about anything. I'm not fearing any man. Mine eyes have seen the glory of the coming of the Lord." Martin Luther King Jr., *A Testament of Hope: The Essential Writings and Speeches of Martin Luther King, Jr.*, ed. James Melvin Washington (San Francisco: HarperSanFrancisco, 1991), 286.

2. Barbara Allen, "Martin Luther King's Civil Disobedience and the American Covenant Tradition," *Publius: The Journal of Federalism* 30, no. 4 (2000): 71–113; Daniel J. Elazar, *Covenant and Constitutionalism: The Great Frontier and the Matrix of Federal Democracy*, The Covenant Tradition in Politics, vol. 3 (New Brunswick: Transaction Publishers, 1998).

3. Danielle S. Allen, *Talking to Strangers: Anxieties of Citizenship Since Brown v. Board of Education* (Chicago: University of Chicago Press, 2004); George M. Shulman, *American Prophecy: Race and Redemption in American Political Culture* (Minneapolis: University of Minnesota Press, 2008).

4. Taylor Branch, *Parting the Waters: America in the King Years, 1954–1963* (New York: Simon and Schuster, 1988), 107–112.

5. King, *Testament of Hope*, 8.

6. The end of violence or the aftermath of violence is bitterness. The aftermath of nonviolence is reconciliation and the creation of a beloved community. A boycott is never an end within itself. It is merely a means to awaken a sense of shame within the oppressor but the end is reconciliation, the end is redemption. (Ibid., 12)

It was a marvelous thing to see the amazing results of a nonviolent campaign. The aftermath of hatred and bitterness that usually follows a violent campaign was found nowhere in India. Today a mutual friendship based on complete equality exists between the Indian and British people within the commonwealth. The way of acquiescence leads to moral and spiritual suicide. The way of violence leads to bitterness in the survivors and brutality in the destroyers. But, the way of nonviolence leads to redemption and the creation of the beloved community. (Ibid., 25)

The nonviolent resister must often express his protest through noncooperation or boycotts, but he realizes that these are not ends in themselves; they are merely means to awaken a sense of moral shame in the opponent. The end is redemption and reconciliation. The aftermath of nonviolence is the creation of the beloved community, while the aftermath of violence is tragic bitterness. (Martin Luther King Jr., *Stride Toward Freedom: The Montgomery Story* [New York: Harper and Brothers, 1958; repr., Boston: Beacon Press, 2010], 90–91)

Citations of *Stride Toward Freedom* refer to Beacon edition.

7. King, *Testament of Hope*, 57–58.

8. Martin Luther King Jr., *Strength to Love* (New York: Harper and Row, 1963; gift ed., Minneapolis: Fortress Press, 2010), 50. Citations of *Strength to Love* refer to the Fortress edition.

9. Ibid.

10. Martin Luther King Jr., *Where Do We Go from Here: Chaos or Community?* (New York: Harper and Row, 1967; repr., Boston: Beacon Press, 2010), 201. Citations refer to the Beacon edition.

11. H. Richard Niebuhr, "The Idea of Covenant and American Democracy," *Church History* 23, no. 2 (1954): 126–135, 127.

12. Ibid.

13. Elazar, *Covenant and Constitutionalism*, 7–10.

14. "For as the body is one, and hath many members, and all the members of that one body, being many, are one body: so also is Christ. For by one Spirit are we all baptized into one body, whether we be Jews or Gentiles, whether we be bond or free; and have been all made to drink into one Spirit. For the body is not one member, but many." I Corinthians 12:12–14 (King James Version).

15. H. Richard Niebuhr, *The Kingdom of God in America* (New York: Harper and Row, 1937; repr., Middletown: Wesleyan University Press, 1988).

16. Barbara Allen explains how covenants actually served this purpose in practice for centuries before the founding of the United States:

While church covenants were obviously religious, many civil covenants also developed from religious foundations. Some civil agreements known as covenants were purposely separated from the polity's religious authority and were, in this sense, akin to the generally secular compact form. Secular and sacred agreements coexisted under the same covenantal rubric, indicating not so much a fusion of church and state as an acknowledgement of the simultaneity of distinct but interrelated arenas of life. Covenants and compacts did not always enjoy the status of law; nevertheless, they often acted as founding documents influencing a community's public activity, including the establishment of a "due form of government." (B. Allen, "Martin Luther King's Civil Disobedience," 76)

17. Niebuhr, *Kingdom of God in America*, 197–198.

18. Arguably, King repeated the cycle, by stripping covenant theology even of its Protestantism; however, he had little choice, due to the decline of Protestant hegemony during the first half of the twentieth century.

19. King, *Stride Toward Freedom*, 125.

20. Martin Luther King Jr., *Why We Can't Wait* (New York: Harper and Row, 1963; repr., New York: Signet Classics, 2000), 148. Citations refer to the Signet edition.

21. Richard Lischer observes a "conflation of two covenants" in mid-career King, one favoring the prophetic tradition of the black church and the other appealing to a broader civil religion. See Richard Lischer, *The Preacher King: Martin Luther King Jr. and the Word That Moved America* (New York: Oxford University Press, 1995), 178–180. On the contrary, the covenant remains the same, but King's representation of it depends on his sense of audience.

22. Martin Luther King Jr., *The Papers of Martin Luther King Jr.*, vol. 2, *Rediscovering Precious Values, July 1951–November 1955*, ed. Clayborne Carson et al. (Berkeley: University of California Press, 1994), 261.

23. Martin Luther King Jr., "Address of Reverend Dr. Martin Luther King Jr." (Speech Before New York State Civil War Centennial Commission, New York City, September 12, 1962), https://www.nps.gov/anti/learn/historyculture/mlk-ep.htm.

24. Lischer, *Preacher King*, 180–184; Shulman, *American Prophecy*, 104–105. Giorgi Areshidze offers an excellent interpretation of King along similar lines in "The Theological Foundations of Martin Luther King, Jr.'s Legacy of Racial Equality and Civil Disobedience," *Democratic Religion from Locke to Obama: Faith and the Civic Life of Democracy* (Lawrence: University Press of Kanas, 2016), 92–112.

25. B. Allen, "Martin Luther King's Civil Disobedience," 73–81.

26. Ibid., 97–100.

27. Ibid., 107–111.

28. Elazar, *Covenant and Constitutionalism*, 2.

29. B. Allen, "Martin Luther King's Civil Disobedience," 76.

30. Elazar, *Covenant and Constitutionalism*, 2.

31. B. Allen, "Martin Luther King's Civil Disobedience," 73–81.

32. Ibid.; Elazar, *Covenant and Constitutionalism*, 17–100.

33. John J. Ansbro, *Martin Luther King Jr.: The Making of a Mind* (Maryknoll: Orbis Books, 1982); Rufus Burrow Jr., *God and Human Dignity: The Personalism, Theology, and Ethics of Martin Luther King Jr.* (South Bend: University of Notre Dame Press, 2006); Kenneth L. Smith and Ira G. Zepp Jr., *Search for the Beloved Community: The Thinking of Martin Luther King Jr.* (Valley Forge: Judson Press, 1974).

34. Patrick Parr, *The Seminarian: Martin Luther King Jr. Comes of Age* (Chicago: Lawrence Hill Books, 2018), 202–203.

35. Ibid., 198–201.

36. "The New Covenant," The King Center Digital Online Archive, n.d., http://www .thekingcenter.org/archive/document/new-covenant.

37. King, *Strength to Love*, 34, 114.

38. "We must see the cross as the magnificent symbol of love conquering hate and of light overcoming darkness. But in the midst of this glowing affirmation, let us never forget that our Lord and Master was nailed to that cross because of human blindness. Those who crucified him knew not what they did." Ibid., 41.

39. Ibid., 19.

40. King, *Testament of Hope*, 265.

41. K. Smith and Zepp, *Search for the Beloved Community*, 121; Burrow, *God and Human Dignity*, 156.

42. Founding Reformed theologians were divided on the issue of resistance to tyranny but were overall far more conservative than King. Even if King had drawn from the covenant tradition, he would have had to resolve his tensions with John Calvin. See Glenn A. Moots, *Politics Reformed: The Anglo-American Legacy of Covenant Theology* (Columbia: University of Missouri Press, 2010), 56–62. As it happened, King did not appeal to Reformed theology but to St. Augustine and St. Thomas Aquinas, arguing that an unjust law was no law at all. See King, *Testament of Hope*, 293–294; Justin Buckley Dyer and Kevin E. Stuart, "Rawlsian Public Reason and the Theological Framework of Martin Luther King's 'Letter from Birmingham City Jail,'" *Politics and Religion* 6, no. 1 (2013): 145–163; Vincent W. Lloyd, *Black Natural Law* (New York: Oxford University Press, 2016), 88–117.

43. K. Smith and Zepp, *Search for the Beloved Community*, 99–118; Ansbro, *Martin Luther King Jr.*, 187–197; Burrow, *God and Human Dignity*, 159–170. Chappell claims that King's personalism was insufficient to explain King's persuasiveness. King's prophetic persona and innovations on personalist ideas allowed King to transcend the limits of academic theology and provoke Americans to seek racial redemption and reconciliation. See David L. Chappell, *A Stone of Hope: Prophetic Religion and the Death of Jim Crow* (Chapel Hill: University of North Carolina Press, 2004), 307–309.

44. Ansbro, *Martin Luther King Jr.*, 228–229; Burrow, *God and Human Dignity*, 173–179.

45. Ansbro, *Martin Luther King Jr.*, 8–28; Martin Luther King Jr., *The Papers of Martin Luther King Jr.*, vol. 4, *Symbol of the Movement, January 1957–December 1958*, ed. Clayborne Carson et al. (Berkeley: University of California Press, 2000), 321–327; Preston N. Williams, "An Analysis of the Conception of Love and Its Influence on Justice in the Thought of Martin Luther King Jr.," *Journal of Religious Ethics* 18, no. 2 (1990): 15–31.

46. King, *Testament of Hope*, 46–47.

47. Lewis V. Baldwin, *Toward the Beloved Community: Martin Luther King and South Africa* (Cleveland: Pilgrim Press, 1995).

48. King, *Strength to Love*, 51.

49. King used the term "sacrifice" to describe the love Christians showed when neglecting self-interest for the interest of the whole. When describing the early Christians, he said, "Willingly they sacrificed fame, fortune, and life itself in behalf of a cause they knew to be right." King, *Strength to Love*, 16. Alternately, he used the word "surrender" to mean the same thing: "As Christians we must never surrender our supreme loyalty to any time-bound custom or

earth-bound idea, for at the heart of our universe is a higher reality—God and his kingdom of love—to which we must be conformed." Ibid., 12. King did not see Christianity as resignation to sin but as a call to suffer for personal and political redemption through *agape* revealed in Jesus.

50. King wrote an entire sermon dedicated to this theme, in which he praised three types of altruism: universal altruism ("the piercing insight into that which is beyond the external accidents of race, religion, and nationality"); dangerous altruism ("If I do not stop to help this man, what will happen to him?" instead of "If I stop to help this man, what will happen to me?"); and excessive altruism ("Pity may arise from interest in an abstraction called humanity, but sympathy grows out of a concern for a particular needy human being who lies at life's roadside"). King, *Strength to Love*, 23–27.

51. King, *Testament of Hope*, 41.

52. Ibid., 292–295.

53. While the structure coheres with Niebuhr's broader understanding of the American covenant, King came to this position through Edgar S. Brightman. See K. Smith and Zepp, *Search for the Beloved Community*, 104–113; Burrow *God and Human Dignity*, 186–201.

54. King explained that members of the beloved community would allow the spirit of *agape* to direct all their individual and social relationships; hence they would manifest a persistent willingness to sacrifice for the good of the community and for their own spiritual and temporal good. In their private lives and as members of a caring community, they would regard each person as an image of God and an heir to a legacy of dignity and worth with rights that are not derived from the state but from God. Inspired by a vision of "total interrelatedness" and of the solidarity of the human family, they would be aware that what directly affects one person affects all persons indirectly. By their laws, actions, and attitudes they would never reduce persons to mere means but always treat them as ends-in-themselves with the right of rational self-determination. . . . Their governments would concentrate on developing moral power, would arrange to share political power with their citizens, and would recognize that their resources, when possible, should be compassionately used as instruments of service for all their citizens and for the rest of humanity. (Ansbro, *Martin Luther King Jr.*, 187–188)

55. This is not to say that love plays no role in Reformed theology and politics but to say that Reformed theology only played an indirect role in King's conception of the Beloved Community. In his book on Reformed theology and political theory, Glenn Moots concludes,

It is no coincidence that the biblical tradition is marked by its emphasis on both love and covenanting and on the relationship between the two. Love is not simply the foundation of the covenant. It is the basis of the sweetest human relationships and therefore of all things political. The prophet Hosea asserts that God desires mercy and not sacrifice. Christ repeats this, adding that love (*agape*) is the sum of the law and that love distinguishes his disciples. Saint Paul argues that the greatest of the virtues is love. The federal liberty of the covenant requires us to transcend the love of self. The model of love is divine love, and covenant love begins with the love of God rather than the love of self. God is *chesed* in the biblical tradition, what some English Bibles translated as "loving-kindness." The ultimate end of this loving-kindness is shalom, meaning peace and wholeness.

> Shalom is the greatest contribution of the covenant tradition, and the possibility
> of loving-kindness in communities holds out hope for a truly humane political
> order. (Moots, *Politics Reformed*, 161)

Scholars quickly tied King's understanding of *agape* to the Beloved Community. See Harvey Cox, *God's Revolution and Man's Responsibility* (Valley Forge: Judson Press, 1965), 58–70; K. Smith and Zepp, *Search for the Beloved Community*, 131.

56. King, *Testament of Hope*, 291–292.

57. Ansbro copies the text from one of the Birmingham Campaign Commitment Cards signed by demonstrators (*Martin Luther King Jr.*, vii):

> I HEREBY PLEDGE MYSELF—MY PERSON AND BODY—TO THE NON-
> VIOLENT MOVEMENT. THEREFORE I WILL KEEP THE FOLLOWING
> TEN COMMANDMENTS:
> 1. MEDITATE daily on the teachings and life of Jesus.
> 2. REMEMBER always that the nonviolent movement in Birmingham seeks
>   justice and reconciliation, not victory.
> 3. WALK and TALK in the manner of love, for God is love.
> 4. PRAY daily to be used by God in order that all men might be free.
> 5. SACRIFICE personal wishes in order that all men might be free.
> 6. OBSERVE with both friend and foe the ordinary rules of courtesy.
> 7. SEEK to perform regular service for others and for the world.
> 8. REFRAIN from the violence of fist, tongue, or heart.
> 9. STRIVE to be in good spiritual and bodily health.
> 10. FOLLOW the directions of the movement and of the captain on a
>   demonstration.

58. King, *Testament of Hope*, 218.

59. Ibid., 292–293.

60. King, *Testament of Hope*, 208–219; K. Smith and Zepp, *Search for the Beloved Community*, 125–128.

61. King, *Testament of Hope*, 217; Martha Solomon, "Covenanted Rights: The Metaphoric Matrix of 'I Have a Dream,'" *Martin Luther King Jr. and the Sermonic Power of Public Discourse*, ed. Carolyn Calloway-Thomas and John Louis Lucaites (Tuscaloosa: University of Alabama Press, 1993), 66–84.

62. Charles Marsh provides an excellent interpretation of the Montgomery Bus Boycott through the lens of the Beloved Community. See Charles Marsh, *The Beloved Community: How Faith Shapes Social Justice, from the Civil Rights Movement to Today* (New York: Basic Books, 2005), 11–50.

63. Ibid., 126–127.

64. John David Smith and J. Vincent Lowery, eds., *The Dunning School: Historians, Race, and the Meaning of Reconstruction* (Lexington: University Press of Kentucky, 2013).

65. King, *Symbol of the Movement*, 317.

66. Ibid., 316.

67. Ibid., 319.

68. Ibid., 318.

69. Ibid. For more on the relationship between the Beloved Community and King's treatment of *imago Dei*, see Richard Wayne Wills Sr., *Martin Luther King Jr. and the Image of God* (New York: Oxford University Press, 2009), 139–191.

70. Personal dignity was a prerequisite to broader political action. King said in "Paul's Letter to America," "You must continue to work passionately and vigorously for your God-given and constitutional rights. . . . But as you continue your righteous protest always be sure that you struggle with Christian methods and Christian weapons. Be sure the means you employ are as pure as the end you seek. . . . As you press on for justice, be sure to move with dignity and discipline, using love as your chief weapon." *Strength to Love*, 150.

71. Martin Luther King Jr., *A Knock at Midnight: Inspiration from the Great Sermons of Reverend Martin Luther King Jr.*, ed. Clayborne Carson and Peter H. Holloran (New York: Warner Books, 2001), 1017–1033, eBook.

72. In *Preacher King*, Lischer argues, "As King's social idealism was succeeded by more realistic appraisals of human evil, references to the Beloved Community gradually disappeared from his sermons, their place taken by the theological symbol, 'the Kingdom of God.' On the basis of King's published writings and utterances, scholars have debated the question of the kingdom's this-worldly as opposed to other-worldly character, but they have not commented on the radical conversion implicit in the shift from the humanism of the 'Community' to the ideology of the 'Kingdom.' The former carries overtones of utopian idealism; the latter acknowledges God's claim upon all human achievements." *Preacher King*, 234. See also Ansbro, *Martin Luther King Jr.*, 187–197; Marsh, *Beloved Community*, 207–214.

73. King, *A Knock at Midnight*, 1017–1033.

74. King, *Strength to Love*, 12.

75. Ibid., 16.

76. Ibid.; King, *Testament of Hope*, 349.

77. Lewis V. Baldwin, *The Voice of Conscience: The Church in the Mind of Martin Luther King Jr.* (New York: Oxford University Press, 2010), 81.

78. King, *Testament of Hope*, 51.

79. King, *Strength to Love*, 152.

80. Ibid., 21.

81. Baldwin, *Voice of Conscience*, 20.

82. King, *Testament of Hope*, 20.

83. As for atheism proper, King offered Nietzsche as an example and tied his views of power to Black Power:

> And one of the great problems of history is that the concepts of love and power have usually been contrasted as opposites—polar opposites—so that love is identified with a resignation of power, and power with a denial of love. It was this misinterpretation that caused Nietzsche, who was a philosopher of the will to power, to reject the Christian concept of love. It was this same misinterpretation which induced Christian theologians to reject the Nietzschean philosophy of the will to power in the name of the Christian idea of love. Now, we've got to get this thing right. What is needed is a realization that power without love is reckless and abusive, and love without power is sentimental and anemic. Power at its best is love implementing the demands of justice, and justice at its best is power correcting everything that stands against love. (*Testament of Hope*, 247)

Therefore, the only way to commit to nonviolence was to confess, on some level, the possibility of loving relationships among neighbors, which, for King, is itself an admission of an openness to a personal, Christian God. The only alternative is to deny the possibility of love and proclaim to the will to power. King concluded, "What has happened is that we have had [the relationship of love and power] wrong in this country, and this has led Negro Americans in the past to seek their goals through power devoid of love and conscience. This is leading a few extremists today to advocate for Negroes the same destructive and conscienceless power that they have justly abhorred in whites. It is precisely this collision of immoral power with the powerless morality which constitutes the major crisis of our times." King, *Testament of Hope*, 247. See also King, *Where Do We Go from Here*, 37–38.

84. King, *Testament of Hope*, 297–298.

85. Ibid., 89–90, 279.

86. Ibid., 457.

87. Ibid., 296–297.

88. Ibid., 302.

89. Ibid., 51.

90. Ibid., 48–51.

91. Ibid., 160–166.

92. Ibid., 292.

93. Ibid., 178.

94. Ibid.

95. Ibid., 180.

96. D. Allen, *Talking to Strangers*, 93.

97. King, *A Knock at Midnight*, 1825.

98. S. Jonathan Bass, *Blessed Are the Peacemakers: Martin Luther King Jr., Eight White Religious Leaders, and the "Letter from Birmingham Jail"* (Baton Rouge: Louisiana State University Press, 2001), 121–134; Stewart Burns, *To the Mountaintop: Martin Luther King Jr.'s Sacred Mission to Save America, 1955–1968* (New York: HarperCollins, 2004), 181–187; James A. Colaiaco, "The American Dream Unfulfilled: Martin Luther King Jr. and the 'Letter from Birmingham Jail,' " *Phylon* 45, no. 1 (Spring 1984): 1–18; Scott W. Hoffman, "Holy Martin: The Overlooked Canonization of Dr. Martin Luther King Jr.," *Religion and American Culture: A Journal of Interpretation* 10, no. 2 (Summer 2000): 123–148; Malinda Snow, "Martin Luther King's 'Letter from Birmingham Jail' as a Pauline Epistle," *Quarterly Journal of Speech* 71, no. 3 (August 1985): 318–334, 319–320; Lischer, *Preacher King*, 184–187; Susan Tiefenbrun, "Semiotics and Martin Luther King's 'Letter from Birmingham Jail,' " *Cardozo Studies in Law and Literature* 4, no. 2 (Autumn 1992): 255–287.

99. King, *Strength to Love*, 138–147.

100. Ibid., 153.

101. The relationship between King's political thought and Thoreau's is uncertain. See Ansbro, *Martin Luther King Jr.*, 110–114; George E. Carter, "Martin Luther King: Incipient Transcendentalist," *Phylon* 40, no. 4 (1979): 318–324; Stephen B. Oates, "The Intellectual Odyssey of Martin Luther King," *Massachusetts Review* 22, no. 2 (Summer 1981): 301–320; Brent Powell, "Henry David Thoreau, Martin Luther King Jr., and the American Tradition of Protest," *OAH Magazine of History* 9, no. 2 (Winter 1995): 26–29; Donald H. Smith, "An Exegesis of Martin Luther King Jr.'s Social Philosophy," *Phylon* 31, no. 1 (1970): 89–97.

102. King, "My Trip to the Land of Gandhi," *Testament of Hope*, 23–30; Ansbro, *Martin Luther King Jr.*, 3–7; Adam Fairclough, *To Redeem the Soul of America: The Southern Christian Leadership Conference and Martin Luther King Jr.*, 2nd ed. (Athens: University of Georgia Press, 2001), 23–26; David J. Garrow, *Bearing the Cross: Martin Luther King Jr., and the Southern Christian Leadership Conference* (New York: HarperCollins, 1986), 66–73; James P.

Hanigan, *Martin Luther King Jr. and the Foundations of Nonviolence* (Lanham: University Press of America, 1984).

103. King, "My Trip to the Land of Gandhi," 24. Karuna Mantena provides an insightful analysis of King's reinterpretation of satyagraha in "Showdown for Nonviolence: The Theory and Practice of Nonviolent Politics," *To Shape a New World: Essays on the Political Philosophy of Martin Luther King, Jr.*, ed. Tommie Shelby and Brandon M. Terry (Cambridge: Belknap Press, 2018), 78–101.

104. King, "Letter from Birmingham City Jail," *Testament of Hope*, 290.

105. Ansbro, *Martin Luther King Jr.*, 8.

106. King, *Stride Toward Freedom*, 84.

107. Ibid., 85.

108. Ibid.

109. Ibid.

110. Burns, *To the Mountaintop*, 129.

111. Lischer, *Preacher King*, 55.

112. Lincoln as "the Great Emancipator" is one of five roles assigned to Lincoln in popular representation, that is, a figure from American collective memory. See Merrill Peterson, *Abraham Lincoln in American Memory* (New York: Oxford University Press, 1994). Among other categories, such as "Man of the People" or "Savior of the Union," Barry Schwartz and Howard Schuman find "the Great Emancipator" as the most popular, since it fits with how identity groups root their collective memory in trauma: "History, Commemoration, and Belief: Abraham Lincoln in American Memory," *American Sociological Review* 70, no. 2 (April 2005): 183–203, 184.

113. Bass, *Blessed Are the Peacemakers*, 131–162.

114. In *Blessed Are the Peacemakers*, Bass describes the strategy and process behind generating and distributing the "Letter from Birmingham Jail," ibid. Drew D. Hansen examines the strategy behind the March on Washington for Jobs and Freedom in *The Dream: Martin Luther King Jr. and the Speech That Inspired a Nation* (New York: HarperCollins, 2003). Richard Lentz explains the SCLC strategy in interfacing with editors of news magazines in *Symbols, the News Magazines, and Martin Luther King* (Baton Rouge: Louisiana State University Press, 1990).

115. David Howard-Pitney, *The African American Jeremiad: Appeals for Justice in America* (Philadelphia: Temple University Press, 2005), 139–160.

116. King, *Testament of Hope*, 218.

117. King, *Testament of Hope*, 41.

118. Eddie S. Glaude Jr., *Exodus! Religion, Race, and Nation in Early Nineteenth-Century Black America* (Chicago: University of Chicago Press, 2000); Gary S. Selby, *Martin Luther King and the Rhetoric of Freedom: The Exodus Narrative in America's Struggle for Civil Rights* (Waco: Baylor University Press, 2010).

119. King, *Strength to Love*, 78 (emphasis in original).

120. Ibid., 80.

121. Ibid., 83.

122. Ibid., 86.

123. King, *Stride Toward Freedom*, 206–207.

124. King, *Symbol of the Movement*, 163.

125. Ibid., 166.

126. Lischer, *Preacher King*, 203–204.

127. Charles Marsh, *God's Long Summer: Stories of Faith and Civil Rights* (Princeton: Princeton University Press, 1997), 50.

128. Ibid., 80 (emphasis in original).

129. Ibid., 93. See also Stephen R. Haynes, *Noah's Curse: The Biblical Justification of American Slavery* (Princeton: Princeton University Press, 2002).

130. Marsh, *God's Long Summer*, 107–109.

131. Ibid., 109.

132. Perry Deane Young, *God's Bullies: Power, Politics, and Religious Tyranny* (New York: Holt, Rinehart and Winston, 1982), 311.

133. Ibid., 310.

134. Ibid., 312.

135. Ibid.

136. Ibid.

137. Ibid., 313.

138. Other counternarratives include those of L. Nelson Bell, "A Southern Evangelical on Integration," and Carl McIntire, "A Minister Denounces the Civil Rights Act," *Jerry Falwell and the Rise of the Religious Right: A Brief History with Documents*, ed. Matthew Avery Sutton (Boston: Bedford/St. Martin's, 2013), 51–54, 54–56.

139. George M. Marsden, *Fundamentalism and American Culture*, 2nd ed. (New York: Oxford University Press, 2006), 232–233.

140. Sidney M. Milkis and Daniel J. Tichenor, "Reform's Mating Dance: Presidents, Social Movements, and Racial Realignments," *Journal of Policy History* 23, no. 4 (2011): 451–490.

141. Steven Levingston, *Kennedy and King: The President, The Pastor, and the Battle Over Civil Rights* (New York: Hatchett, 2017), 96–97.

142. "President Urged to End Race Laws, King Wants Proclamation for a 2d 'Emancipation,'" *New York Times*, June 6, 1961; "Dr. King Asks New Laws, Urges Kennedy to Initiate Civil Rights Measure," *New York Times*, October 28, 1961; "JFK's Action on Civil Rights Lagging, Says Rev. Dr. King," *Washington Post*, April 10, 1962; "Kennedy Finds 'Good Deal Left Undone' in Field of Civil Rights but Hopes for Progress," *New York Times*, May 18, 1962. For the original text, see Martin Luther King Jr., "Appeal to the President of the United States," May 17, 1962, The King Center Digital Archive, accessed November 22, 2017, http://www.thekingcenter.org/archive/document/appeal-president-united-states.

143. King, "Address of Reverend Dr. Martin Luther King Jr.," September 12, 1962.

144. King's 1962 *Nation* article "Bold Design for a New South" directly challenged the Kennedy administration for its failure to make the necessary steps for full integration: see King, *Testament of Hope*, 112–116. See Adam Fairclough, *Martin Luther King Jr.* (Athens: University of Georgia Press, 1995), 70; Levingston, *Kennedy and King*, 202–206; Nicholas Bryant, *The Bystander: John F. Kennedy and the Struggle for Black Equality* (New York: Basic Books, 2006), Kindle.

145. Fairclough, *Martin Luther King Jr.*, 67–70; Bryant, *Bystander*, 4023–4416; Levingston, *Kennedy and King*, 207–256.

146. Bass, *Blessed Are the Peacemakers*, 145–146.

147. Bryant, *Bystander*, 6010.

148. Ibid., 6047.

149. Ibid., 6092.

150. Ibid., 6337–6350.

151. Lyndon B. Johnson, "Remarks of Vice President Lyndon B. Johnson on Memorial Day, Gettysburg, Pennsylvania," May 30, 1963, Lyndon Baines Johnson Presidential Library Archives, accessed August 2, 2018, http://www.lbjlibrary.net/collections/selected-speeches/pre -presidential/05-30-1963.html.

152. Ibid.

153. Ibid.

154. Robert A. Caro, *Means of Ascent* (repr., New York: Vintage, 1991), xvii–xix.

155. John F. Kennedy, "Radio and Television Report to the American People on Civil Rights," June 11, 1963, accessed August 2, 2018, https://www.jfklibrary.org/Asset-Viewer /Archives/JFKWHA-194-001.aspx.

156. Ibid.

157. Ibid.

158. Ibid.

159. Ibid.

160. The two newspapers featuring negative views were the *Chicago Tribune* and *Wall Street Journal*. The *Chicago Tribune* ran a story the day of the March on Washington featuring a secondary headline that read "Rights Marchers Invade Capital Today" and discussed at length Washington, DC, resident concerns for safety and the efforts to prevent activists from the purchase of alcohol. See Michael Pakenham, "Capital Ready for Big Rights March Today," *Chicago Tribune*, August 28, 1963. The *Wall Street Journal* covered the event with a story describing white Americans as opposed to the rally and unlikely to change their minds after it, largely because of African American violence. See "Action and Reaction, Most White in North, West Say They Oppose Rights Demonstrations," *Wall Street Journal*, August 28, 1963.

161. "Kennedy Asks Speedup in Civil Rights Drive," *Los Angeles Times*, August 29, 1963.

162. Ibid.

163. E. W. Kenworthy, "200,000 March for Civil Rights in Orderly Washington Rally; President Sees Gain for Negro," *New York Times*, August 29, 1963.

164. Ibid.

165. Ibid.

166. Irving Spiegel, "Three Faiths Join in Rights Demand," *New York Times*, August 29, 1963.

167. Ibid.

168. Ibid.

169. "Equality Is Their Right," *New York Times*, August 29, 1963.

170. Ibid.

171. Ibid.

172. Lischer, *Preacher King*, 123. The editorial's metonym is poorly constructed. In battle, one does not wear armor to defend against walls but against enemy weapons.

173. Kenworthy, "200,000 March for Civil Rights in Orderly Washington Rally."

174. "Texts of the President's Statements on Rights and on Labor Day," *New York Times*, August 29, 1963.

175. William Moore, "Talks with Lawmakers Please Civil Rights Leaders," *Chicago Tribune*, August 29, 1963.

176. Lyndon Baines Johnson, "Address Before a Joint Session of the Congress, November 27, 1963," accessed August 2, 2018, http://www.lbjlibrary.net/collections/selected-speeches /november-1963-1964/11-27-1963.html.

177. "Transcript of President Johnson's Address Before the Joint Session of Congress," *New York Times*, November 28, 1963, accessed October 23, 2017. http://www.nytimes.com/books/98 /04/12/specials/johnson-63address.html.

178. Ibid.

179. Senator Humphrey (MN), speaking on H.R. 7152 on March 30, 1964, 88th Cong., 2nd sess., *Congressional Record* 110, Pt. 5:6528.

180. Ibid., 6529.

181. Senator Keating (NY), speaking on H.R. 7152 on April 1, 1964, 88th Cong., 2nd sess., *Congressional Record* 110, Pt. 5:6721.

182. Senator Ervin (NC), speaking on H.R. 7152 on April 1, 1964, 88th Cong., 2nd sess., *Congressional Record* 110, Pt. 5:6721.

183. Senator Keating (NY), speaking on H.R. 7152 on April 1, 1964, 88th Cong., 2nd sess., *Congressional Record* 110, Pt. 5:6721.

184. Senator Ervin (NC), speaking on H.R. 7152 on April 1, 1964, 88th Cong., 2nd sess., *Congressional Record* 110, Pt. 5:6721.

185. Senator Keating (NY), speaking on H.R. 7152 on April 1, 1964, 88th Cong., 2nd sess., *Congressional Record* 110, Pt. 5:6721.

186. Senator Ervin (NC), speaking on H.R. 7152 on April 1, 1964, 88th Cong., 2nd sess., *Congressional Record* 110, Pt. 5:6721.

187. Senator Ellender (LA), speaking on H.R. 7152, on April 1, 1964, 88th Cong., 2nd sess., *Congressional Record* 110, Pt. 5:6749.

188. Ibid.

189. Ibid.

190. Ibid.

191. Senator Morse (OR), speaking on H.R. 7152 on April 2, 1964, 88th Cong., 2nd sess., *Congressional Record* 110, Pt. 5:6796.

192. Ibid.

193. Ibid.

194. Ibid.

195. Senator Clark (PA), speaking on H.R. 7152 on April 9, 1964, 88th Cong., 2nd sess., *Congressional Record* 110, Pt. 6:7203.

196. Ibid.

197. Ibid.

198. Ibid.

199. Senator Kennedy (MA), speaking on H.R. 7152 on April 9, 1964, 88th Cong., 2nd sess., *Congressional Record* 110, Pt. 6:7375–S7380.

200. Ibid., S7375.

201. Ibid.

202. Ibid., S7376.

203. Ibid.

204. Ibid., S7380.

205. Lyndon B. Johnson, "Radio and Television Remarks upon Signing the Civil Rights Bill," July 2, 1964 (broadcast from the East Room at the White House at 6:45 p.m.), Lyndon Baines Johnson Library and Museum National Archives and Records Administration, accessed August 2, 2018, http://www.lbjlibrary.net/collections/selected-speeches/november-1963-1964 /07-02-1964.html.

206. Ibid.

207. Ibid.

208. George Lardner Jr., "King Plans Accommodations Tests to Bring Law Home to the South," *Washington Post*, July 2, 1964; James C. Tanner, "Civil Rights Test, Negroes in South Ready Immediate, Broad Drive to Try Out New Law," *Wall Street Journal*, July 2, 1964; Homer Bigart, "Dr. King Outlines Rights Law Tests," *New York Times*, July 2, 1964.

209. Lyndon Baines Johnson, "The Inaugural Address," January 20, 1965, Lyndon Baines Johnson Presidential Library Archives, accessed August 2, 2018, http://www.lbjlibrary.net /collections/selected-speeches/1965/01-20-1965.html.

210. Ibid.

211. Ibid.

212. King, *Where Do We Go from Here*, 143–176.

Chapter 3

1. Jon A. Shields, *The Democratic Virtues of the Christian Right* (Princeton: Princeton University Press, 2009).

2. David G. Bromley and Anson Shupe, eds., *New Christian Politics* (Macon: Mercer University Press, 1984); Thomas M. Gannon, "The New Christian Right in America: As a Social and Political Force," *Archives de sciences sociales des religions* 26, no. 52.1 (July–September 1981): 69–83; Sharon Linzey Georgianna, *The Moral Majority and Fundamentalism: Plausibility and Dissonance* (Lewiston: Edwin Mellen Press, 1989); Joseph B. Tamney and Stephen D. Johnson, "The Moral Majority in Middletown," *Journal for the Scientific Study of Religion* 22, no. 2 (June 1983): 145–157; Charles L. Harper and Kevin Leicht, "Religious Awakenings and Status Politics: Sources of Support for the New Religious Right," *Sociological Analysis* 45, no. 4 (Winter 1984): 339–353; Arthur H. Miller and Martin P. Wattenberg, "Politics from the Pulpit: Religiosity and the 1980 Elections," *Public Opinion Quarterly* 48, no. 1b (Spring 1984): 301–317; Stephen D. Johnson and Joseph B. Tamney, "The Christian Right and the 1980 Presidential Election," *Journal for the Scientific Study of Religion* 21, no. 2 (June 1982): 123–131; Stephen D. Johnson and Joseph B. Tamney, "Support for the Moral Majority: A Test of a Model," *Journal for the Scientific Study of Religion* 23, no. 2 (June 1984): 183–196; Carol Mueller, "In Search of a Constituency for the 'New Religious Right,'" *Public Opinion Quarterly* 47, no. 2 (Summer 1983): 213–229; Richard V. Pierard, "Religion and the 1984 Election Campaign," *Review of Religious Research* 27, no. 2 (December 1985): 98–114; Wade Clark Roof and William McKinney, "Denominational America and the New Religious Pluralism," *Annals of the American Academy of Political and Social Science* 480 (July 1985): 24–38; John H. Simpson, "Socio-Moral Issues and Recent Presidential Elections," *Review of Religious Research* 27, no. 2 (December 1985): 115–123; Corwin Smidt and James M. Penning, "Religious Commitment, Political Conservatism, and Political and Social Tolerance in the United States," *Sociological Analysis* 43, no. 3 (Autumn 1982): 231–245.

3. D. G. Hart, "Mainstream Protestantism, 'Conservative' Religion, and Civil Society," *Religion Returns to the Public Square: Faith and Policy in America*, ed. Hugh Heclo and Wilfred M. McClay (Baltimore: Johns Hopkins University Press, 2003), 195–226; James Davison Hunter, *To Change the World: The Irony, Tragedy, and Possibility of Christianity in the Late Modern World* (New York: Oxford University Press, 2010), 3–93, 276–278; George M. Marsden, *Fundamentalism and American Culture*, 2nd ed. (New York: Oxford University Press, 2006), 239–257; Susan Friend Harding, *The Book of Jerry Falwell: Fundamentalist Language and Politics* (Princeton:

Princeton University Press, 2000), 34–61; Daniel K. Williams, *God's Own Party: The Making of the Christian Right* (New York: Oxford University Press, 2010).

4. Ed Dobson, Ed Hindson, and Jerry Falwell, *The Fundamentalist Phenomenon: The Resurgence of Conservative Christianity*, 2nd ed. (Grand Rapids: Baker Books Press, 1981), 157–164.

5. Jerry Falwell, "The Sins of America," *Old-Time Gospel Hour (OTGH)* 418; Series 5: *OTGH* Transcripts 400's, Sub-Group 4, Cassette Tape Series; *Old-Time Gospel Hour*, Record Group 3; Falwell Ministries; Liberty University Archive, Lynchburg, VA.

6. Marsden, *Fundamentalism and American Culture*, 43–71; Harding, *The Book of Jerry Falwell*, 234–246.

7. Jerry Falwell, "Responsible Christian Citizenship," *OTGH* 395; Series 4: *OTGH* Transcripts 400's, Sub-Group 4, Cassette Tape Series; *Old-Time Gospel Hour*, Record Group 3; Falwell Ministries; Liberty University Archive, Lynchburg, VA. The "exalted nation" is an old theme in American Protestant preaching. See Daniel L. Dreisbach, *Reading the Bible with the Founding Fathers* (New York: Oxford University Press, 2017), 145–158.

8.   Through it all [the programs dedicated to studying the Book of Proverbs] we have said that we believe America to be a nation founded by our forefathers as a Christian nation, and as a base for world evangelization. There is much evidence to support that statement. No wonder that for 200 years God has blessed this country beyond all others, simply because here in our environment of freedom and liberty, America has, for two centuries, been allowed to give the Gospel out to a world for whom Jesus died, more so than any nation in history. And yet we begin to see our country, our republic, crumbling. We see a moving away from God and away from the principles responsible for her greatness. We therefore feel that it's high time for the people of God to awaken out of their sleep. (Jerry Falwell, "Conditions Corrupting America," *OTGH* 192; Series 2: *OTGH* Transcripts 100's, Sub-Group 4, Cassette Tape Series; *Old-Time Gospel Hour*, Record Group 3; Falwell Ministries; Liberty University Archive, Lynchburg, VA)

9. Jerry Falwell, "The Millennial Reign of Christ," *OTGH* 416; Series 5: *OTGH* Transcripts 400's, Sub-Group 4, Cassette Tape Series; *Old-Time Gospel Hour*, Record Group 3; Falwell Ministries; Liberty University Archive, Lynchburg, VA.

10. Jerry Falwell, *Listen, America!* (New York: Bantam Books, 1980), 177–194.

11. Francis A. Schaeffer, *The God Who Is There* (Downers Grove: Inter-Varsity Press, 1968), 17.

12. D. Williams, *God's Own Party*, 155–156; Harding, *The Book of Jerry Falwell*, 149–152; Neil J. Young, *We Gather Together: The Religious Right and the Problem of Interfaith Politics* (New York: Oxford University Press, 2016), 172–173.

13. Randall Balmer, *Thy Kingdom Come: How the Religious Right Distorts the Faith and Threatens America: An Evangelical's Lament* (New York: Basic Books, 2006), 88.

14. Randall Balmer, "The Real Origins of the Religious Right," *Politico*, May 27, 2014, https://www.politico.com/magazine/story/2014/05/religious-right-real-origins-107133?o=2.

15. Jerry Falwell, *Falwell: An Autobiography* (Lynchburg: Liberty Hill Publishers, 1997), 357–360.

16. Ibid., 316–321.

17. Michael Sean Winters, *God's Right Hand: How Jerry Falwell Made God a Republican and Baptized the American Right* (New York: HarperOne, 2012), 124.

18. One typical piece of Moral Majority propaganda campaigned explicitly on opposition to LGBT issues and deployed a jeremiad, "With God as my witness, I pledge that I will continue to expose the sin of homosexuality to the people of this nation. I believe that the massive homosexual revolution is always a symptom of a nation coming under the judgement of God." Perry Deane Young, *God's Bullies: Power, Politics and Religious Tyranny* (New York: Holt, Rinehart and Winston, 1982), 307.

19. Ibid., 125.

20. D. Williams, *God's Own Party*, 176–177; Philip Gorski, *American Covenant: A History of Civil Religion from the Puritans to the Present* (Princeton: Princeton University Press, 2017), 180–181; Harding, *The Book of Jerry Falwell*, 161–164.

21. Falwell, "The Sins of America," *OTGH* 418; Record Group (RG) 3-4-5; Liberty University Archive (LUA).

22. Falwell, "Conditions Corrupting America," *OTGH* 192; RG 3-4-2; LUA.

23. For this reason, it is problematic to call Falwell an "American exceptionalist." See D. Williams, *God's Own Party*, 176–177.

24. Falwell, "The Millennial Reign of Christ," *OTGH* 416; RG 3-4-5; LUA.

25. One final strike against America as a uniquely covenanted nation with God was the reemergence of the state of Israel, which played a significant role in Falwell's eschatology. See Samuel Goldman, *God's Country: Christian Zionism in America* (Philadelphia: University of Pennsylvania Press, 2018), 168–170.

26. Gorski, *American Covenant*, 180.

27. See Isaac Backus, *An Appeal to the Public for Religious Liberty* (Boston: John Boyle, 1773), reprinted in *The Sacred Rights of Conscience: Selected Readings on Religious Liberty and Church-State Relations in the American Founding*, ed. Daniel L. Dreisbach and Mark David Hall (Indianapolis: Liberty Fund, 2009), 204–211; William G. McLoughlin, "Isaac Backus and the Separation of Church and State in America," *American Historical Review* 73, no. 5 (June 1968): 1392–1413; Mark A. Noll, *America's God: From Jonathan Edwards to Abraham Lincoln* (New York: Oxford University Press, 2002), 149–152; J. Judd Owen, "The Struggle Between 'Religion and Nonreligion': Jefferson, Backus, and the Dissonance of America's Founding Principles," *American Political Science Review* 101, no. 3 (August 2007): 493–503; Randolph Ferguson Scully, *Religion and the Making of Nat Turner's Virginia* (Charlottesville: University of Virginia Press, 2008), 19–133.

28. Perry Miller, *The New England Mind: From Colony to Province*, vol. 2 (Cambridge: Beacon Press, 1960).

29. Harding, *The Book of Jerry Falwell*, 157.

30. D. Williams, *God's Own Party*, 11–48.

31. Marsden, *Fundamentalism and American Culture*, 63–66, 86–93.

32. Ibid., 62–71.

33. Ibid., 118–138.

34. Harding, *The Book of Jerry Falwell*, 62–82.

35. The story is considerably more complicated than what can be offered here, and some new historical work has offered new insight into the more standard narrative provided. See Heath W. Carter and Laura Rominger Porter, eds., *Turning Points in the History of American Evangelicalism* (Grand Rapids: Wm. B. Eerdmans, 2017); Darren Dochuk, Thomas S. Kidd, and Kurt W. Peterson, eds., *American Evangelicalism: George Marsden and the State of American Religious History* (South Bend: University of Notre Dame Press, 2014).

36. Dobson, Hindson, and Falwell, *Fundamentalist Phenomenon*, 113–148.

37. Hart, "Mainstream Protestantism, 'Conservative' Religion, and Civil Society," 201.

38. Walter H. Capps, *The New Religious Right: Piety, Patriotism, and Politics* (Columbia: University of South Carolina Press, 1990), 205–210; Robert Wuthnow, *The Restructuring of American Religion: Society and Faith Since World War II* (Princeton: Princeton University Press, 1988), 133–172.

39. Hart, "Mainstream Protestantism, 'Conservative' Religion, and Civil Society," 199–201.

40. Nehemiah 9:6–37.

41. Very few scholars have noticed Falwell's preference for Nehemiah over Jeremiah when discussing the relationship between Christianity and American politics. Donald Heinz happened upon Falwell's treatment of Nehemiah but made no sustained inquiry into it. See Donald Heinz, "The Struggle to Define America," *The New Christian Right: Mobilization and Legitimation*, ed. Robert C. Liebman and James L. Guth (New York: Aldine, 1983), 133–148, 145.

42. See James M. Patterson, "The American Nehemiad, or the Tale of Two Walls," *Journal of Church and State* 57, no. 3 (2015): 450–468; James M. Patterson, "'I Am Doing a Great Work, So That I Cannot Come Down': The American Nehemiad and the 'Great Work of Religion' in the Early Republic," *Anamnesis* 5, no. 1 (2016): 68–98.

43. Jerry Falwell, "America Needs Spiritual Awakening," *OTGH* 294; Series 3: *OTGH* Transcripts 200's, Sub-Group 4, Cassette Tape Series; *Old-Time Gospel Hour*, Record Group 3; Falwell Ministries; Liberty University Archive, Lynchburg, VA.

44. Jerry Falwell, "Our Citizenship as Americans," *OTGH* 200; Series 3: *OTGH* Transcripts 200's, Sub-Group 4, Cassette Tape Series; *Old-Time Gospel Hour*, Record Group 3; Falwell Ministries; Liberty University Archive, Lynchburg, VA.

45. Falwell, "The Sins of America," *OTGH* 418; RG 3-4-5; LUA.

46. Falwell, "Our Citizenship as Americans," *OTGH* 200; RG 3-4-3; LUA 3; LUA.

47. Jerry Falwell, "A Biblical Perspective on Church/State Relations," *OTGH* 627; Series 9: Evening Transcripts, Sub-Group 4, Cassette Tape Series; *Old-Time Gospel Hour*, Record Group 3; Falwell Ministries; Liberty University Archive, Lynchburg, VA.

48. Falwell used this term as part of the church-growth strategy he cowrote with Elmer Towns (Elmer L. Towns and Jerry Falwell, *Church Aflame* [Kirkwood: Impact Books, 1971]). He applied the strategy to moral revival in American politics later, for instance, in a 1976 saying, "Finally, if we're going to turn the world upside down like the Jerusalem church did, we've got to use the principle of saturation. They preached the Gospel day and night and night and day, Acts 5:28, says they filled Jerusalem with their doctrine. They gave the Gospel to everybody. Everybody. And you and I, dear friends, have got to use every available means at every available time to reach every available person." Jerry Falwell, "How Christians Can Best Serve Their Country," *OTGH* 208; Series 3: *OTGH* Transcripts 200's, Sub-Group 4, Cassette Tape Series; *Old-Time Gospel Hour*, Record Group 3; Falwell Ministries; Liberty University Archive, Lynchburg, VA.

49. Jerry Falwell, "America . . . You're Too Young to Die," *OTGH* 401; Series 5: *OTGH* Transcripts 400's, Sub-Group 4, Cassette Tape Series; *Old-Time Gospel Hour*, Record Group 3; Falwell Ministries; Liberty University Archive, Lynchburg, VA.

50. Falwell, "The Sins of America," *OTGH* 418; RG 3-4-5; LUA.

51. Ibid.

52. Falwell, "Responsible Christian Citizenship," *OTGH* 395; RG 3-4-4; LUA.

53. Falwell, "America . . . You're Too Young to Die," *OTGH* 401; RG 3-4-5; LUA.

54. Jerry Falwell, "When Will America Sit Down and Cry?" *OTGH* 591; Series 6: *OTGH* Transcripts 500's, Sub-Group 4, Cassette Tape Series; *Old-Time Gospel Hour*, Record Group 3; Falwell Ministries; Liberty University Archive, Lynchburg, VA.

55. Falwell was not alone in looking to Nehemiah as a source for Christian patriotism. See Michael Lienisch, *Redeeming America: Piety and Politics in the New Christian Right* (Chapel Hill: University of North Carolina Press, 1993), 156, 216.

56. Falwell, "How Christians Can Best Serve Their Country," *OTGH* 208; RG 3-4-4; LUA.

57. Falwell, "The Sins of America," *OTGH* 418; RG 3-4-5; LUA.

58. Ibid.

59. Falwell, "America Needs Spiritual Awakening," *OTGH* 294; RG 3; LUA.

60. Falwell, "A Biblical Perspective on Church/State Relations," *OTGH* 627; RG 3-4-9; LUA.

61. I've never heard so much comment as I hear today about religion and politics. Nobody said very much when ministers were leading the civil rights march 30 years ago. No one said very much when ministers were leading the anti–Vietnam War protests 15–20 years ago. No one was saying very much when ministers were involved in the anti-draft and anti-registration campaigns of days gone by. The World Council of Churches and its American counterpart, the National Council of Churches has been involved in political activity for years and years. William Sloane Coffin, the Berrigan Brothers, Father Drinan, Reverend Jesse Jackson ran for the presidency. Gave a public address at the Democratic National Convention. But when a few of the conservative Catholic archbishops and a Baptist preacher who's also a conservative named Jerry Falwell speak up and out on issues of moral and social concern, the liberals have hernias. They write stories, they do protests. They absolutely fall apart. Well, it was our Lord Jesus who said once: we're to render to God that which is God's, that's always first. That's what we're doing here today. Two: we're to render to Caesar that which is Caesar's, that's good citizenship. And of course registering voters, getting people involved and getting people informed, that's all a part of good citizenship as I see it. (Falwell, "A Biblical Perspective on Church/State Relations," *OTGH* 627; RG 3-4-9; LUA)

62. D. Williams, *God's Own Party*, 38–39, 114–115; Markku Ruotsila, *Fighting Fundamentalist: Carl McIntire and the Politicization of American Fundamentalism* (New York: Oxford University Press, 2015).

63. As Daniel Williams points out, McIntire disapproved of Falwell's efforts, believing that Falwell had committed "the mistake of separating his moral standards from the Bible and the word of God," quoted from *God's Own Party*, 174.

64. "God Almighty established three institutions and three institutions only. God established the home. There is no question that God has placed his sanction upon the home. Is it any wonder then that Satan's most vicious attack today is against that institution called the home. . . . Secondly, God established the church. There is no question that this heavenly institution with earthly members is of divine origin. . . . No wonder today we have such an assault against the church, because it is of God's origin and therefore the archenemy of Satan. But likewise, God established the state." Falwell, "Our Citizenship as Americans," *OTGH* 200; RG 3-4-3; LUA. See also Lienisch, *Redeeming America*, 138.

65. Jerry Falwell, *America Can Be Saved* (Murfreesboro: Sword of the Lord Publishers, 1979), 138.

66. D. Williams, *God's Own Party*, 167–179.

67. Linda Kintz and Julia Lesage, eds., *Media, Culture, and the Religious Right* (Minneapolis: University of Minnesota Press, 1998).

68. Harding, *The Book of Jerry Falwell*, 125–182; Capps, *New Religious Right*, 36–37.

69. Hart, "Mainstream Protestantism, 'Conservative' Religion, and Civil Society," 195–226.

70. Wilfred M. McClay, "Two Concepts of Secularism," *Religion Returns to the Public Square: Faith and Policy in America*, ed. Hugh Heclo and Wilfred M. McClay (Baltimore: Johns Hopkins University Press, 2003), 31–62.

71. The then newly elected pope John Paul II reaffirmed the doctrine found in *In Humanae Vitae* in 1978. See George Weigel, *Witness to Hope: The Biography of Pope John Paul II* (New York: HarperCollins, 1999), 336; James Davison Hunter, *Culture Wars: The Struggle to Define America* (New York: Basic Books, 1991), 176–196.

72. Richard John Neuhaus, *The Naked Public Square: Religion and Democracy in America*, 2nd ed. (Grand Rapids: Wm. B. Eerdmans, 1996).

73. Paul G. Kengor, "Ronald Reagan: The Anti–Nixon/Kissinger," The Center for Vision and Values at Grove City College, February 7, 2011, accessed July 14, 2011, http://www.visionandvalues.org/2011/02/ronald-reagan-the-anti-nixon-kissinger/.

74. Cal Thomas and Ed Dobson, *Blinded by the Might: Why the Religious Right Can't Save America* (Grand Rapids: Zondervan, 2000); D. Williams, *God's Own Party*, 159–179.

75. Falwell, *Falwell: An Autobiography*, 357–379. See also D. Williams, *God's Own Party*, 173.

76. Megan Rosenfeld, "The New Moral America and the War of the Religicos," *Washington Post*, August 24, 1980.

77. P. Young, *God's Bullies*, 310–317.

78. Falwell, *Falwell: An Autobiography*, 309–321, 359–361.

79. Tamney and S. Johnson, "Moral Majority in Middletown," 145–157; S. Johnson and Tamney, "Support for the Moral Majority," 183–196; J. Shields, *Democratic Virtues of the Christian Right*, 1–45.

80. Helen A. Moore and Hugh P. Whitt, "Multiple Dimensions of the Moral Majority Platform: Shifting Interest Group Coalitions," *Sociological Quarterly* 27, no. 3 (Autumn 1986): 423–439; Clyde Wilcox, "Evangelicals and the Moral Majority," *Journal for the Scientific Study of Religion* 28, no. 4 (December 1989): 400–414; Clyde Wilcox, Sharon Linzey, and Ted G. Jelen, "Reluctant Warriors: Premillennialism and Politics in the Moral Majority," *Journal for the Scientific Study of Religion* 30, no. 3 (September 1991): 245–258.

81. Dobson, Hindson, and Falwell, *Fundamentalist Phenomenon*, 47–77.

82. Falwell, *Listen, America!*, 177–194.

83. Glenn Frankel, "Guy Farley Emerges as Party Leader," *Washington Post*, July 15, 1980.

84. Margot Hornblower, "'Pro-Family' Push: Political Mine Field," *Washington Post*, July 25, 1980; Leslie Bennetts, "Conservatives Join on Social Concerns," *New York Times*, July 30, 1980.

85. Ronald Reagan, "Acceptance of the Republican Nomination for President," July 17, 1980, accessed August 3, 2018, https://www.reaganlibrary.gov/7-17-80.

86. Bennetts, "Conservatives Join on Social Concerns."

87. John Herbers, "Ultraconservative Evangelicals a Surging New Force in Politics," *New York Times*, August 17, 1980; Dudley Clendinen, "Christian New Right's Rush to Power," *New*

York Times, August 18, 1980; Kenneth A. Briggs, "Evangelicals Turning to Politics Fear Moral Slide Imperils Nation," *New York Times*, August 19, 1980.

88. Briggs, "Evangelicals Turning to Politics Fear Moral Slide Imperils Nation."

89. Kenneth A. Briggs, "Evangelical Preachers Gather to Polish Their Politics," *New York Times*, August 21, 1980; Richard Bergholz, "Reagan Tries to Cement His Ties with TV Evangelicals," *Los Angeles Times*, August 23, 1980; Bill Stall, "Part of New Right: Evangelicals on Their Faith in Political Action," *Los Angeles Times*, August 24, 1980; Kathy Sawyer, "Linking Religion and Politics," *Washington Post*, August 24, 1980. All articles mentioned that the event was nominally nonpartisan, but Carter declined to attend—with good reason.

90. Bergholz, "Reagan Tries to Cement His Ties."

91. Kenneth A. Briggs, "Evangelicals Hear Plea: Politics Now," *New York Times*, August 24, 1980.

92. Howell Raines, "Reagan Backs Evangelicals in Their Political Activities," *New York Times*, August 23, 1980.

93. George Skelton, "The Times Poll: Reagan Gains with Some Evangelicals," *Los Angeles Times*, September 17, 1980.

94. "Poll: Carter Best for Peace: But Not Prosperity," *Washington Post*, September 27, 1980.

95. Albert R. Hunt, "Reagan and 'Depth,'" *Wall Street Journal*, November 3, 1980.

96. Karlyn Barker, "Churches Press Va. Senate," *Washington Post*, February 16, 1980; Glenn Frankel, "In GOP's Mainstream," *Washington Post*, June 10, 1980.

97. "Ally of Thomas T. Byrd, Is Elected to Virginia GOP Post," *Washington Post*, September 29, 1980.

98. Falwell also benefited from the demise of the Byrd Machine, which had controlled the Democratic Party and, with it, the entire Commonwealth of Virginia (except the "Fighting Ninth" at the western tip) for seventy years.

99. Megan Rosenfeld, "Miller and Warner Attend a Lynchburg Happening," *Washington Post*, October 23, 1980. Elizabeth Taylor was married to Warner at the time, and she attended services, making for one of the more unlikely congregants in Falwell's church.

100. Ibid.

101. Karlyn Barker, "Favorite Faces Challenge in Va.'s 10th," *Washington Post*, June 7, 1980; Kerry Dougherty, "Candidate Wolf: Shaking Each Hand," *Washington Post*, August 21, 1980; Ed Bruske, "There's a Hungry Wolf at Rep. Joe Fisher's Door," *Washington Post*, October 11, 1980.

102. Smith only served one term. He was defeated by Ben Erdreich, who was Jewish.

103. "'Moral Majority' Forces Help Fell Rep. Buchanan," *Washington Post*, September 4, 1980; "Outflanked on the Right," *New York Times*, September 7, 1980; "Mr. Buchanan's 'Doggone Truth,'" *Washington Post*, September 7, 1980; "Evangelical Group Quietly and Angrily Upsets Alabama Primary," *New York Times*, September 8, 1980; Ward Sinclair, "Special-Interest Shock Troops: All-Out War," *Washington Post*, October 25, 1980.

104. Art Harris, "In the 'Heart of Dixie,' a Conservative Clash," *Washington Post*, October 21, 1980; Sinclair, "Special-Interest Shock Troops"; "Alabama Race: Ex-POW Running for Seat in Senate," *Los Angeles Times*, September 21, 1980. Denton had also worked for Robertson's Christian Broadcasting Network, giving him ties to two conservative preachers who would support him.

105. Bob Baker, "Verbal Battle Between Dornan, Peck Heats Up," *Los Angeles Times*, August 28, 1980.

106. Jerry Falwell, "Enforcing God's Law in the Voting Booth," *Los Angeles Times*, September 7, 1980.

107. Falwell, *Listen, America!*, 162–170; Falwell, *America Can Be Saved*, 39–60; Cal Thomas, "How You Can Help Clean Up America: The Press," *How You Can Help Clean Up America*, ed. Jerry Falwell (Lynchburg: Liberty Press, 1981), 69–76.

108. Myra MacPherson, "Evangelicals Seen Cooling on Carter," *Washington Post*, September 27, 1976.

109. Timothy McNulty, "From Tent to Tube: Religion Takes Its Message Through Channels," *Chicago Tribune*, April 4, 1979; Megan Rosenfeld, "The Evangelist and His Empire: Cleaning Up America with Jerry Falwell," *Washington Post*, April 28, 1979; Jim Montgomery, "The Electric Church: Religious Broadcasting Becomes Big Business, Spreading Across U.S.," *Wall Street Journal*, May 19, 1979; Jeff Prugh and Russell Chandler, "Old-Time Religion in the Big Time," *Los Angeles Times*, May 20, 1979; Jean Peters, "Religious TV Finds a Niche in Manassas," *Washington Post*, September 25, 1979; John Dart, "'New Face' Emerging in Protestant Fundamentalism: With 325 Stations, Jerry Falwell Is No. 1 TV Preacher," *Los Angeles Times*, October 13, 1979; Ernest Holsendolph, "Religious Broadcasts Bring Rising Revenues and Create Rivalries," *New York Times*, December 2, 1979.

110. Outside, the church is the very model of Williamsburg antiquity, right down to its redbrick walls, Colonial windows and tall steeple. But then you walk through the front doors and past a tiny foyer—and suddenly you feel as if you have spanned three centuries and 3000 miles to an almost perfect copy of an NBC television studio in Burbank. Beneath a tangle of overhead cables and lights are 350 plush theatre-type seats and folding chairs filled with mostly elderly worshipers who arrive by tour bus and private car from all over the country. There are also four $100,000 color cameras, a 30-monitor control booth and four tiers of men and women who sit beneath a world-map wall mural with twinkling lights, answering 60 pale-blue telephones that ring again and again. (Prugh and Chandler, "Old-Time Religion in the Big Time")

It's a typical Sunday morning at Thomas Road Baptist Church here. Pastor Jerry Falwell is preaching to a full house of 3200 parishioners—and to four television cameras. In the control room overhead, a dozen technicians scanning 14 screens select the succession of images that will become an "Old-Time Gospel Hour" videotape to be broadcast in a few weeks on 327 stations. (Montgomery, "The Electric Church")

"Are we ready, Mr. Cameraman?" asked the Rev. Jerry Falwell, as though addressing the horizon. Behind him were arrayed the I Love America Singers, dressed in red, white, and blue, and a row of American flags. Below him fanning out from the Capitol Steps, were thousands of rain-drenched Christians. "We're ready, Dr. Falwell," said the voices of Mr. Cameraman [*sic*] from somewhere in the electronic cosmos. It was time for the show to begin. (M. Rosenfeld, "The Evangelist and His Empire")

111. Laxalt described Falwell as part of a broader conservative wing that, regardless of its small number, had an outsized effect on setting the political agenda and mobilization: "They were a squeaking wheel, aggravating, but boy, it's great to have them on your side. It's just like the left. I mean, the left, they're the squeaking wheel, too, and I suppose a lot of the people like Carter and even Clinton probably said, Get rid of those lefties." Paul Laxalt, interview by

Stephen F. Knott, James Sterling Young, and Erwin Hargrove, transcript of an oral history conducted October 9, 2001, Miller Center of Public Affairs Presidential Oral History Project, University of Virginia, 2005, http://millercenter.org/president/reagan/oralhistory/paul-laxalt.

112. Dart, " 'New Face' Emerging in Protestant Fundamentalism"; George Vecsey, "Militant Television Preachers Try to Weld Fundamentalist Christians' Political Power," *New York Times*, January 21, 1980; George Vecsey, "Church and State: Moral Issues Are Drawing Clergy into Politics," *Chicago Tribune*, January 23, 1980.

113. Prugh and Chandler, "Old-Time Religion in the Big Time." Chandler later described these charges as common to all such televangelists: Russell Chandler, "The Electronic Church— Big Time Religion," *Los Angeles Times*, February 25, 1980.

114. Peter Weaver, "Mind Your Money: Taking Religion into Account," *Los Angeles Times*, March 13, 1980.

115. "Evangelist Falwell, Va. City Argue over $67,000 in Taxes," *Washington Post*, June 27, 1980; "Falwell Must Provide Property Information," *Washington Post*, October 7, 1980.

116. Falwell held a fundraiser in which he raised $11,000 in cash and an additional $20,000 in pledges. He handed the full amount over to Citizens for Decency and Morality—evidently without concern for recouping the pledges first. Falwell claimed he later recouped the money for the pledges, though he also upset donors by putting their names on the fundraising mailing list for Thomas Road Baptist Church despite promising he would not. State senator John Briggs, who ran the investigation and originally sponsored Proposition 6, later claimed that Falwell offered "zero cooperation" on the matter. Falwell had been one of the most high profile supporters of the initiative, but his activism had failed to unite California denominations behind the measure, with many mainline Protestant, Catholic, and Jewish groups publicly denouncing it to the frustration of the Catholic-gone-evangelical sponsor, state house representative John Briggs, and Falwell himself. Robert Welkos, "Briggs Initiative Transactions Investigated," *Los Angeles Times*, October 3, 1979; Robert Welkos, "Briggs Pins Probe Blame on Minister," *Los Angeles Times*, October 4, 1979; Holsendolph, "Religious Broadcasts Bring Rising Revenues and Create Rivalries"; Bud Lembke, "4 Religious Leaders Urge Rejection of Proposition 6," *Los Angeles Times*, November 1, 1978; Russell Chandler and John Dart, "Many Church Leaders Oppose Prop. 6," *Los Angeles Times*, November 3, 1978.

117. Ellen Goodman, "The Right-Wingers May Be out of Control," *Los Angeles Times*, July 21, 1980. The column also ran as "Gaining Control," *Washington Post*, July 23, 1980.

118. Goodman, "The Right-Wingers May Be out of Control."

119. Ibid.

120. Ibid.

121. Stephen S. Rosenfeld, "Policy by The Book," *Washington Post*, July 25, 1980; Jimmy Breslin, "Born-Again Unease over Born-Again Pols," *Los Angeles Times*, August 25, 1980; Anthony Lewis, "Abroad at Home: Religion and Politics," *New York Times*, September 18, 1980.

122. Meg Greenfield, "The Feds and the Family," *Washington Post*, September 3, 1980.

123. Ibid.

124. Ellen Goodman, "Underneath the Present Politics of Morality Is Religious Strife," *Los Angeles Times*, September 24, 1980. Also published as "As If God Were a Ward Heeler," *Washington Post*, September 24, 1980.

125. Anthony Lewis, "Political Religion," *New York Times*, September 25, 1980.

126. "Harris Criticizes 'Moral Absolutism,' " *Washington Post*, September 25, 1980. Coincidentally, it was an unfavorable comparison like one made during the original split between

modernist and Fundamentalist Protestants. Rev. Harry Emerson Fosdick made the compari-
son in the classic critique of 1920s Protestant Fundamentalism, "Shall the Fundamentalists
Win?" May 21, 1922, published in *American Sermons: The Pilgrims to Martin Luther King Jr.*, ed.
Michael Warner (New York: Library of America, 1999), 780–781.

127. "Private Religion," *New York Times*, October 5, 1980.

128. Andrew Young, "New Guise for Old Right," *Los Angeles Times*, October 22, 1980.

129. "N. Y. Activist Chastises Right-Wing Preachers," *Washington Post*, October 6, 1980;
Marjorie Hyer, "Outflanking the Right: Mainline Clerics Oppose the Evangelicals," *Washington
Post*, October 21, 1980; Timothy L. Smith, "Protestants Falwell Does Not Represent," *New York
Times*, October 22, 1980.

130. "Church Bells, Alarm Bells," *Los Angeles Times*, October 3, 1980; Mark Shields, "A Difference in Ministers," *Washington Post*, October 3, 1980; Jon Margolis, "In the South, Morality
Means Votes," *Chicago Tribune*, October 15, 1980.

131. "The Amoral Minority," *Wall Street Journal*, October 20, 1980.

132. Kevin Phillips, *The Emerging Republican Majority* (New Rochelle: Arlington House,
1969).

133. Charles Kirbo, interview by Charles Jones et al., transcript of an oral history conducted
January 5, 1983, Miller Center of Public Affairs Presidential Oral History Project, University of
Virginia, 2003.

134. C. Thomas, "How You Can Help Clean Up America," 71.

135. Harding, *The Book of Jerry Falwell*, 153–182.

136. Falwell, *America Can Be Saved*, 61, 71.

137. Ibid., 71.

138. Ibid., 102–103.

139. Ibid., 140.

140. Ibid., 149.

141. Ronald Reagan, "Remarks at a White House Ceremony in Observance of a National
Day of Prayer," May 6, 1982, accessed August 3, 2018, https://www.reaganlibrary.gov/research
/speeches/50682c.

142. According to Reagan's former campaign advisor Stuart Spencer, Reagan was ambivalent about Falwell. In a 2005 interview, Spencer said,

> He wasn't close to any of them. He had a very basic attitude: I'm not buying into
> their philosophy. They're buying into mine. He had that attitude about anybody.
> I had Ralph Abernathy and Hosea Williams with him, and he acted and worked
> and treated them just the way he did Jerry Falwell when he was in the room, no
> damn difference. He acted in the same way with the air traffic controllers as he
> did with those. He was glad that people were buying in, that they were a part of
> it. He didn't make deals with them. He didn't sell out to them.
>
> The bottom line with the moral majority, or whatever it was called that was
> started by Falwell, was that they had no place to go. They had to go with Reagan.
> He could have even dumped on them a little and they had no place to go, right?
> He knew that. He accepted people for what they were and went on about his
> business. (Stuart Spencer, interview by Paul B. Freedman et al., transcript of an
> oral history conducted November 15–16, 2001, Miller Center of Public Affairs
> Presidential Oral History Project, University of Virginia.

This reading of Reagan is plausible but perhaps underestimates the importance of obvious concessions Reagan made. For example, as governor of California, Reagan had signed legislation liberalizing access to abortion, yet he went on to place his name on a book, *Abortion and the Conscience of the Nation*, that repudiated the practice, perhaps out of guilt for signing the bill in the first place. Reagan published the book nearing the end of his first term in office with his decision to run for reelection not at all in doubt. Spencer's reading of Falwell and the Religious Right, then, may reflect Spencer's opinion of them rather than their relationship with Reagan. See Paul G. Kengor and Patricia Clark Doerner, "Reagan's Darkest Hour," *National Review*, January 28, 2008.

143. 374 US 203 (1963). This Bill Murray is not the same Bill Murray of *Saturday Night Live*, *Ghostbusters*, or later fame.

144. Jerry Falwell, "America's Children—Free to Pray?" *OTGH* 440; Series 5; Sub-Group 4; *Old-Time Gospel Hour*, Record Group 3; Falwell Ministries; Liberty University Archive, Lynchburg, VA.

145. Ibid.

146. The transcription here is not the official remarks from the White House but those provided by the Falwell archives. *Old-Time Gospel Hour* (Falwell, "America's Children—Free to Pray?" *OTGH* 440; RG: 3-4-5; LUA).

147. Falwell, "America's Children—Free to Pray?" *OTGH* 440; RG 3-4-5; LUA.

148. The interview was apparently taped the same day of Reagan's speech and edited for use in this episode of *OTGH*, which was three months after the speech. Both men had attended the event.

149. Falwell, "America's Children—Free to Pray?" *OTGH* 440; RG 3-4-5; LUA.

150. Ibid.

151. Ibid.

152. Ibid.

153. Ibid.

154. Ibid.

155. Ibid.

156. Well I was 14 when the case started, and of course we had just come back from Europe where my mother had attempted and failed to gain citizenship in the Soviet Union, first applying in—attempting to obtain that here in Washington, DC, just a short way away at the Soviet embassy and then again in Paris at the Soviet embassy there, and it was when we returned to the United States and she had to enroll me late in . . . [the] first week of October in 1960 that for the first time she discovered that there were prayers in public schools and she fumed at the idea that there was a Pledge Allegiance [sic] and prayer going on. She literally accidentally took me up there to register me at the time when this was going on. Five minutes later and there would probably still have been prayer in school. . . .

She denounced her citizenship. I'm sure if the state department will look back through their files for July and August of 1960 if they have them on microfilm they'll find a letter from her that—telling the Secretary of State exactly what to do with his U.S. citizenship, she was never coming back, and of course when changed her mind when the Soviet Union informed her that they weren't going to let her in to Russia because of her poor work history. She hadn't held down a job for more than six months in the previous ten years and that they didn't have any welfare programs, food stamps or unemployment in the Soviet Union and that they believed that she would probably starve to death over there, that you either worked or starved in that country.

She was manager of the New Era Bookstore in Baltimore, Maryland, which was then and still is the official Communist Party bookstore. You can call the Communist Party Headquarters, New York. They'll tell you it's their bookstore.

... like most dissidents she has made a good deal of money out of tearing the nation down, and it isn't my mother—I love her and I pray for her, Jerry, and it—it isn't her I'm sure that we're aware that is really doing this, but she like many of the other distracted from our society have made large fortunes in tearing down the country. Gus Hall, the chairman of the Communist Party of the United States, has a chauffeured limousine that he goes to work in every morning, and my mother, Madalyn Murray O'Hair, gets her brand new Cadallac [*sic*] every six months ... from her own organization [American Atheists].

Well, I was raised, again, in a Marxist home, Jerry, and one of the presets [*sic*] of Marxism is that religion is the opiate of the people. It was also the opinion of the Communist Party at the time that religion was one of the tripod of supports that the free enterprise system had and the other being democratic structure and the mobility of society. And—in America. And they believed that—and my mother believed in particular—that though probably the weakest leg to that tripod was organized religion and with the destruction of organized religion the corrupt, as they called it, free enterprise system or capitalist society would collapse, bringing about a workers' general rebellion and revolution and a dictatorship of the proletariat. (William J. Murray, interview by Jerry Falwell, "America's Children—Free to Pray?" *OTGH* 440; RG 3-4-5; LUA)

157. Ibid.

158. Jerry Falwell, "The Healing of America," *OTGH* 553; Series 6: *OTGH* Transcripts 500's, Sub-Group 4, Cassette Tape Series; *Old-Time Gospel Hour*, Record Group 3; Falwell Ministries; Liberty University Archive, Lynchburg, VA.

159. As a matter of fact, all the polls indicate that we have bottomed out, and our young people today are more conservative on moral and spiritual values than are their parents generally speaking. That's exciting. I find myself speaking on campuses. I was invited to come to Yale and spoke to a packed house there. Young people who in the main part, in my opinion, were saying yes to many of those values that made this great nation and that caused those ten prominent ministers to establish Yale University over 200 years ago. And in—I was invited to Harvard to speak to the young people there, and the young people at Dartmouth and now U.C.L.A., and I—as I travel to university campuses, as I speak to leaders in Washington, as I talk to alcoholics and drug addicts and so on through our own ministries here I find that it's true everywhere. There is a moving at the grass roots level back towards God, back towards morality, and the question is who's causing that. Well I think there are a lot of people responsible for it. Number one, I would say congratulations to the hundred and ten thousand pastors in America who believing in the inerrancy of the Word of God, Fundamentalist preachers

of the sacrificial death of Christ on the cross, who believe in His bodily resurrection, who believe in His eminent [*sic*] return and preach that and believe in
world evangelization and are practicing the carrying out of the great commission.
(Falwell, "The Healing of America," *OTGH* 553; RG 3-4-6; LUA)

160.   This is the July/August issue of *Fundamentalist Journal*, and the lead story is
       "What Is Happening to Our Freedom?" Religious freedom in this country is
       being challenged, and everywhere the American Civil Liberties Union, in jerk-
       ing manger scenes out of city halls and prayer out of public schools, and many,
       many other things are being challenged now, even the right of our little children
       to have prayer before or after in a voluntary meeting in property. All that's being
       challenged. As a matter of fact, in Lakeworth, Florida, the school principal down
       there actually cut a page out of the year book, of the Lakeworth High School
       year book, because on one side of the page the Bible Club in the school had put
       a verse of Scripture and a picture of a Bible there. The Spanish Club advertised
       on the back side of that sheet of paper, and they have that reprinted and pasted
       back in the book, but no room for God or the Bible. That's America, not Russia,
       and this entire July/August issue of some 65 or 70 pages is devoted to religious
       freedom in the United States of America. Many, many articles and issues. A lot
       of family articles here, and we—we send this out monthly. The July/August issue
       is merged, but there are eleven issues a year. "What Is Happening to Our Free-
       dom" by Norman Geisler (?), "The Church and Her Rights," by J. Adams. There's
       an interview with Richard Halverson, the Chaplain of the U.S. Senate. There's a
       feature book report by Frankie Schaeffer on Cal Thomas' book, *Book Burning*,
       that I hope you will purchase in your bookstore somewhere. There's successful
       teaching ideas for the Sunday school teacher. Bible Study, this time by Don-
       ald Rickards, on how to live with decisions beyond your control. There's a story
       of my meeting at Harvard with the students there and the National Education
       Association's indoctrination of their teachers and students. There's an article in
       there on that by Cal Thomas, and on and on. Many articles. (Jerry Falwell, "The
       Law of Sowing and Reaping," *OTGH* 561; Series 6: *OTGH* Transcripts 500's, Sub-
       Group 4, Cassette Tape Series; *Old-Time Gospel Hour*, Record Group 3; Falwell
       Ministries; Liberty University Archive, Lynchburg, VA)

161. Sarah Pulliam Bailey, " 'God Is Not Against Building Walls!' The Sermon Trump Heard
from Robert Jeffress Before His Inauguration," *Washington Post*, January 20, 2017, accessed
November 15, 2017, https://www.washingtonpost.com/news/acts-of-faith/wp/2017/01/20/god-is
-not-against-building-walls-the-sermon-donald-trump-heard-before-his-inauguration/?utm
_term=.baee814896a5.

162. Ibid.

163. Ibid.

164. Ibid.

Conclusion

1. Paul A. Djupe, Jacob R. Neiheisel, and Anand E. Sokhey, "Reconsidering the Role of Politics in Leaving Religion: The Importance of Affiliation," *American Journal of Political Science* 62,
no. 1 (January 2018): 161–175; Michael Hout and Claude S. Fischer, "Why More Americans Have

No Religious Preferences: Politics and Generations," *American Sociological Review* 67, no. 2 (April 2002): 165–190; Robert D. Putnam and David E. Campbell, *American Grace: How Religion Divides and Unites Us* (New York: Simon and Schuster, 2010), 91–133; Michael Hout and Claude S. Fischer, "Explaining Why More Americans Have No Religious Preference: Political Backlash and Generational Succession, 1987–2012," *Sociological Science* 1, no. 24 (October 2014): 423–447.

2. Matthew Sitman, "Against Moral Austerity: On the Need for a Christian Left," *Dissent*, Summer 2017, https://www.dissentmagazine.org/article/moral-austerity-need-christian-left.

3. Elizabeth Bruenig, "How Augustine's Confessions and Left Politics Inspired My Conversion to Catholicism," *America: The Jesuit Review*, August 7, 2017, https://www.americamagazine.org/faith/2017/07/25/how-augustines-confessions-and-left-politics-inspired-my-conversion-catholicism.

4. Laura R. Olson, "The Religious Left in Contemporary American Politics," *Politics, Religion and Ideology* 1, no. 3 (September 2011): 271–294.

5. Kimberly H. Conger, "Same Battle, Different War: Religious Movements in American State Politics," *Politics and Religion* 7, no. 2 (June 2014): 395–417.

6. Patrick J. Deneen, *Why Liberalism Failed* (New Haven: Yale University Press, 2018).

7. Rod Dreher, *The Benedict Option: A Strategy for Christians in a Post-Christian Nation* (New York: Sentinel, 2014).

8. Russell R. Reno, "The Spirit of Democratic Capitalism," *First Things*, October 2017, https://www.firstthings.com/article/2017/10/the-spirit-of-democratic-capitalism.

9. Adrian Vermeule, "The Ark of Tradition," *University Bookman*, November 19, 2017, http://www.kirkcenter.org/bookman/article/the-ark-of-tradition.

10. Adrian Vermeule, "As Secular Liberalism Attacks the Church, Catholics Can't Afford to Be Nostalgic," *Catholic Herald*, January 5, 2018, http://www.catholicherald.co.uk/commentandblogs/2018/01/05/as-secular-liberalism-attacks-the-church-catholics-cant-afford-to-be-nostalgic/.

11. Alexis de Tocqueville, *Democracy in America*, ed. and trans. Harvey C. Mansfield and Delba Winthrop (Chicago: University of Chicago Press, 2000), 280.

12. Tocqueville, *Democracy in America*, 426.

13. Ibid.

14. Ibid., 411.

15. Ibid.

16. Ibid.

17. Ibid., 415.

18. Ibid.

19. Ibid., 414.

20. Congregation for the Doctrine of the Faith, Letter *Placuit Deo*, February 22, 2018, http://www.vatican.va/roman_curia/congregations/cfaith/documents/rc_con_cfaith_doc_20180222_placuit-deo_en.html.

21. Tocqueville, *Democracy in America*, 485.

22. Ibid.

BIBLIOGRAPHY

Adams, Frank S. "Youth Congress Moves on Turbulent Course." *New York Times*, February 11, 1940.

Allan, Robert Tate. "U.S. Marks Holiday with Emphasis on Sharing." *Washington Post*, November 28, 1947.

Allen, Barbara. "Martin Luther King's Civil Disobedience and the American Covenant Tradition." *Publius: The Journal of Federalism* 30, no. 4 (2000): 71–113.

Allen, Danielle S. *Our Declaration: A Reading of the Declaration of Independence in Defense of Equality*. New York: Liveright, 2014.

———. *Talking to Strangers: Anxieties of Citizenship Since* Brown v. Board of Education. Chicago: University of Chicago Press, 2004.

Ansbro, John J. *Martin Luther King Jr.: The Making of a Mind*. Maryknoll: Orbis Books, 1982.

Areshidze, Giorgi. *Democratic Religion from Locke to Obama: Faith and the Civic Life of Democracy*. Lawrence: University Press of Kansas, 2016.

Ariel, Yaakov. "It's All in the Bible: Evangelical Christians, Biblical Literalism, and Philosemitism in Our Times." *Philosemitism in History*. Edited by Jonathan Karp and Adam Sutcliffe. Cambridge: Cambridge University Press, 2012.

Backus, Isaac. *An Appeal to the Public for Religious Liberty*. Boston: John Boyle, 1773. Reprinted in *The Sacred Rights of Conscience: Selected Readings on Religious Liberty and Church-State Relations in the American Founding*. Edited by Daniel L. Dreisbach and Mark David Hall. Indianapolis: Liberty Fund, 2009.

Baker, Bob. "Verbal Battle Between Dornan, Peck Heats Up." *Los Angeles Times*, August 28, 1980.

Baldwin, Lewis V. *Toward the Beloved Community: Martin Luther King and South Africa*. Cleveland: Pilgrim Press, 1995.

———. *The Voice of Conscience: The Church in the Mind of Martin Luther King Jr.* New York: Oxford University Press, 2010.

Balmer, Randall. *Thy Kingdom Come: How the Religious Right Distorts the Faith and Threatens America: An Evangelical's Lament*. New York: Basic Books, 2006.

———. "The Real Origins of the Religious Right." *Politico*, May 27, 2014, https://www.politico.com/magazine/story/2014/05/religious-right-real-origins-107133?o=2.

Barker, Karlyn. "Churches Press Va. Senate." *Washington Post*, February 16, 1980.

———. "Favorite Faces Challenge in Va.'s 10th." *Washington Post*, June 7, 1980.

Bass, S. Jonathan. *Blessed Are the Peacemakers: Martin Luther King Jr., Eight White Religious Leaders, and the "Letter from Birmingham Jail."* Baton Rouge: Louisiana State University Press, 2001.

Bates, Keith, Liam J. Atchison, and Darin D. Lenz, eds. *Civil Religion and American Christianity*. Mountain Home: BorderStone Press, 2015.

Bauman, Mark K., and Berkley Kalen, eds. *The Quiet Voices: Southern Rabbis and Black Civil Rights, 1880s to 1990s.* Tuscaloosa: University of Alabama Press, 1997.

Bauman, Mark K., and Stephen Krause, eds. *To Stand Aside or Stand Alone: Southern Reform Rabbis and the Civil Rights Movement.* Tuscaloosa: University of Alabama Press, 2017.

Bell, L. Nelson. "A Southern Evangelical on Integration." *Jerry Falwell and the Rise of the Religious Right: A Brief History with Documents.* Edited by Matthew Avery Sutton. Boston: Bedford/St. Martin's, 2013.

Bellah, Robert N. "Civil Religion in America." *Daedalus* 96, no. 1 (Winter 1967): 1–21.

Bennetts, Leslie. "Conservatives Join on Social Concerns." *New York Times,* July 30, 1980.

Bercovitch, Sacvan. *The American Jeremiad.* Madison: University of Wisconsin Press, 1978.

Bergholz, Richard. "Reagan Tries to Cement His Ties with TV Evangelicals." *Los Angeles Times,* August 23, 1980.

Bigart, Homer. "Dr. King Outlines Rights Law Tests." *New York Times,* July 2, 1964.

Blanshard, Paul. *American Freedom and Catholic Power.* Reprint, Santa Barbara: Greenwood Press, 1984. First published 1949 by Beacon Press (Boston).

———. *Communism, Democracy, and Catholic Power.* Boston: Beacon Press, 1951.

Branch, Taylor. *Parting the Waters: America in the King Years, 1954–1963.* New York: Simon and Schuster, 1988.

Breidenbach, Michael. "Conciliarism and the American Founding." *William and Mary Quarterly* 73, no. 3 (Summer 2016): 467–500.

Breslin, Jimmy. "Born-Again Unease over Born-Against Pols." *Los Angeles Times,* August 25, 1980.

Briggs, Kenneth A. "Evangelical Preachers Gather to Polish Their Politics." *New York Times,* August 21, 1980.

———. "Evangelicals Hear Plea: Politics Now." *New York Times,* August 24, 1980.

———. "Evangelicals Turning to Politics Fear Moral Slide Imperils Nation." *New York Times,* August 19, 1980.

Bromley, David G., and Anson Shupe, eds. *New Christian Politics.* Princeton: Princeton University Press, 1984.

Bruenig, Elizabeth. "How Augustine's Confessions and Left Politics Inspired My Conversion to Catholicism." *America: The Jesuit Review,* August 7, 2017, https://www.americamagazine.org /faith/2017/07/25/how-augustines-confessions-and-left-politics-inspired-my-conversion -catholicism.

Bruske, Ed. "There's a Hungry Wolf at Rep. Joe Fisher's Door." *Washington Post,* October 11, 1980.

Bryant, Nicholas. *The Bystander: John F. Kennedy and the Struggle for Black Equality.* New York: Basic Books, 2006. Kindle.

Burns, Stewart. *To the Mountaintop: Martin Luther King Jr.'s Sacred Mission to Save America, 1955–1968.* New York: HarperCollins, 2004.

Burrow, Rufus, Jr. *God and Human Dignity: The Personalism, Theology, and Ethics of Martin Luther King Jr.* South Bend: University of Notre Dame Press, 2006.

Byrd, James P. *Sacred Scripture, Sacred War: The Bible and the American Revolution.* New York: Oxford University Press, 2013.

Capps, Walter H. *The New Religious Right: Piety, Patriotism, and Politics.* Columbia: University of South Carolina Press, 1990.

Caro, Robert A. *Means of Ascent.* Reprint, New York: Vintage, 1991.

Carter, George E. "Martin Luther King: Incipient Transcendentalist." *Phylon* 40, no. 4 (1979): 318–324.

Carter, Heath W., and Laura Rominger Porter, eds. *Turning Points in the History of American Evangelicalism*. Grand Rapids: Wm. B. Eerdmans, 2017.

Ceaser, James W. "Foundational Concepts and American Political Development." *Nature and History in American Political Development*. Cambridge: Harvard University Press, 2006.

Chandler, Russell. "The Electronic Church—Big Time Religion." *Los Angeles Times*, February 25, 1980.

Chandler, Russell, and John Dart. "Many Church Leaders Oppose Prop. 6." *Los Angeles Times*, November 3, 1978.

Chapman, James L. *Americanism versus Romanism, or the Cis-Atlantic Battle Between Sam and the Pope*. Nashville: printed by the author, 1856.

Chappell, David L. *A Stone of Hope: Prophetic Religion and the Death of Jim Crow*. Chapel Hill: University of North Carolina Press, 2004.

Chase, John W. "Expanded Articles." *New York Times*, May 15, 1949.

Chicago Daily Tribune. "Dominant Red Symbol at Fair Hit by Prelate," May 22, 1939.

———. "Reds Call Pope Pro-Fascist; Fascists Say He's Red: Sheen," February 2, 1944.

———. "Assails Soviet Cry of 'Fascist' Against Pope," February 4, 1944.

———. "Blast Fails—Prelate," February 9, 1944.

———. "Red Editor Quits to Go Back to His Catholic Faith," October 11, 1945.

———. "Revealed House Aid Quizzed on Smear Attack," March 26, 1946.

———. "Miss Bentley, Former Red Spy Ring Aid, in Catholic Retreat," November 16, 1948.

———. "Elizabeth Bentley, Former Soviet Spy Becomes a Catholic," November 17, 1948.

———. "Sees Parallel in Catholic, Russian Policy," February 2, 1951.

———. "Catholics Put to Red Torture, Sheen Charges," February 22, 1951.

———. "23,000 Vow Patriotism at Catholic Parley," November 12, 1951.

———. " 'I Love Lucy,' Bishop Sheen Win TV Emmies," February 6, 1953.

Clark, Victoria. *Allies for Armageddon: The Rise of Christian Zionism*. New Haven: Yale University Press, 2007.

Clendinen, Dudley. "Christian New Right's Rush to Power." *New York Times*, August 18, 1980.

Colaiaco, James A. "The American Dream Unfulfilled: Martin Luther King Jr. and the 'Letter from Birmingham Jail.' " *Phylon* 45, no. 1 (Spring 1984): 1–18.

Conger, Kimberly H. "Same Battle, Different War: Religious Movements in American State Politics." *Politics and Religion* 7, no. 2 (June 2014): 395–417.

Congregation for the Doctrine of the Faith. *Placuit Deo*, February 22, 2018. http://www.vatican .va/roman_curia/congregations/cfaith/documents/rc_con_cfaith_doc_20180222_placuit -deo_en.html.

Cox, Harvey. *God's Revolution and Man's Responsibility*. Valley Forge: Judson Press, 1965.

Craiutu, Aurelian, and Matthew N. Holbreich. "On Individualism, Authority, and Democracy as a New Form of Religion: A Few Tocquevillian Reflections." *The Spirit of Religion and the Spirit of Liberty: The Tocqueville Thesis Revisited*. Edited by Michael P. Zuckert. Chicago: University of Chicago Press, 2017.

Crosby, Donald F. *God, Church, and Flag: Senator Joseph R. McCarthy and the Catholic Church, 1950–1957*. Chapel Hill: University of North Carolina Press, 1978.

Dart, John. " 'New Face' Emerging in Protestant Fundamentalism: With 325 Stations, Jerry Falwell Is No. 1 TV Preacher." *Los Angeles Times*, October 13, 1979.

Decatur Daily Review. "Clare Boothe Luce Chooses Not to Run," January 30, 1946.

Deneen, Patrick J. *Conserving America? Essays on Present Discontents.* South Bend: St. Augustine's Press, 2016.

——. *Why Liberalism Failed.* New Haven: Yale University Press, 2018.

Djupe, Paul A., Jacob R. Neiheisel, and Anand E. Sokhey. "Reconsidering the Role of Politics in Leaving Religion: The Importance of Affiliation." *American Journal of Political Science* 62, no. 1 (January 2018): 161–175.

Dobson, Ed, Ed Hindson, and Jerry Falwell. *The Fundamentalist Phenomenon: The Resurgence of Conservative Christianity.* 2nd ed. Grand Rapids: Baker Books Press, 1981.

Dochuk, Darren, Thomas S. Kidd, and Kurt W. Peterson, eds. *American Evangelicalism: George Marsden and the State of American Religious History.* South Bend: University of Notre Dame Press, 2014.

Dodd, Bella V. *School of Darkness: The Record of a Life and of a Conflict Between Two Faiths.* New York: Devine Adair, 1954.

Dole, Kenneth. "Bishop Sheen Hails Loyalty of Catholics." *Washington Post,* November 26, 1951.

——. "Truman Pastor Tried to Halt Naming of Envoy, He Revealed." *Washington Post,* October 22, 1951.

Dougherty, Kerry. "Candidate Wolf: Shaking Each Hand." *Washington Post,* August 21, 1980.

Dreher, Rod. *The Benedict Option: A Strategy for Christians in a Post-Christian Nation.* New York: Sentinel, 2014.

Dreisbach, Daniel L. *Reading the Bible with the Founding Fathers.* New York: Oxford University Press, 2017.

Dyer, Justin Buckley, and Kevin E. Stuart. "Rawlsian Public Reason and the Theological Framework of Martin Luther King's 'Letter from Birmingham City Jail.'" *Politics and Religion* 6, no. 1 (2013): 145–163.

Edwards, William. "Bishop Oxnam Defends Red Front Links." *Chicago Daily Tribune,* July 22, 1953.

Eisenach, Eldon J. *The Next Religious Establishment: National Identity and Political Theology in Post-Protestant America.* Lanham: Rowman and Littlefield, 2000.

Elazar, Daniel J. *Covenant and Constitutionalism: The Great Frontier and the Matrix of Federal Democracy.* The Covenant Tradition in Politics, vol. 3. New Brunswick: Transaction Publishers, 1998.

Fairclough, Adam. *Martin Luther King Jr.* Athens: University of Georgia Press, 1995.

——. *To Redeem the Soul of America: The Southern Christian Leadership Conference and Martin Luther King Jr.* 2nd ed. Athens: University of Georgia Press, 2001.

Falwell, Jerry. "Conditions Corrupting America." *Old-Time Gospel Hour (OTGH)* 192. Series 2: *OTGH* Transcripts 100's, Sub-Group 4, Cassette Tape Series. *Old-Time Gospel Hour,* Record Group 3. Falwell Ministries. Liberty University Archive (LUA). Lynchburg, VA.

——. "Our Citizenship as Americans." *OTGH* 200. Series 3: *OTGH* Transcripts 200's, Sub-Group 4, Cassette Tape Series. *Old-Time Gospel Hour,* Record Group 3. Falwell Ministries. Liberty University Archive. Lynchburg, VA.

——. "How Christians Can Best Serve Their Country." *OTGH* 208. Series 3: *OTGH* Transcripts 200's, Sub-Group 4, Cassette Tape Series. *Old-Time Gospel Hour,* Record Group 3. Falwell Ministries. Liberty University Archive. Lynchburg, VA.

——. "America Needs a Spiritual Awakening." *OTGH* 294. Series 3: *OTGH* Transcripts 200's, Sub-Group 4, Cassette Tape Series. *Old-Time Gospel Hour,* Record Group 3. Falwell Ministries. Liberty University Archive. Lynchburg, VA.

———. "Responsible Christian Citizenship." *OTGH* 395. Series 4: *OTGH* Transcripts 400's, Sub-Group 4, Cassette Tape Series. *Old-Time Gospel Hour*, Record Group 3. Falwell Ministries. Liberty University Archive. Lynchburg, VA.

———. "America . . . You're Too Young to Die." *OTGH* 401. Series 5: *OTGH* Transcripts 400's, Sub-Group 4, Cassette Tape Series. *Old-Time Gospel Hour*, Record Group 3. Falwell Ministries. Liberty University Archive. Lynchburg, VA.

———. "The Millennial Reign of Christ." *OTGH* 416. Series 5: *OTGH* Transcripts 400's, Sub-Group 4, Cassette Tape Series. *Old-Time Gospel Hour*, Record Group 3. Falwell Ministries. Liberty University Archive. Lynchburg, VA.

———. "The Sins of America." *OTGH* 418. Series 5: *OTGH* Transcripts 400's, Sub-Group 4, Cassette Tape Series. *Old-Time Gospel Hour*, Record Group 3. Falwell Ministries. Liberty University Archive. Lynchburg, VA.

———. "America's Children—Free to Pray?" *OTGH* 440. Series 5, Sub-Group 4. *Old-Time Gospel Hour*, Record Group 3. Falwell Ministries. Liberty University Archive. Lynchburg, VA.

———. "The Healing of America." *OTGH* 553. Series 6: *OTGH* Transcripts 500's, Sub-Group 4, Cassette Tape Series. *Old-Time Gospel Hour*, Record Group 3. Falwell Ministries. Liberty University Archive. Lynchburg, VA.

———. "The Law of Sowing and Reaping." *OTGH* 561. Series 6: *OTGH* Transcripts 500's, Sub-Group 4, Cassette Tape Series. *Old-Time Gospel Hour*, Record Group 3. Falwell Ministries. Liberty University Archive. Lynchburg, VA.

———. "When Will America Sit Down and Cry?" *OTGH* 591. Series 6: *OTGH* Transcripts 500's, Sub-Group 4, Cassette Tape Series. *Old-Time Gospel Hour*, Record Group 3. Falwell Ministries. Liberty University Archive. Lynchburg, VA.

———. "A Biblical Perspective on Church/State Relations." *OTGH* 627. Series 9: Evening Transcripts, Sub-Group 4, Cassette Tape Series. *Old-Time Gospel Hour*, Record Group 3. Falwell Ministries. Liberty University Archive. Lynchburg, VA.

———. *America Can Be Saved*. Murfreesboro: Sword of the Lord Publishers, 1979.

———. "Enforcing God's Law in the Voting Booth." *Los Angeles Times*, September 7, 1980.

———. *Falwell: An Autobiography*. Lynchburg: Liberty Hill Publishers, 1997.

———. *Listen, America!* New York: Bantam Books, 1980.

Feinberg, Alexander. "Budenz Calls Santo a Leader in Red Infiltration of Unions." *New York Times*, September 13, 1947.

———. "No U.S. Alliances." *New York Times*, March 17, 1946.

Fessenden, Tracy. *Culture and Redemption: Religion, the Secular, and American Literature*. Princeton: Princeton University Press, 2007.

Finke, Roger, and Rodney Stark. *The Churching of America, 1776–2005: Winners and Losers in Our Religious Economy*. 6th ed. New Brunswick: Rutgers University Press, 2014.

Follard, Edward T. "President Speaks at Catholic U." *Washington Post*, November 20, 1953.

Fosdick, Harry Emerson. "Shall the Fundamentalists Win?" *American Sermons: The Pilgrims to Martin Luther King Jr.* Edited by Michael Warner. New York: Library of America, 1999.

Frankel, Glenn. "Guy Farley Emerges as Party Leader." *Washington Post*, July 15, 1980.

———. "In GOP's Mainstream." *Washington Post*, June 10, 1980.

Gallup, George. "Eisenhower Rated as Most Admired." *Los Angeles Times*, December 30, 1956.

Gannon, Thomas M. "The New Christian Right in America: As a Social and Political Force." *Archives de sciences sociales des religions* 26, no. 52.1 (July–September 1981): 69–83.

Gardella, Peter. *American Civil Religion: What Americans Hold Sacred*. New York: Oxford University Press, 2013.

Garrow, David J. *Bearing the Cross: Martin Luther King Jr., and the Southern Christian Leadership Conference*. New York: HarperCollins, 1986.

Gaul, Anita Talsma. "John Ireland, St. Eloi Parish, and the Dream of an American Catholic Church." *American Catholic Studies* 123, no. 3 (Fall 2013): 21–43.

Georgianna, Sharon Linzey. *The Moral Majority and Fundamentalism: Plausibility and Dissonance*. Lewiston: Edwin Mellen Press, 1989.

Glaude, Eddie S., Jr. *Exodus! Religion, Race, and Nation in Early Nineteenth-Century Black America*. Chicago: University of Chicago Press, 2000.

Gleason, Philip. *Contending with Modernity: Catholic Higher Education in the Twentieth Century*. New York: Oxford University Press, 1995.

———. *Keeping the Faith: American Catholicism Past and Present*. South Bend: University of Notre Dame Press, 1987.

Goldman, Samuel. *God's Country: Christian Zionism in America*. Philadelphia: University of Pennsylvania Press, 2018.

Goodman, Ellen. "The Right-Wingers May Be out of Control." *Los Angeles Times*, July 21, 1980.

———. "Gaining Control." *Washington Post*, July 23, 1980.

———. "Underneath the Present Politics of Morality Is Religious Strife." *Los Angeles Times*, September 24, 1980.

———. "As If God Were a Ward Heeler." *Washington Post*, September 24, 1980.

Gorski, Philip. *American Covenant: A History of Civil Religion from the Puritans to the Present*. Princeton: Princeton University Press, 2017.

Greenfield, Meg. "The Feds and the Family." *Washington Post*, September 3, 1980.

Grutzner, Charles. "1,500 U.S. Teachers Red, Dr. Dodd Says." *New York Times*, September 9, 1952.

———. "Teachers Union Witnesses Assail Senate Red Inquiry." *New York Times*, September 24, 1952.

Hamburger, Philip. *Separation of Church and State*. Cambridge: Harvard University Press, 2002.

Handy, Robert T. *A Christian America: Protestant Hopes and Historical Realities*. 2nd ed. New York: Oxford University Press, 1984.

Hanigan, James P. *Martin Luther King Jr. and the Foundations of Nonviolence*. Lanham: University Press of America, 1984.

Hansen, Drew D. *The Dream: Martin Luther King Jr. and the Speech That Inspired a Nation*. New York: HarperCollins, 2003.

Harding, Susan Friend. *The Book of Jerry Falwell: Fundamentalist Language and Politics*. Princeton: Princeton University Press, 2000.

Harper, Charles L., and Kevin Leicht. "Religious Awakenings and Status Politics: Sources of Support for the New Religious Right." *Sociological Analysis* 45, no. 4 (Winter 1984): 339–353.

Harris, Art. "In the 'Heart of Dixie,' a Conservative Clash." *Washington Post*, October 21, 1980.

Hart, D. G. "Mainstream Protestantism, 'Conservative' Religion, and Civil Society." *Religion Returns to the Public Square: Faith and Policy in America*. Edited by Hugh Heclo and Wilfred M. McClay. Baltimore: Johns Hopkins University Press, 2003.

Hatch, Nathan O. *The Democratization of American Christianity*. New Haven: Yale University Press, 1990.

Haynes, John Earl, and Harvey Klehr. *Venona: Decoding Soviet Espionage in America*. New Haven: Yale University Press, 2000.

Haynes, Stephen R. *Noah's Curse: The Biblical Justification of American Slavery*. Princeton: Princeton University Press, 2002.

Heclo, Hugh. "Christianity and Democracy in America." *Christianity and American Democracy*. Cambridge: Harvard University Press, 2007.

Hedstrom, Matthew S. *The Rise of Liberal Religion: Book Culture and American Spirituality in the Twentieth Century*. New York: Oxford University Press, 2013.

Heinz, Donald. "The Struggle to Define America." *The New Christian Right: Mobilization and Legitimation*. Edited by Robert C. Liebman and James L. Guth. New York: Aldine, 1983.

Herberg, Will. *Protestant, Catholic, Jew: An Essay in American Religious Sociology*. Garden City: Doubleday, 1955.

Herbers, John. "Ultraconservative Evangelicals a Surging New Force in Politics." *New York Times*, August 17, 1980.

Herrera, Robert A. "Orestes Brownson's Vision of American Life." *Modern Age* 43, no. 2 (Spring 2001): 133–145.

Herzog, Jonathan P. *The Spiritual-Industrial Complex: America's Religious Battle Against Communism in the Early Cold War*. New York: Oxford University Press, 2011.

Higham, John. *Strangers in the Land: Patterns of American Nativism, 1860–1925*. New Brunswick: Rutgers University Press, 1983.

Hoffman, Scott W. "Holy Martin: The Overlooked Canonization of Dr. Martin Luther King Jr." *Religion and American Culture: A Journal of Interpretation* 10, no. 2 (Summer 2000): 123–148.

Hofstadter, Richard. "The Paranoid Style in American Politics." *Harper's*, November 1964.

Holsendolph, Ernest. "Religious Broadcasts Bring Rising Revenues and Create Rivalries." *New York Times*, December 2, 1979.

Hornblower, Margot. " 'Pro-Family' Push: Political Mine Field." *Washington Post*, July 25, 1980.

Hout, Michael, and Claude S. Fischer. "Explaining Why More Americans Have No Religious Preference: Political Backlash and Generational Succession, 1987–2012." *Sociological Science* 1, no. 24 (October 2014): 423–447.

———. "Why More Americans Have No Religious Preferences: Politics and Generations." *American Sociological Review* 67, no. 2 (April 2002): 165–190.

Howard-Pitney, David. *The African American Jeremiad: Appeals for Justice in America*. Philadelphia: Temple University Press, 2005.

Hunt, Albert R. "Reagan and 'Depth.' " *Wall Street Journal*, November 3, 1980.

Hunter, James Davison. *Culture Wars: The Struggle to Define America*. New York: Basic Books, 1991.

———. *To Change the World: The Irony, Tragedy, and Possibility of Christianity in the Late Modern World*. New York: Oxford University Press, 2010.

Hyer, Marjorie. "Outflanking the Right: Mainline Clerics Oppose the Evangelicals." *Washington Post*, October 21, 1980.

Jenkins, Philip. *The New Anti-Catholicism: The Last Acceptable Prejudice*. New York: Oxford University Press, 2004.

Johnson, Lyndon Baines. "The Inaugural Address." January 20, 1965. Lyndon Baines Johnson Presidential Library Archives. http://www.lbjlibrary.net/collections/selected-speeches/1965/01-20-1965.html.

———. "Remarks of Vice President Lyndon B. Johnson on Memorial Day, Gettysburg, Pennsylvania." May 30, 1963. Lyndon Baines Johnson Presidential Library Archives. http://www.lbjlibrary.net/collections/selected-speeches/pre-presidential/05-30-1963.html.

————. "Address Before a Joint Session of the Congress," November 27, 1963. Lyndon Baines Johnson Presidential Library Archives. http://www.lbjlibrary.net/collections/selected-speeches /november-1963-1964/11-27-1963.html.

Johnson, Stephen D., and Joseph B. Tamney. "The Christian Right and the 1980 Presidential Election." *Journal for the Scientific Study of Religion* 21, no. 2 (June 1982): 123–131.

————. "Support for the Moral Majority: A Test of a Model." *Journal for the Scientific Study of Religion* 23, no. 2 (June 1984): 183–196.

Jordan, Ryan P. *Church, State and Race: The Discourse of American Religious Liberty, 1750–1900.* Lanham: University Press of America, 2012.

Kahan, Alan S. *Tocqueville, Democracy, and Religion: Checks and Balances for Democratic Souls.* New York: Oxford University Press, 2015.

Kaplan, Edward K. *Spiritual Radical: Abraham Joshua Heschel in America, 1940–1972.* New Haven: Yale University Press, 2009.

Kengor, Paul G. "Ronald Reagan: The Anti–Nixon/Kissinger." The Center for Vision and Values at Grove City College. February 7, 2011. http://www.visionandvalues.org/2011/02/ronald -reagan-the-anti-nixon-kissinger/.

Kengor, Paul G., and Patricia Clark Doerner. "Reagan's Darkest Hour." *National Review*, January 28, 2008.

Kennedy, John F. "Radio and Television Report to the American People on Civil Rights." June 11, 1963. John F. Kennedy Presidential Library Archives. https://www.jfklibrary.org/Asset -Viewer/Archives/JFKWHA-194-001.aspx.

Kenworthy, E. W. "200,000 March for Civil Rights in Orderly Washington Rally; President Sees Gain for Negro." *New York Times*, August 29, 1963.

Kidd, Thomas S. *God of Liberty: A Religious History of the American Revolution.* Philadelphia: Basic Books, 2010.

King, Martin Luther, Jr. "Address of Reverend Dr. Martin Luther King Jr." Speech Before New York State Civil War Centennial Commission, New York City, September 12, 1962. http:// www.nysm.nysed.gov/mlk1.

————. "Appeal to the President of the United States." May 17, 1962. The King Center Digital Archive. http://www.thekingcenter.org/archive/document/appeal-president-united-states.

————. *A Knock at Midnight: Inspiration from the Great Sermons of Reverend Martin Luther King Jr.* Edited by Clayborne Carson and Peter H. Holloran. New York: Warner Books, 2001. eBook.

————. "The New Covenant." The King Center Digital Online Archive, n.d. http://www .thekingcenter.org/archive/document/new-covenant.

————. *The Papers of Martin Luther King Jr.* Vol. 2, *Rediscovering Precious Values, July 1951– November 1955.* Edited by Clayborne Carson, Ralph E. Luker, Penny A. Russell, and Peter H. Holloran. Berkeley: University of California Press, 1994.

————. *The Papers of Martin Luther King Jr.* Vol. 4, *Symbol of the Movement, January 1957– December 1958.* Edited by Clayborne Carson, Susan Carson, Adrienne Clay, Virginia Shadron, and Kieran Taylor. Berkeley: University of California Press, 2000.

————. *Strength to Love.* Gift ed., Minneapolis: Fortress Press, 2010. First published 1963 by Harper and Row (New York).

————. *Stride Toward Freedom: The Montgomery Story.* Reprint, Boston: Beacon Press, 2010. First published 1958 by Harper and Brothers (New York).

————. *A Testament of Hope: The Essential Writings and Speeches of Martin Luther King Jr.* Edited by James Melvin Washington. San Francisco: HarperSanFrancisco, 1991.

———. *Where Do We Go from Here: Chaos or Community?* Reprint, Boston: Beacon Press, 2010. First published 1967 by Harper and Row (New York).

———. *Why We Can't Wait.* Reprint, New York: Signet Classics, 2000. First published 1963 by Harper and Row (New York).

Kintz, Linda, and Julia Lesage, eds. *Media, Culture, and the Religious Right.* Minneapolis: University of Minnesota Press, 1998.

Kirbo, Charles. Interview by Charles Jones, Robert Strong, James Sterling Young, Erwin Hargrove, and David Truman. Transcript of an oral history conducted January 5, 1983. Miller Center of Public Affairs Presidential Oral History Project. University of Virginia, 2003.

Klein, Felix. *Americanism: A Phantom Heresy.* Atchison: Aquin Book Shop, 1951.

Kruse, Kevin M. *One Nation Under God: How Corporate America Invented Christian America.* New York: Basic Books, 2015.

Lardner, George, Jr. "King Plans Accommodations Tests to Bring Law Home to the South." *Washington Post,* July 2, 1964.

Lawler, Peter Augustine. "Introduction: The Civilization of the Pluralist Society." *We Hold These Truths: Catholic Reflections on the American Proposition.* By John Courtney Murray. Lanham: Rowman and Littlefield, 2005.

Laxalt, Paul. Interview by Stephen F. Knott, James Sterling Young, and Erwin Hargrove. Transcript of an oral history conducted October 9, 2001. Miller Center of Public Affairs Presidential Oral History Project. University of Virginia, 2005.

Lembke, Bud. "4 Religious Leaders Urge Rejection of Proposition 6." *Los Angeles Times,* November 1, 1978.

Lentz, Richard. *Symbols, the News Magazines, and Martin Luther King.* Baton Rouge: Louisiana State University Press, 1990.

Lewis, Anthony. "Abroad at Home: Religion and Politics." *New York Times,* September 18, 1980.

———. "Political Religion." *New York Times,* September 25, 1980.

Lienisch, Michael. *Redeeming America: Piety and Politics in the New Christian Right.* Chapel Hill: University of North Carolina Press, 1993.

Lischer, Richard. *The Preacher King: Martin Luther King Jr. and the Word That Moved America.* New York: Oxford University Press, 1995.

Livingston, Steven. *Kennedy and King: The President, The Pastor, and the Battle Over Civil Rights.* New York: Hatchett Books, 2017.

Lloyd, Vincent W. *Black Natural Law.* New York: Oxford University Press, 2016.

Los Angeles Times. "Al Smith Sails for Europe; Plans Audience with Pope," May 16, 1937.

———. "American Flag Display at Fair Attacked," May 22, 1939.

———. "Henry Ford's Grandson Becomes Bridegroom," July 14, 1940.

———. "Self-Sacrifice Call Sounded," October 14, 1940.

———. "Russian Paper Says Vatican Aiding Fascism," February 2, 1944.

———. "Prelate Scores New Red Charge," February 9, 1944.

———. "Communist Daily Head Quits, Rejoins Church," October 11, 1945.

———. "Rep. Clare Luce Received into Catholic Church," February 17, 1946.

———. "In Retreat," November 16, 1948.

———. "Eisenhower Invites 21 to Private Stag Dinner," October 27, 1953.

———. "Kennedy Asks Speedup in Civil Rights Drive," August 29, 1963.

———. "Alabama Race: Ex-POW Running for Seat in Senate," September 21, 1980.

———. "Church Bells, Alarm Bells," October 3, 1980.

Lutz, Donald S. *The Origins of American Constitutionalism*. Baton Rouge: Louisiana State University Press, 1988.

Lynch, Christopher. *Selling Catholicism: Bishop Sheen and the Power of Television*. Lexington: University of Kentucky Press, 1998.

MacPherson, Myra. "Evangelicals Seen Cooling on Carter." *Washington Post*, September 27, 1976.

Mansfield, Harvey C. "Tocqueville on Religion and Liberty." *The Spirit of Religion and the Spirit of Liberty: The Tocqueville Thesis Revisited*. Edited by Michael P. Zuckert. Chicago: University of Chicago Press, 2017.

Mantena, Karuna. "Showdown for Nonviolence: The Theory and Practice of Nonviolent Politics." *To Shape a New World: Essays on the Political Philosophy of Martin Luther King, Jr.* Edited by Tommie Shelby and Brandon M. Terry. Cambridge: Belknap Press, 2018.

Margolis, Jon. "In the South, Morality Means Votes." *Chicago Tribune*, October 15, 1980.

Mariano, Marco. "Fear of a Nonwhite Planet: Clare Boothe Luce, Race, and American Foreign Policy." *Prospects* 29 (October 2005): 373–394.

Marsden, George M. *Fundamentalism and American Culture*. 2nd ed. New York: Oxford University Press, 2006.

Marsh, Charles. *The Beloved Community: How Faith Shapes Social Justice, from the Civil Rights Movement to Today*. New York: Basic Books, 2005.

———. *God's Long Summer: Stories of Faith and Civil Rights*. Princeton: Princeton University Press, 1997.

Marty, Martin E. *Pilgrims in Their Own Land: 500 Years of Religion in America*. Boston: Little, Brown, 1984.

Massa, Mark S. *Anti-Catholicism in America: The Last Acceptable Prejudice*. New York: Crossroad Publishing, 2005.

———. *Catholics and American Culture: Fulton Sheen, Dorothy Day, and the Notre Dame Football Team*. New York: Crossroad Publishing, 1999.

May, Gary. *Un-American Activities: The Trials of William Remington*. New York: Oxford University Press, 1994.

McClay, Wilfred M. "Two Concepts of Secularism." *Religion Returns to the Public Square: Faith and Policy in America*. Edited by Hugh Heclo and Wilfred M. McClay. Baltimore: Johns Hopkins University Press, 2003.

McIntire, Carl. "A Minister Denounces the Civil Rights Act." *Jerry Falwell and the Rise of the Religious Right: A Brief History with Documents*. Edited by Matthew Avery Sutton. Boston: Bedford/St. Martin's, 2013.

McLoughlin, William G. "Isaac Backus and the Separation of Church and State in America." *American Historical Review* 73, no. 5 (June 1968): 1392–1413.

McNulty, Timothy. "From Tent to Tube: Religion Takes Its Message Through Channels." *Chicago Tribune*, April 4, 1979.

Merlin, Milton. "Books." *Los Angeles Times*, March 19, 1950.

Milkis, Sidney M., and Daniel J. Tichenor. "Reform's Mating Dance: Presidents, Social Movements, and Racial Realignments." *Journal of Policy History* 23, no. 4 (2011): 451–490.

Miller, Arthur H., and Martin P. Wattenberg. "Politics from the Pulpit: Religiosity and the 1980 Elections." *Public Opinion Quarterly* 48, no. 1b (Spring 1984): 301–317.

Miller, Perry. *The New England Mind: From Colony to Province*. Vol. 2. Cambridge: Beacon Press, 1960.

Montgomery, Jim. "The Electric Church: Religious Broadcasting Becomes Big Business, Spreading Across U.S." *Wall Street Journal*, May 19, 1979.

Moore, Helen A., and Hugh P. Whitt. "Multiple Dimensions of the Moral Majority Platform: Shifting Interest Group Coalitions." *Sociological Quarterly* 27, no. 3 (Autumn 1986): 423–439.

Moore, William. "Talks with Lawmakers Please Civil Rights Leaders." *Chicago Tribune*, August 29, 1963.

Moots, Glenn A. *Politics Reformed: The Anglo-American Legacy of Covenant Theology.* Columbia: University of Missouri Press, 2010.

Morone, James A. *Hellfire Nation: The Politics of Sin in American History.* New Haven: Yale University Press, 2003.

Mueller, Carol. "In Search of a Constituency for the 'New Religious Right.'" *Public Opinion Quarterly* 47, no. 2 (Summer 1983): 213–229.

Murphy, Andrew R. *Prodigal Nation: Moral Decline and Divine Punishment from New England to 9/11.* New York: Oxford University Press, 2009.

Neal, Steve. *Dark Horse: A Biography of Wendell Willkie.* Garden City: Doubleday, 1984.

Neuhaus, Richard John. *The Naked Public Square: Religion and Democracy in America.* 2nd ed. Grand Rapids: Wm. B. Eerdmans, 1996.

New York Times. "Assails Einstein's Views on Religion," November 16, 1930.

———. "Pontifical Mass Sung in Cathedral," March 18, 1933.

———. "Bolshevism Traced to Atheism by Sheen," April 3, 1933.

———. "Dr. Sheen Scores Rise of Paganism," February 5, 1934.

———. "Communist 'Faith' Defined by Sheen," May 25, 1935.

———. "Mgr. Sheen Warns of Godless World," December 16, 1935.

———. "Capital Is Divided on Smith Threat," January 27, 1936.

———. "New Catholic Stand on Communism Urged," March 9, 1936.

———. "Neglect of God Held Cause of Reds' Rise," March 15, 1936.

———. "Catholics Urged to Convert Reds," March 30, 1936.

———. "Cardinal Bestows Papal Blessing on Throng at Mass in St. Patrick's," April 13, 1936.

———. "Sheen Says World Robs Man of Soul," May 2, 1936.

———. "Action by Catholics Urged," September 20, 1936.

———. "Smith Sails May 15 on First Trip Abroad," April 13, 1937.

———. "No Bias in Relief, Mayor Declares," April 19, 1937.

———. "Smith Denies Report of Vatican Summons," May 11, 1937.

———. "Al Smith Sets Sail in a Brown Derby," May 16, 1937.

———. "Smith Is Greeted by Pope as an Old Friend; Amazed, at First Audience, by Pontiff's Vigor," May 27, 1937.

———. "Words Failed Smith for the First Time in Audience with Pope, He Confesses," May 29, 1937.

———. "Smith Reiterates Dig at New Deal," August 16, 1937.

———. "Sees French Revolution," August 24, 1937.

———. "The Reply of 175 Catholic Clergy and Laymen to Protestant Letter on Spain," October 14, 1937.

———. "Sheen Says Man Is Being Crucified," March 7, 1938.

———. "Catholic Charities Opens Conference," March 14, 1938.

———. "6,000 Attend Mass at St. Patrick's," April 18, 1938.

———. "Wallace to Attend Protest Rally Here," December 8, 1938.

———. "La Guardia Rally Warns of Danger of Hatreds in U.S.," December 10, 1938.

———. "Catholics Invited to Loyalist Spain," January 9, 1939.

———. "Rival Camps Open Embargo Battles," January 10, 1939.

———. "Flight from Cross Held Trend Today," March 27, 1939.

———. "Fusion of Hitler and Stalin Feared," May 20, 1939.

———. "Catholics Denounce Russian Fair Statue," May 22, 1939.

———. "Youth Congress Members in Anti-War Demonstration," February 5, 1940.

———. "Mgr. Sheen Scores Youth Congress," March 4, 1940.

———. "Emphasis on Guilt Is Urged by Sheen." March 11, 1940.

———. "Ford's Grandson May Become a Catholic; Receiving Instruction from Mgr. Sheen," March 25, 1940.

———. "Fair Not Courting a 'Chief Speaker,'" May 7, 1940.

———. "Temple Dedicated to True Freedom," May 12, 1940.

———. "States Friendly to Soviet Scored by Sheen; Not Fighting for Kingdom of God, He Says," March 3, 1949.

———. "Sheen Finds Peril in a Static Nation," March 10, 1941.

———. "75,000 Irish Parade Here Tomorrow," March 16, 1941.

———. "Lehman Appeals for Catholic Fund," March 23, 1941.

———. "Mgr. Sheen Says Nazi Paganism Menaces World Christianity," November 17, 1941.

———. "Willkie to Aid Hospital," January 11, 1942.

———. "Sheen Condemns False Tolerance," February 23, 1942.

———. "Gethsemane Spirit Held Need of U.S.," March 2, 1942.

———. "War Called Knight of 'Great Surgeon,'" March 23, 1942.

———. "Mgr. Sheen Assails Worldly Philosophy," November 16, 1942.

———. "Views War as Judgment," November 30, 1942.

———. "Dewey Promises Move to End Crisis on Farms of State," February 13, 1943.

———. "Our 'Naïve Trust in Japan' Is Assailed by Sheen as 'False Optimism' of the West," March 15, 1943.

———. "Sheen Assails Russia," February 9, 1944.

———. "Prayers for Stalin Said by Mgr. Sheen," April 23, 1944.

———. "Mgr. Sheen Predicts Conversion of China," July 17, 1944.

———. "Msgr. Sheen Hails Spirit of Russians," April 2, 1945.

———. "Daily Worker Editor Renounces Communism for Catholic Faith," October 11, 1945.

———. "Foster Calls Budenz 'Deserter' from Labor; Sheen Tells How Editor Rejoined Church," October 12, 1945.

———. "Farley Stresses Legislative Duty," May 27, 1946.

———. "Romulo Warns U.S. to Cultivate East," January 27, 1947.

———. "Sheen Asks Prayers to Win Communists," March 24, 1947.

———. "Worry Is Atheism, Msgr. Sheen Says," February 23, 1948.

———. "Miss Bentley, Ex-Spy, Becomes a Catholic," November 16, 1948.

———. "Sheen Calls for Action," February 7, 1949.

———. "Sheen Lauds Mindszenty," February 14, 1949.

———. "Stalin's Fear Held Persecution Basis," March 21, 1949.

———. "30,000 Catholics Protest on Reds," May 2, 1949.

———. "The Best Sellers," June 26, 1949.

——. "The Best Books I Read This Year—Twelve Distinguished Opinions," December 4, 1949.

——. "Bishop Reports Torture," December 6, 1951.

——. "Bella Dodd Back in Catholic Fold," August 6, 1952.

——. "President Gives Dinner," October 27, 1953.

——. "U.S. Will Hear President on 'Back to God' Appeal," January 28, 1954.

——. "Why Foreign Aid? What Eight Leaders Say," March 2, 1958.

——. "President Urged to End Race Laws, King Wants Proclamation for a 2d 'Emancipation,'" June 6, 1961.

——. "Dr. King Asks New Laws, Urges Kennedy to Initiate Civil Rights Measure," October 28, 1961.

——. "Kennedy Finds 'Good Deal Left Undone' in Field of Civil Rights but Hopes for Progress," May 18, 1962.

——. "Equality Is Their Right," August 29, 1963.

——. "Texts of the President's Statements on Rights and on Labor Day," August 29, 1963.

——. "Transcript of President Johnson's Address Before the Joint Session of Congress," November 28, 1963. http://www.nytimes.com/books/98/04/12/specials/johnson-63address.html.

——. "Outflanked on the Right," September 7, 1980.

——. "Evangelical Group Quietly and Angrily Upsets Alabama Primary," September 8, 1980.

——. "Private Religion," October 5, 1980.

Niebuhr, H. Richard. *Christ and Culture*. New York: Harper and Brothers, 1951.

——. "The Idea of Covenant and American Democracy." *Church History* 23, no. 2 (1954): 126–135.

——. *The Kingdom of God in America*. Reprint, Middletown: Wesleyan University Press, 1988. First published 1937 by Harper and Row (New York).

Noll, Mark A. *America's God: From Jonathan Edwards to Abraham Lincoln*. New York: Oxford University Press, 2002.

Nordstrom, Justin. *Danger on the Doorstep: Anti-Catholicism and American Print Culture in the Progressive Era*. South Bend: University of Notre Dame Press, 2006.

Oates, Stephen B. "The Intellectual Odyssey of Martin Luther King." *Massachusetts Review* 22, no. 2 (Summer 1981): 301–320.

O'Brien, David J. "American Catholicism and American Religion." *Journal of the American Academy of Religion* 40, no. 1 (March 1972): 36–53.

——. *American Catholics and Social Reform*. New York: Oxford University Press, 1968.

——. *The Renewal of American Catholicism*. New York: Oxford University Press, 1972.

——. *Isaac Hecker: An American Catholic*. Mahwah: Paulist Press, 1992.

Olson, Laura R. "The Religious Left in Contemporary American Politics." *Politics, Religion and Ideology* 1, no. 3 (September 2011): 271–294.

Owen, J. Judd. *Making Religion Safe for Democracy: Transformation from Hobbes to Tocqueville*. New York: Cambridge University Press, 2015.

——. "The Struggle Between 'Religion and Nonreligion': Jefferson, Backus, and the Dissonance of America's Founding Principles." *American Political Science Review* 101, no. 3 (August 2007): 493–503.

Pakenham, Michael. "Capital Ready for Big Rights March Today." *Chicago Tribune*, August 28, 1963.

Parr, Patrick. *The Seminarian: Martin Luther King Jr. Comes of Age*. Chicago: Lawrence Hill Books, 2018.

Patterson, James M. "The American Nehemiad, or the Tale of Two Walls." *Journal of Church and State* 57, no. 3 (2015): 450–468.

———. "'I Am Doing a Great Work, So That I Cannot Come Down': The American Nehemiad and the 'Great Work of Religion' in the Early Republic." *Anamnesis* 5, no. 1 (2016): 68–98.

Peters, Jean. "Religious TV Finds a Niche in Manassas." *Washington Post*, September 25, 1979.

Peterson, Merrill. *Abraham Lincoln in American Memory*. New York: Oxford University Press, 1994.

Phillips, Bessie. "Miss Anne McDonnell Is Wd to Henry Ford 2d at Shore." *New York Times*, July 14, 1940.

Phillips, Kevin. *The Emerging Republican Majority*. New Rochelle: Arlington House, 1969.

Pierard, Richard V. "Religion and the 1984 Election Campaign." *Review of Religious Research* 27, no. 2 (December 1985): 98–114.

Pinheiro, John C. *Missionaries of Republicanism: A Religious History of the Mexican-American War*. New York: Oxford University Press, 2014.

Portier, William L. *Divided Friends: Portraits of the Roman Catholic Modernist Crisis in the United States*. Washington, DC: Catholic University of America Press, 2013.

Powell, Brent. "Henry David Thoreau, Martin Luther King Jr., and the American Tradition of Protest." *OAH Magazine of History* 9, no. 2 (Winter 1995): 26–29.

Prugh, Jeff, and Russell Chandler. "Old-Time Religion in the Big Time." *Los Angeles Times*, May 20, 1979.

Putnam, Robert D., and David E. Campbell. *American Grace: How Religion Divides and Unites Us*. New York: Simon and Schuster, 2010.

Raines, Howell. "Reagan Backs Evangelicals in Their Political Activities." *New York Times*, August 23, 1980.

Raskin, A. H. "Presenting the Phenomenon Called Quill." *New York Times*, March 5, 1950.

Reagan, Ronald. "Acceptance of the Republican Nomination for President." July 17, 1980. Ronald Reagan Presidential Library Archives. https://www.reaganlibrary.gov/7-17-80.

———. "Remarks at a White House Ceremony in Observance of a National Day of Prayer." May 6, 1982. Ronald Reagan Presidential Library Archives. https://www.reaganlibrary.gov /research/speeches/50682c.

Reeves, Thomas C. *America's Bishop: The Life and Times of Fulton J. Sheen*. San Francisco: Encounter Books, 2001.

Reher, Margaret M. "Phantom Heresy: A Twice-Told Tale," *U.S. Catholic Historian* 11, no. 3 (Summer 1993): 93–105.

Reinsch, Richard M., II. "Introduction: Orestes Brownson's American Search for the Truth." *Seeking the Truth: An Orestes Brownson Anthology*. Edited by Richard M. Reinsch II. Washington, DC: Catholic University of America Press, 2016.

Reno, Russell R. "The Spirit of Democratic Capitalism." *First Things*, October 2017. https://www .firstthings.com/article/2017/10/the-spirit-of-democratic-capitalism.

Richard, Carl J. *The Founders and the Bible*. Lanham: Rowman and Littlefield, 2016.

Riley, Kathleen L. *Fulton J. Sheen: An American Catholic Response to the Twentieth Century*. Staten Island: Alba House, 2004.

Roof, Wade Clark, and William McKinney. "Denominational America and the New Religious Pluralism." *Annals of the American Academy of Political and Social Science* 480 (July 1985): 24–38.

Rosenfeld, Megan. "The Evangelist and His Empire: Cleaning Up America with Jerry Falwell." *Washington Post*, April 28, 1979.

———. "Miller and Warner Attend a Lynchburg Happening." *Washington Post*, October 23, 1980.

———. "The New Moral America and the War of the Religicos." *Washington Post*, August 24, 1980.

Rosenfeld, Stephen S. "Policy by The Book." *Washington Post*, July 25, 1980.

Roy, Jody M. *Rhetorical Campaigns of the Nineteenth Century Anti-Catholics and Catholics in America*. Lewiston: Edwin Mellen Press, 2000.

Ruotsila, Markku. *Fighting Fundamentalist: Carl McIntire and the Politicization of American Fundamentalism*. New York: Oxford University Press, 2015.

Ryan, Edward F. "Mrs. Luce Appointed Ambassador to Italy." *Washington Post*, February 8, 1953.

Sawyer, Kathy. "Linking Religion and Politics." *Washington Post*, August 24, 1980.

Schaeffer, Francis A. *The God Who Is There*. Downers Grove: Inter-Varsity Press, 1968.

Schleifer, James T. "Tocqueville, Religion, and *Democracy in America*: Some Essential Questions." *The Spirit of Religion and the Spirit of Liberty: The Tocqueville Thesis Revisited*. Edited by Michael P. Zuckert. Chicago: University of Chicago Press, 2017.

Schrecker, Ellen. *Many Are the Crimes: McCarthyism in America*. New York: Little, Brown, 1998.

Schultz, Debra L. *Going South: Jewish Women in the Civil Rights Movement*. New York: New York University Press, 2002.

Schultz, Kevin Michael. *Tri-Faith America: How Catholics and Jews Held Postwar America to Its Protestant Promise*. New York: Oxford University Press, 2011.

Schwartz, Barry, and Howard Schuman. "History, Commemoration, and Belief: Abraham Lincoln in American Memory." *American Sociological Review* 70, no. 2 (April 2005): 183–203.

Schwarz, Jordan A. "Al Smith in the Thirties." *New York History* 45, no. 4 (October 1964): 316–330.

Scully, Randolph Ferguson. *Religion and the Making of Nat Turner's Virginia*. Charlottesville: University of Virginia Press, 2008.

Selby, Gary S. *Martin Luther King and the Rhetoric of Freedom: The Exodus Narrative in America's Struggle for Civil Rights*. Waco: Baylor University Press, 2010.

Sheen, Fulton J. Appearance on *What's My Line?* Aired October 21, 1956. New York: Columbia Broadcasting System. Footage located at https://www.youtube.com/watch?v=T74qnT7WFZw&t=1257s.

———. *Communism and the Conscience of the West*. Indianapolis: Bobbs-Merrill, 1948.

———. *Declaration of Dependence*. Milwaukee: Bruce Publishing, 1941.

———. "Educating for a Catholic Renaissance." *National Catholic Educational Association Bulletin* 26 (1929): 45–54.

———. "Evil Has Its Hour." *The Catholic Hour*, March 14, 1943.

———. *For God and Country*. New York: P. J. Kennedy and Sons, 1941.

———. *Freedom Under God*. Milwaukee: Bruce Publishing, 1940.

———. "The Last of the Enemies." *The Prodigal World*. Washington, DC: National Council of Catholic Men, 1936.

———. *Life Is Worth Living*. First Series. New York: McGraw-Hill, 1953.

———. *Life Is Worth Living*. Fourth Series. New York: McGraw-Hill, 1956.

———. *Life Is Worth Living*. Fifth Series. New York: McGraw-Hill, 1957.

———. *Thinking Life Through*. New York: McGraw-Hill, 1955.

———. *Moods and Truths: How to Solve the Problems of Modern Life*. Reprint, New York: Popular Library, 1956. First published 1932 by Century (New York).

———. *Treasure in Clay: The Autobiography of Fulton J. Sheen*. Garden City: Doubleday, 1980.

Shields, Jon A. *The Democratic Virtues of the Christian Right*. Princeton: Princeton University Press, 2009.

Shields, Mark. "A Difference in Ministers." *Washington Post*, October 3, 1980.

Shulman, George M. *American Prophecy: Race and Redemption in American Political Culture*. Minneapolis: University of Minnesota Press, 2008.

Silk, Mark. "Notes on the Judeo-Christian Tradition in America." *American Quarterly* 36, no. 1 (Spring 1984): 65–85.

Simon, Merrill. *Jerry Falwell and the Jews*. Middle Village: Jonathan David Publishers, 1984.

Simpson, John H. "Socio-Moral Issues and Recent Presidential Elections." *Review of Religious Research* 27, no. 2 (December 1985): 115–123.

Sinclair, Ward. "Special-Interest Shock Troops: All-Out War." *Washington Post*, October 25, 1980.

Sitman, Matthew. "Against Moral Austerity: On the Need for a Christian Left." *Dissent*, Summer 2017. https://www.dissentmagazine.org/article/moral-austerity-need-christian-left.

Skelton, George. "The Times Poll: Reagan Gains with Some Evangelicals." *Los Angeles Times*, September 17, 1980.

Smidt, Corwin, and James M. Penning. "Religious Commitment, Political Conservatism, and Political and Social Tolerance in the United States." *Sociological Analysis* 43, no. 3 (Autumn 1982): 231–245.

Smith, Donald H. "An Exegesis of Martin Luther King Jr.'s Social Philosophy." *Phylon* 31, no. 1 (1st Qtr. 1970): 89–97.

Smith, John David, and J. Vincent Lowery, eds. *The Dunning School: Historians, Race, and the Meaning of Reconstruction*. Lexington: University Press of Kentucky, 2013.

Smith, Kenneth L., and Ira G. Zepp Jr. *Search for the Beloved Community: The Thinking of Martin Luther King Jr*. Valley Forge: Judson Press, 1974.

Smith, Rogers M. "What If God Was One of Us?" *Nature and History in American Political Development*. Cambridge: Harvard University Press, 2006.

Smith, Timothy L. "Protestants Falwell Does Not Represent." *New York Times*, October 22, 1980.

Snow, Malinda. "Martin Luther King's 'Letter from Birmingham Jail' as a Pauline Epistle." *Quarterly Journal of Speech* 71, no. 3 (August 1985): 318–334.

Solomon, Martha. "Covenanted Rights: The Metaphoric Matrix of 'I Have a Dream.'" *Martin Luther King Jr. and the Sermonic Power of Public Discourse*. Edited by Carolyn Calloway-Thomas and John Louis Lucaites. Tuscaloosa: University of Alabama Press, 1993.

Spencer, Stuart. Interview by Paul B. Freedman, Stephen F. Knott, Russell L. Riley, and James Sterling Young. Transcript of an oral history conducted November 15–16, 2001. Miller Center of Public Affairs Presidential Oral History Project. University of Virginia, 2005.

Spiegel, Irving. "Three Faiths Join in Rights Demand." *New York Times*, August 29, 1963.

Stall, Bill. "Part of New Right: Evangelicals on Their Faith in Political Action." *Los Angeles Times*, August 24, 1980.

Tamney, Joseph B., and Stephen D. Johnson. "The Moral Majority in Middletown." *Journal for the Scientific Study of Religion* 22, no. 2 (June 1983): 145–157.

Tanner, James C. "Civil Rights Test, Negroes in South Ready Immediate, Broad Drive to Try Out New Law." *Wall Street Journal*, July 2, 1964.

Tessitore, Aristide. "Tocqueville's American Thesis and the New Science of Politics." *The Spirit of Religion and the Spirit of Liberty: The Tocqueville Thesis Revisited*. Edited by Michael P. Zuckert. Chicago: University of Chicago Press, 2017.

Thomas, Cal. "How You Can Help Clean Up America: The Press." *How You Can Help Clean Up America.* Edited by Jerry Falwell. Lynchburg: Liberty Press, 1981.

Thomas, Cal, and Ed Dobson. *Blinded by the Might: Why the Religious Right Can't Save America.* Grand Rapids: Zondervan, 2000.

Thomas, Samuel J. "Mugwump Cartoonists, the Papacy, and Tammany Hall in America's Gilded Age." *Religion and American Culture: A Journal of Interpretation* 14, no. 2 (Summer 2004): 213–250.

Tiefenbrun, Susan. "Semiotics and Martin Luther King's 'Letter from Birmingham Jail.'" *Cardozo Studies in Law and Literature* 4, no. 2 (Autumn 1992): 255–287.

Time. "Religion: Conversion," May 22, 1939.

———. "Religion: Biography of Sheen," January 1, 1940.

———. "Religion: Converter on Wax," May 6, 1946.

———. "Religion: How to Win a Convert," July 12, 1948.

———. "Microphone Missionary," April 14, 1952.

Tocqueville, Alexis de. *Democracy in America.* Edited and translated by Harvey C. Mansfield and Delba Winthrop. Chicago: University of Chicago Press, 2000.

Towns, Elmer L and Jerry Falwell. *Church Aflame.* Kirkwood: Impact Books, 1971.

United Press. "Religious Freedom Guarantee Urged as Basis for Assistance." *Washington Post,* October 8, 1941.

US Congress. *Congressional Record.* 88th Cong., 2nd sess., 1964. Vol. 110, pt. 5.

Vecsey, George. "Church and State: Moral Issues Are Drawing Clergy into Politics." *Chicago Tribune,* January 23, 1980.

———. "Militant Television Preachers Try to Weld Fundamentalist Christians' Political Power." *New York Times,* January 21, 1980.

Vermeule, Adrian. "The Ark of Tradition." *University Bookman,* November 19, 2017. https://kirkcenter.org/uncategorized/the-ark-of-tradition/

———. "As Secular Liberalism Attacks the Church, Catholics Can't Afford to Be Nostalgic." *Catholic Herald,* January 5, 2018. http://www.catholicherald.co.uk/commentandblogs/2018/01/05/as-secular-liberalism-attacks-the-church-catholics-cant-afford-to-be-nostalgic/.

Wall Street Journal. "Action and Reaction, Most White in North, West Say They Oppose Rights Demonstrations," August 28, 1963.

———. "The Amoral Minority," October 20, 1980.

Wall, Wendy L. *Inventing the "American Way": The Politics of Consensus from the New Deal to the Civil Rights Movement.* New York: Oxford University Press, 2008.

Washington Post. "Friendly Sons Hold St. Patrick's Event," March 19, 1933.

———. "Mgr. Sheen Sees Man Losing Self in Materialism," October 24, 1934.

———. "Pope Is Leader in World Drive Against Reds," December 14, 1936.

———. "Dr. Sheen Cites Anti-Fascists as 'Slummers,'" November 11, 1937.

———. "Catholics Fight Lifting Ban on Arms to Spain," December 31, 1938.

———. "2 Parleys Set Tomorrow on Arms Embargo," January 8, 1939.

———. "Father Sheen Asks Exposure of 'Isms' in U.S. Schools," April 23, 1939.

———. "Pope Foresaw Nazi, Red Pact, Sheen Reveals," December 11, 1939.

———. "Mrs. Roosevelt Denies Youth Follows Reds," February 6, 1940.

———. "Roosevelt Condemns Russia Before 5,000 Youth Delegates," February 11, 1940.

———. "America Is Nation Falling in Decay, Says Msgr. Sheen," March 10, 1940.

———. "Msgr. Sheen Says 'Sense of Guilt' Oppresses U.S.," March 11, 1940.

———. "Msgr. Sheen Instructs Ford Scion in Bride-to-Be's Faith," March 25, 1940.

———. "A Challenge: Msgr. Sheen Asks Backing for President," December 15, 1941.

———. "End of False War Ideas Is Urged," January 4, 1943.

———. "Sheen Cites Three Dogmas at War Today," January 11, 1943.

———. "Peace Without Morals Can't Last, Prelate Asserts," April 12, 1943.

———. "Nazi and Soviet Ideologies Identical, Msgr. Sheen Asserts," October 29, 1943.

———. "Msgr. Sheen Says Soviet Agent Was 'Picked Up' in Congress," March 25, 1946.

———. "25,000 Rally to Pray for World Peace," May 2, 1947.

———. "Sheen in Australia, Gives Red Antidotes," May 8, 1948.

———. "Miss Bentley, Self-Styled Spy, Becomes a Catholic," November 17, 1948.

———. "Sheen Sees Better Soviet-U.S. Relations," January 23, 1949.

———. "Religion-Red War On, Says Msgr. Sheen," February 14, 1949.

———. "Priests and Nuns Tortured in China, Says Msgr. Sheen," February 22, 1951.

———. "JFK's Action on Civil Rights Lagging, Says Rev. Dr. King," April 10, 1962.

———. "Evangelist Falwell, Va. City Argue over $67,000 in Taxes," June 27, 1980.

———. "'Moral Majority' Forces Help Fell Rep. Buchanan," September 4, 1980.

———. "Mr. Buchanan's 'Doggone Truth,'" September 7, 1980.

———. "Harris Criticizes 'Moral Absolutism,'" September 25, 1980.

———. "Poll: Carter Best for Peace: But Not Prosperity," September 27, 1980.

———. "Ally of Thomas T. Byrd, Is Elected to Virginia GOP Post," September 29, 1980.

———. "N. Y. Activist Chastises Right-Wing Preachers," October 6, 1980.

———. "Falwell Must Provide Property Information," October 7, 1980.

Weaver, Peter. "Mind Your Money: Taking Religion into Account." *Los Angeles Times*, March 13, 1980.

Weigel, George. *Witness to Hope: The Biography of Pope John Paul II*. New York: HarperCollins, 1999.

Welkos, Robert. "Briggs Initiative Transactions Investigated." *Los Angeles Times*, October 3, 1979.

———. "Briggs Pins Probe Blame on Minister." *Los Angeles Times*, October 4, 1979.

Wilcox, Clyde. "Evangelicals and the Moral Majority." *Journal for the Scientific Study of Religion* 28, no. 4 (December 1989): 400–414.

Wilcox, Clyde, Sharon Linzey, and Ted G. Jelen. "Reluctant Warriors: Premillennialism and Politics in the Moral Majority." *Journal for the Scientific Study of Religion* 30, no. 3 (September 1991): 245–258.

Williams, Daniel K. *God's Own Party: The Making of the Christian Right*. New York: Oxford University Press, 2010.

Williams, Preston N. "An Analysis of the Conception of Love and Its Influence on Justice in the Thought of Martin Luther King Jr." *Journal of Religious Ethics* 18, no. 2 (1990): 15–31.

Wills, Richard Wayne, Sr. *Martin Luther King Jr. and the Image of God*. New York: Oxford University Press, 2009.

Wilsey, John D. *American Exceptionalism and Civil Religion: Reassessing the History of an Idea*. Downers Grove: IVP Academic, 2015.

Winsboro, Irvin D. S. and Michael Epple, "Religion, Culture, and the Cold War: Bishop Fulton J. Sheen and America's Anti-Communist Crusade of the 1950s," *The Historian* 71, no. 2 (Summer 2009): 209–233.

Winters, Michael Sean. *God's Right Hand: How Jerry Falwell Made God a Republican and Baptized the American Right*. New York: HarperOne, 2012.

Wuthnow, Robert. *The Restructuring of American Religion: Society and Faith Since World War II.* Princeton: Princeton University Press, 1988.

Young, Andrew. "New Guise for Old Right." *Los Angeles Times*, October 22, 1980.

Young, Neil J. *We Gather Together: The Religious Right and the Problem of Interfaith Politics.* New York: Oxford University Press, 2016.

Young, Perry Deane. *God's Bullies: Power, Politics and Religious Tyranny.* New York: Holt, Rinehart and Winston, 1982.

INDEX

Abernathy, Walter, 97

abortion, 119–21, 126, 130–31, 134, 136, 138, 140, 144, 147, 203–4n142; Planned Parenthood, 130, 134

activist, 64, 77, 90, 97–98, 103, 138, 144, 152, 163, 191n160, 201n116; political activism, 74; public activism, 87. *See also* civil rights

agape, 19, 65–66, 68, 72, 75–80, 82–83, 86–89, 100–101, 103, 113, 184–85n49, 185n54, 185–86n55

Ahmann, Matthew, 102

Allen, Barbara, 66, 72–73, 75, 78

Allen, Danielle S., 2, 66, 78–80, 82, 86

amendment, 155; Equal Rights Amendment, 137; First Amendment, 6, 48, 154; Fourteenth Amendment, 105, 109

American Civil Liberties Union (ACLU), 130, 134, 153–54, 157, 205n160

American civil religion, 10–13, 171n45, 183n21

American Civil War, 15, 98, 100, 103, 113

American Constitution, 1, 11, 32, 78, 87, 99, 102, 105–9, 111, 129, 153

Americanism, 18, 20–32, 36–38, 43, 46, 48, 53, 58, 161

Anderson, John B., 150

anti-: anti-American, 147, 156; anti-Catholic, 12, 15, 17–18, 21–26, 28, 43, 47–48, 51, 54–55, 161; anti-Christ, 28, 31–35, 41; anti-Christian, 33–34, 156; anti-Communist, 23, 36–37, 42, 44, 51, 53–57, 60, 140, 179–80n150; antidemocratic, 60; antihuman, 30; antiliberal, 164; anti-Mormon, 12, 15; antipatriotic, 45; antipolitical, 141; antireligious, 30, 60, 162; anti-Semitism, 18, 167; antitotalitarianism, 21, 44

Arafat, Yasser, 139

Armstrong, William L., 155

Artaxerxes. *See* Nehemiad

assassination: of Julius Caesar, 35; of Abraham Lincoln, 104; of John F. Kennedy, 104, 110; of Martin Luther King Jr., 113

atheist, 48, 119, 144, 153, 156, 187n83, 203–4n156

Augustine of Hippo, 163, 184n42

authority, 7–8, 38, 45, 62, 65–66, 72–73, 78, 86, 95, 131, 143, 171n45; apostolic authority, 36; authority of the Government, 48; Church authority, 38, 41, 43, 66, 80; democratic authority, 86; divine authority, 14, 74, 86, 161; moral authority, 37–38, 61, 66, 101; political authority, 29, 66; preliberal authority, 2; religious authority, 15, 38, 96, 182–83n16; spiritual authority, 21, 37–38, 43, 49, 81; universal authority, 37

Baker, Ella, 17

Bakker, Jim, 146–48

Bakunin, 166

Baldwin, James, 17

Baldwin, Lewis V., 81–82

Balmer, Randall, 120–21

Barber, Reverend William, 163

Barkley, Vice President Alben W., 46–47

Bass, S. Jonathan, 91

Beatitudes, 107–8. *See* Ten Commandments

Beecher, Lyman, 15, 21, 25

Bellah, Robert N., 11

Beloved Community, 18–19, 64–68, 72, 74–75, 77, 80–87, 89–93, 97–98, 100, 102–3, 106, 110, 112–13, 161, 182n6, 185n54, 185–86n55, 186n62, 187n72

Benedict Option, 2, 164

Bentley, Elizabeth, 52–53

Bercovitch, Sacvan, 10–11

Bible-believing Christians, 117–20, 123–28, 130–32, 134–47, 151–53, 156–58, 161–62

ACKNOWLEDGMENTS

While my name is on this book, a small army of contributors were essential to its completion. I am humbled and grateful for their support, criticism, and expertise. They are so numerous that I will inevitably fail to include all their names here. To those omitted, I extend my apologies.

This book began with a fellowship from The Lynde and Harry Bradley Foundation, which funded both the archival work and the initial composition of the manuscript at the University of Virginia. The mentors during that time—James W. Ceaser, Lawrie Balfour, Melvin Rogers, and Charles Mathewes—were each essential to its completion. I would like to thank Sr. Connie Derby, RSM, for her help with the Fulton J. Sheen Archives in the Rochester Diocese Library and Abigail Sattler at the Liberty University Jerry Falwell Archives for such organized archives and their help sorting through them.

Multiple institutions provided the time and resources for transforming my initial project into a proper book. The Program in American Values and Institutions at Duke University provided me a fellowship during which I revised the manuscript, as well as work in additional archives. While there, Michael Gillespie, Michael Munger, Ruth Grant, Nora Hanagan, Samuel Bagg, Jonathan Schwartz, and Aaron B. Roberts provided welcoming collegiality and scholarly engagement. During the following year, the politics faculty at Hampden-Sydney College, especially James Pontuso and Warner Winborne, offered me the time and support I needed to present and publish my work. After my time at Hampden-Sydney, the James Madison Program in American Ideals and Institutions at Princeton University offered me an opportunity to complete additional research, attend conferences to improve the manuscript, and work with scholars working on similar subjects. I benefited greatly from friendships with Robby George, Brad Wilson, Charlie and the late Leslie Rubin, Matthew J. Franck, Christopher Kaczor, Aurelian Craiutu, Veronica Roberts, Kody Cooper, and Dominic Burbidge. During the following year at Gettysburg College, my colleagues in the Political Science Department—particularly Bruce Larson, Kathleen Iannello, Shirley Anne

Warshaw, Rob Bohrer, Don Borock, and Roy Dawes—provided generous professional and personal support. Finally, I completed the final manuscript at Ave Maria University, where the faculty and administration have proved tremendously supportive. I am especially grateful to Seana Sugrue, John Colman, Gabriel Martinez, Roger Nutt, Dan Davy, Michael Breidenbach, Brent Johnson, and James and Mary Towey.

I had some excellent experiences presenting this research in a variety of venues. Tony Gill offered me a chance to talk about the early stages of the book on his podcast *Research on Religion*. Bob Subrick, John Robinson, and Zac Gochenour provided me the chance to present a summary of the book to their wonderful students at James Madison University. Finally, I am deeply indebted to Samuel Goldman and the Loeb Institute for Religious Freedom at George Washington University for the seminar where several scholars reviewed the manuscript. The reviewers—Leo Ruffino, Matt Franck, Stephen White, Mark Tooley, Chad Pecknold, and Sam himself—provided excellent advice for improvement.

At the University of Pennsylvania Press, Damon Linker helped this first-time author through the process of publishing a manuscript. He answered all questions patiently, thoroughly, and always with a dash of humor. Two anonymous reviewers provided essential insight into how best to revise and improve the manuscript. Lily Palladino and Ellen Douglas provided excellent help with copyediting.

Finally, my friends offered moral support, advice, and even child care—to name a few: Sara Henary, Josh Bowman, John Wilsey, Bill Batchelder, Nina Barzachka, Ashleen Bagnulo, Daniel J. Mahoney, Carrie Schaeffer, Glenn Moots, Fr. Bob Garrity, Mary and Jacob Blanchard, Daniel and Veronica Lendman, Jeremy and Lily Johnston, and most especially the late Peter Augustine Lawler. Bryan and Suzanne Pfaffenberger provided me, their son-in-law, a second home, and Bryan was something of a "fifth reader" for the manuscript back in its earliest form. My parents Leon and Donna, as well as my sister Gibson, have tolerated entirely too many long lectures on my research and missed holidays on account of one deadline or another. Finally, my wife Julia has shown tremendous grace as she endured several moves, changing living arrangements, and all the other peculiarities of a contemporary academic lifestyle even while she carried and cared for our children. She is the rock on which our family is built.

Printed in the USA
CPSIA information can be obtained
at www.ICGtesting.com
JSHW021444070924
69456JS00002B/17